D1780905

Quantitative Research in Archaeology

Quantitative Research in Archaeology

PROGRESS and PROSPECTS

—— EDITED BY ——
Mark S. Aldenderfer

SAGE PUBLICATIONS
The Publishers of Professional Social Science
Newbury Park Beverly Hills London New Delhi

Copyright © 1987 by Sage Publications, Inc.

All rights reserved. No part of this book may be reproduced or utilized in any form or by any means, electronic or mechanical, including photocopying, recording, or by any information storage and retrieval system, without permission in writing from the publisher.

For information address:

SAGE Publications, Inc.
2111 West Hillcrest Drive
Newbury Park, California 91320

SAGE Publications Inc.  SAGE Publications Ltd.
275 South Beverly Drive   28 Banner Street
Beverly Hills   London EC1Y 8QE
California 90212   England

SAGE PUBLICATIONS India Pvt. Ltd.
M-32 Market
Greater Kailash I
New Delhi 110 048 India

Printed in the United States of America

Library of Congress Cataloging-in-Publication Data

Main entry under title:

Quantitative research in archaeology.

   Papers presented at the 50th Annual Meeting of the Society for American Archaeology, held in Denver in 1985.
   1. Archaeology—Statistical methods—Congresses.
I. Aldenderfer, Mark S. II. Society for American Archaeology. Meeting (50th : 1985 : Denver, Colo.)
CC80.6.Q82   1987   930.1   85-15564
ISBN 0-8039-2844-0

Contents

Preface 7

1. Assessing the Impact of Quantitative Thinking on Archaeological Research: Historical and Evolutionary Insights
   Mark S. Aldenderfer 9

2. Paradigms and Paradoxes in Contemporary Archaeology
   G. A. Clark 30

3. Formal and Statistical Models in Archaeology
   A. Voorrips 61

4. Anthropological Archaeology, Computational Modeling, and Expert Systems
   Jim Doran 73

5. On the Structure of Archaeological Data
   Mark S. Aldenderfer 89

6. A Consideration of the Role of Quantitative Archaeology in Theory Construction
   Larry R. Kimball 114

7. Quantitative Methods Designed for Archaeological Problems
   Keith W. Kintigh 126

8. Simple Statistics
   Robert Whallon 135

9. Archaeological Theory and Statistical Methods: Discordance, Resolution, and New Directions
   Dwight W. Read 151

10.	Removing Discordance from Quantitative Analysis Christopher Carr	185
11.	Reliability, Validity, and Quantitative Methods in Archaeology Jack D. Nance	244
12.	Quantitative Burial Analyses as Interassemblage Comparison James A. Brown	294
About the Authors		309

Preface

The idea for this book came about in 1984 at the Portland Society for American Archaeology meeting, at which I discussed with some of the participants my idea of a retrospective look at quantitative thinking in archaeology over the past twenty years. The number "twenty" was firmly established in my mind, because 1986 would mark the twentieth anniversary of the publication of Binford and Binford's introduction of factor analysis to the discipline. I see that event as something of a baseline in the appearance of the quantitative idiom in archaeology, and at the time, the idea of reflecting on our progress in the use of these methods was appealing.

As we discussed the idea of a retrospective, however, it became clear that a retrospective, interesting as it might have been, was not really what was needed. What eventually emerged was the idea of a critical evaluation of the "place" of quantitative thinking in archaeological research. Such a discussion would avoid fixing itself on methods per se by putting methods into a series of contexts: epistemological, theoretical, substantive, and practical. The benefits of thinking in terms of contexts is clear; understanding context can help to assess the relevance of a technique or approach to an archaeological problem, and not the reverse.

I therefore charged the participants to think about two different, but related aspects of context: How they would look at the development of quantitative thinking in a theoretical context, and how they would communicate their thoughts to archaeologists who are nonspecialists in the field of statistics or quantitative methods. If the impact of quantitative thinking on archaeological research is to become what many of us would like, then there must be some level of agreement as to the relationships between theory, method, and substance; and furthermore, the concerns of the specialists must be presented effectively to archaeologists who will have to use the results of this thinking even though they may have no interest in developing such models. This is one way of bringing method back to archaeology in a realistic and, above all, practical framework.

These papers were first presented in a "presession" at an afternoon meeting of the Commission 4 (Data Management and Mathematical Methods) of the International Union of the Pre-and-Proto-Historical Sciences that was held just prior to the Denver SAAs in 1985. Although the papers were not formally presented at that time, there was a lively discussion of many of the issues eventually raised in the papers in this book. A good deal of time was spent in thinking about the amount and kind of training archaeologists should have in statistics, units of analysis, and a number of questions seldom discussed in print, but ones nevertheless of great importance. The papers were then formally presented at the Fiftieth Annual Meeting of the SAA.

Despite disagreements in a number of areas, I think there is a great deal of consistency exhibited in these papers on the "place" of quantitative thinking in archaeology and the ways in which archaeologists must first come to grips with archaeological problems to use statistics and quantitative thinking soundly. The papers range the gamut from "head" pieces to ones more concerned with method; but importantly, the thread of the original charge to the participants—how should we place quantitative thinking into the research process—was maintained by all of the authors. The use of these methods is still evolving in archaeology, but these papers give a clear indication that our use is beginning to mature.

Many have helped to make this book come to life. The participants in the original session must be thanked for their efforts and patience. I asked Geoffrey Clark, who was unable to participate in the original sessions, to contribute a paper, and I am pleased he was able to do so. Sandra Parker, the organizer of the Commission 4 meetings in Denver, is owed a special debt of thanks for her help in setting up the presession and helping things to move along smoothly. The audience of the presession is to be especially commended for their commentary and liveliness; their insights were always appreciated. Finally, I must thank my wife, Karen, who drafted all of the figures used in this book with the exception of Geoff Clark's drawings. These were so good it was a shame to have them redone. Karen worked without pay, so I will owe her many hours of child care down the road, a task that I look forward to.

1

Assessing the Impact of Quantitative Thinking on Archaeological Research: Historical and Evolutionary Insights

Mark S. Aldenderfer

An Archaeological Tale

Consider the following story of the introduction and subsequent history of quantitative methods in archaeological research:

Although quantitative methods have long been used in archaeology, they have only risen to importance during the past twenty years. The specific historical factors identified as being responsible for this rise include the desire to make archaeology an objective science, the general intellectual climate of the times that saw the rise of quantitative approaches in many social sciences, such as geography and sociology, and the widespread availability of the digital computer, which for the first time put many formerly computationally tedious, but powerful, statistical methods at the disposal of the scientist (Clark and Stafford 1982). Many archaeologists would agree that the event that really pushed quantitative thinking into the mainstream of modern archaeology was the publication of Binford and Binford's (1966) reanalysis of Mousterian assemblage data from southwestern France and the Middle East. In retrospect, it is easy to see what happened. The use of a statistical procedure by an important archaeologist with a message, combined with the computer, a powerful tool which made it all possible, created an irresistible bandwagon. Statistics were, rightly or wrongly, identified with the "new"; and to many, new meant better. Most of the archaeologists who jumped on the bandwagon had little formal training in mathematics, statistics, and quantitative analysis and were thus prone to make basic mistakes and errors. Those archaeologists who did not jump on the bandwagon were similarly ill-prepared to identify the mistakes being made. To many, statistical analysis became an end in itself; and the reason why it was used in the first place—to obtain a more complete understanding of the past—got lost in the rush to borrow novel methods of analysis.

The use of the computer and statistical methods in contemporary archaeology has become far more respectful. Mistakes are still being made, but most archaeologists now receive some formal training in their use, and as the methods become more fully integrated into research designs, the most blatant errors will disappear. There are still major questions about the "proper" role of statistical methods, especially as regards their articulation with archaeological theory, but new generations of statistically sophisticated archaeologists promise to make substantial contributions toward the solution of this problem. Despite the abuses of the recent past and the serious problems that remain, there seems to be considerable optimism about the prospects of quantitative analysis for making a significant impact on both the conduct and quality of archaeological research. As Clark and Stafford (1982: 107) put it, "If there is at present an uncritical overuse of statistical procedure, it can only be hoped that a more reasonable perspective will be established in the future as the novelty of automated archaeological analysis wears off."

On first reading, the story appears plausible, and it is likely that few archaeologists would dispute its accuracy. Implicit in the argument is that we are passing through a stage in the development and use of quantitative methods, and that sooner or later, preferably sooner, we will find ourselves peacefully coexisting with quantitative methods, and indeed, relying on their benefits rather heavily. Thomas

(1978) has described the late 1970s in terms of a bandwagon effect, and also has described the evolution of use of quantitative methods in the discipline as being similar to the swing of a pendulum. When first pushed, the pendulum swings out to one extreme and then returns to the other. The extremes will eventually dampen; this metaphorical place at which the pendulum centers will presumably indicate the "place" of quantitative methods in archaeological research. Given the pattern of abuses and problems described in the literature, we are probably in one of the initial stages of the evolutionary process. The pendulum is in a backswing, moving toward a dampening.

Another important feature of this story is its emphasis on method. Archaeologists either borrow methods from other disciplines or are forced to develop their own for the unique problems that plague archaeological data. While we may make mistakes in our uses of the methods, and while we may also lack sufficient experience to police ourselves, at least in the short run, as Scheps (1982) has suggested, we have recognized the importance of these tools for archaeological analysis. In effect we have come to agree with Clarke (1972: 44), who predicted that statistics and quantitative methods, as a part of the "New Methodology" that accompanied the appearance of the "New Paradigms," would transform the way in which archaeology was done and, presumably, what was to be learned about the past. It is important to note that the methods were to crosscut all of the paradigms, implying that each one would benefit from their use equally.

What is perhaps most striking about this story is its air of inevitability. Since our present experience with quantitative methods is simply a stage in the evolution of their use, we will eventually move into another, more advanced stage. Although little thought is given to how this evolution might proceed, it is generally assumed that better and more comprehensive training of archaeologists in the use of quantitative methods will eliminate the most glaring abuses, and thus, through familiarity, the methods will find their place in research. The emphasis on method is well justified, since it is through the use of method that we can expect to make significant advances in our understanding of the past.

But is this process inevitable, and is it likely that all areas of archaeology will require the use of quantitative methods, and if not, why not? Thinking in stages and believing in the eventual efficacy of education to help us progress from stage to stage is reminiscent of nineteenth-century tracts on the role of progress in the betterment of mankind. Progress is inevitable, and we must be prepared for it, so this thinking goes. Anthropologists, however, have long abandoned both the idea of unilineal evolution through stages and the concept of inevitable progress, and therefore archaeologists intent on understanding just how quantitative methods have made an impact on archaeological research will have to turn to other, more complex bodies of thought.

Evolutionary Trajectories of Ideas in a Scientific Discipline

One such source is the study of the history and sociology of science. Considerable progress has been made in the analysis of how ideas spread through a discipline, and a number of fascinating regularities have emerged. In general, topics in a scientific discipline follow a predictable course of four stages: early exploration, discovery, consolidation, and accommodation (May 1969; Nowakowska 1973; Rucci and Tweney 1980). During the early exploration phase, the initial ideas concerning a topic are mentioned, often in scattered areas through the scientific literature. These ideas are rarely recognized as important, and little or no follow-up occurs after the initial offering of the ideas. In the discovery phase, the ideas expressed during the early exploration phase are recognized as important by the scientific community, and the literature on the topic suddenly explodes. The topic may well become a fad and may generate a significant bandwagon effect. The idea is a "hot topic" for a period of time. Many of the publications that appear during this phase are either trivial or redundant. The consolidation phase is marked by the appearance of review papers about the idea that generally adopt a critical tone. Considerable skepticism about the topic is often expressed, and the excesses of the discovery phase are identified and castigated. Also, major theoretical works that organize the literature on the topic and systematically explore its ramifications begin to appear. The final phase, accommodation, occurs when the topic has gained sufficient recognition to be integrated into the general store of knowledge of the discipline.

Unlike the simple models of inevitable evolution or pendulum damping, this ideal trajectory is multilineal, and it can be truncated or transformed at any point. Price (1963: Fig. 7) describes a number of possible outcomes of the accommodation phase. Some topics go through a phase of escalation in which the growth of interest in a topic experiences a series of explosions after reaching the plateau of the consolidation phase. Escalation often occurs in disciplines marked by rapid technological advance within a well-defined theoretical context. Other topics suffer a loss of definition, often due to the phenomenon described as paradigm shift. An idea can be literally defined out of existence unless it can be adapted to the new environment. Finally, an idea can suffer divergent oscillation, or rapid swings of growth and decline. This oscillation is often found in situations of considerable disagreement over theoretical and epistemological foundations of a discipline. The oscillation may dampen if progress is made in reconciling these different perspectives.

If these concepts of the evolutionary trajectories of ideas within scientific disciplines are valid, they should dispel the notion that progress in quantitative methods within archaeology is inevitable, and that education alone will not establish the place and subsequent successful use of a method or series of methods within the discipline. Taking the science as a whole, archaeology is still in the discovery phase. The picture is one of exponential growth in citations of quantitative methods in the archaeological literature (Clark and Stafford 1982: Fig. 2), a clear sign of the discovery phase (Price 1963). There are signs that archaeology is beginning to enter the consolidation phase. Thomas's and Scheps's articles are good examples of this trend, as well as the edited volumes by Carr (1985) and Whallon and Brown (1982).

But is this aggregate approach the best way to characterize the evolutionary trajectory of quantitative methods in archaeology? Probably not, simply because it is easy to see that different problem areas within archaeology use quantitative methods more frequently than others. Models of spatial analysis borrowed from human geography are used frequently for the analysis of settlement patterns in state-level societies, and other spatial models are used extensively to explore site structure at sites in the settlement systems of hunters and gatherers. In contrast, quantitative methods are little used to study assemblage variability or to develop classification schemes of archaeological materials, at least in the modern era of the 1980s. We at least have the subjective impression, then, that quantitative methods have penetrated archaeology at different rates in different subject areas. While the aggregate approach can give us some sense of the big picture, it provides us with only a superficial understanding of the details of the process.

The Quantitative Idiom

The aggregate approach has also misled us by its concentration on methods, rather than on the circumstances and context of the archaeological setting into which the methods have been introduced. This focus on methods has been emphasized by the belief that quantitative methods, particularly statistics, are simply tools. What is overlooked, however, is the appearance of a quantitative idiom as a major conceptual approach to archaeological thinking. Simply put, a *quantitative* idiom is one in which measurements and their manipulation are seen as significant ways in which to gain insight into some phenomenon of interest (Kaplan 1964: 212-213). The idiom, however, does not simply consist of the use of some statistical or quantitative procedure but is instead a way of *thinking* about things; a quantitative idiom attempts to express a problem in quantitative terms and seeks solutions through the application of appropriate quantitative methods. The success of the quantitative idiom, while it in part relies on the development of useful methods, is more appropriately evaluated on the basis of how thinking about things in a quantitative way can help us understand what it is we are studying. Measurements must be meaningful. "Too often, we ask how to measure something without raising the question of what we would do with the measurement if we had it" (Kaplan 1964: 214). The assignment of meaning, of course, is an archaeological and anthropological problem and cannot be solved for us by the use of statistics.

How a quantitative idiom appears within a discipline is a topic for another paper, but at least one factor in their evolution seems to be related to the problem of paradigm shift, especially in times when a discipline seeks to achieve "scientific" status. Geography underwent its own scientific revolution in the 1960s and 1970s; proponents of the new orientation saw traditional geography as a natural history, in which description and interpretation were important. A more scientific geography emphasized explanation in a positivist model, and quantification had a strong place in this transformation. The debates between the advocates of "science" and quantification versus the keepers of a traditional, "qualitative" geography were more vituperative (but more humorous) than comparable debates within archaeology (Figure 1.1).

There is clearly a quantitative idiom alive and well in archaeology today. In part, it is reflected by the tremendous surge in publications of quantitative methods in general across the discipline, but it can also be seen in the way in which problems are discussed and framed. Scheps's (1982) example of statistical blight, an article by Isbell and Schreiber (1978), illustrates the presence of the idiom nicely. The goal of the Isbell and Schreiber paper was to determine if Huari was organized at the state level of sociopolitical complexity. One aspect of the argument was to compare "room-shape" factors, quantitative measures of room shape and size, across sites with the use of ANOVA. The authors argued that the traditional way to compare sites on the basis of architecture was intuitive; their room-shape measure was seen as objective and quantified, and thus more reliable. If significant differences could be detected by ANOVA, this would indicate "a rupture of tradition" of an indigenous cultural evolution from an external source (Isbell and Schreiber 1978: 377). What is important about this example is not the use of the statistical method, but the way in which the problem has been framed. Traditional means of assessing cultural continuity or discontinuity based on "intuitive" evaluations of architectural patterns have been rejected in favor of "operationalized" and quantified measures. Many similar examples of this trend can be found throughout the literature.

The concept of a quantitative idiom, coupled with an enhanced understanding of the range of possible trajectories of quantitative methods within the discipline, can help us to explain how and why different areas of archaeology have been penetrated at differential rates by quantitative methods. The trajectories and rate of acceptance are conditioned by the following:

(1) the relevance of quantitative thinking to the problem area in question and the appearance of a quantitative idiom are crucial. Relevance is simply the degree to which meaningful measurements of archaeological phenomena can be made. Meaning, of course, is made within a theoretical context, and therefore, the better developed the theory, the more likely it is that meaningful measures can be made. A lack of theory does not mean that measures cannot be constructed, but under these circumstances, it is likely that the measures will eventually discovered as being meaningless. Methods used within this context are often "labeled" as unreliable or not useful, when in fact the measures themselves are at fault (see 3 below).

Figure 1.1 Quantification. A cartoon of the quantitative revolution tearing geography away from the conventional qualitative traditions. "Geographia" is somewhat older and more able to take care of herself than the cartoonist suggests. [From L. Curry, "Quantitative Geography, 1967." *Canadian Geographer* 11 (1967), 265-279.] Reprinted by permission.

(2) suitable methods must be available; they may be borrowed or constructed within the discipline, but they must be tailored to the phenomena under study, and not vice versa. Fitting method to problem is a subtle and difficult process, and progress in this area has been slow. Once again, methods unsuitable to the problem may well be used, but this will ultimately affect the trajectory of acceptance of the method over time.

(3) historical and sociological factors, especially in the early exploration phase, exert considerable influence over the subsequent progress of the method. The prestige of the authors, the journal in which the first major use of the method is published, and the existence of competing invisible colleges, among other factors, are very important (Price 1963). While scientists are loathe to acknowledge these subjective, irrational factors, they are nevertheless of great importance.

(4) the general status of the discipline and the intellectual climate of the times must also be considered. In stable, "normal" science, new ideas may face considerable opposition if they run contrary to accepted wisdom. Alternatively, if the methods help to explore the structure of the discipline in conformance with the expected norms, they will be accepted more readily. In times of paradigm shift or competition between paradigms, methods may be denied or accepted according to their perceived relevance to both the scientific controversy under way as well as the political and social context in which that controversy takes place.

Although these factors can be separated analytically, they are closely linked in any real-world situation. Furthermore, each factor may wax and wane in influence and may be important at different points in the evolutionary trajectory of an idea in a discipline. Although the following discussion treats each factor individually, their mutual overlap will become clear.

The Evolution of Quantitative Thinking in Classification and Typology Building in Archaeology

The practice of classification and typology building in archaeological research is an excellent forum for the exploration of how scientific, historical, and sociological factors influence the penetration of quantitative methods into a discipline. Classification is a fundamental step in every scientific discipline, and every archaeologist who deals with data at any level must have a sound grasp of the principles of classification as well as a practical knowledge of how classifications are built. Classifications, of course, must be replicable and objective for any progress to be made in the study of the phenomena of interest. We can assume, then, that a large number of archaeologists would be interested in any method, quantitative or not, that is said to enhance the reliability and objectivity of the classificatory process.

Classification and the Quantitative Idiom

Statistical methods of classification have been used in cultural anthropology for some time, at least since the early part of this century. Most of these early attempts to classify cultures were based upon simple matrix ordering procedures. Similarity matrices of trait lists comprised the data, and the theoretical context was one that was grounded in the belief that these methods could discover patterns of diffusion of cultural traits (Driver and Kroeber 1932; see also Driver 1965 and Johnson 1972). The theories upon which this quantitative idiom were based were eventually repudiated by later generations of scholars, but the idiom was later resurrected in modern crosscultural studies.

Archaeological classification of the first half of the twentieth century, by comparison, had no similar quantitative idiom despite the general overlap of the goals of classification between the two subdisciplines. As Hill and Evans (1972: 233-249) have reconstructed the traditional model of classification in this era, it was one based primarily upon hierarchical models that used an imported Linnean taxonomic scheme borrowed from biology. In fact, the Pecos Conference of 1930 codified such analogies as "Kingdom: artifacts; phylum: ceramics; class: pottery," and so on to genus and species (Hargrave 1932: 8). Other variants of this basic hierachical scheme were adopted by others, such as Krieger (1944) and Rouse (1939). Although there was considerable debate about the meaning of types, and how types should best be developed, there was very little consideration about the theoretical place of classifications. They were seen as basic descriptions of the data discovered by archaeology, and they were used primarily to build chronologies and assess historical relationships between cultural areas. Types were created (or discovered, depending on your orientation) through exhaustive description of the materials within the classificatory scheme adopted. This usually involved the visual examination of artifacts as they were sorted into categories. Type creation, then, was a complex combination of exhaustive verbal description and visual assessment and comparison of the features of these verbally described categories.

Sporadic attempts to quantify this research were made by Kroeber (1940, 1942), one of the proponents of the classificatory approach in cultural anthropology, but this orientation never really made much difference in archaeological classification until the 1950s, when the first stirrings of the modern quantitative idiom in archaeology can be seen. The decade of the 1950s was a time of ferment; and as Willey and Sabloff (1974) have noted, there was increasing dissatisfaction with standard cultural historical and descriptive studies. Among other aspects of archaeology, this ferment was reflected in classification research by the debate between Ford and Spaulding on the reality of types. The debate was one between two different conceptions of types; Ford (1954) defended the traditional approach to typology, which reflected its essential historical and chronological dimensions, whereas Spaulding (1954) asserted that types were in fact discovered, and that many different kinds of types, some possibly representing function, with others reflecting time and space, could be found. Although the basic approach used by Spaulding was not significantly different than the technique advocated by Kroeber in the 1940s, the meaning assigned by Spaulding to types, and the context in which types were to be used—the study of human behavior in an anthropological context—made Spaulding's method attractive. However, it took the article by Binford in 1965 to provide real legitimacy to this perspective on classification. Binford extensively discussed the nature of archaeological systematics and placed classificatory practice into a theoretical framework it never really had before. Spaulding's method figured prominently in this discussion. Binford and Binford's reanalysis of the Mousterian data was published a year later, and the quantitative idiom was firmly established.

A parallel development of quantification in classification was taking place in England during the early 1960s. Unlike Spaulding's variable clustering approach, this emphasized cluster analysis and object clustering, and its primary impetus stemmed from numerical taxonomy as practiced in biology (Doran and Hodson 1966; Hodson, Sneath, and Doran 1966). This introduction, as I shall show below, owed less to the development of a quantitative idiom than it did to the sociological factors that surrounded the introduction of the methods to the discipline. The two independent trends were fused in the late 1960s, when the quantitative idiom was well established, and when the discovery phase of the use of quantitative methods in classification really began (Cowgill 1968).

The number of studies that used cluster analysis, and to a lesser extent, variable clustering continued to grow until the late 1970s, when two critical papers were published. Thomas (1978) presented his celebrated paper on the good, bad, and ugly in quantitative research. Although few names were named, studies were generally lumped in the "ugly" category. Thomas correctly pointed out that the use of these methods rarely provided new insight into the items being classified, and in general, they tended to confirm what we already know. Many examples were trivial, as well. If this was the case, what was the point of using methods that rarely improved our knowledge of the past? The second article, by Christenson and Read (1977), criticized clustering methods from a methodological and statistical standpoint. Using one type of clustering method, a variant of single linkage, they showed that application of these methods to raw data simply failed to produce meaningful results when compared to a known classification. They further demonstrated that this clustering method, and by implication all clustering methods, was strongly affected by a number of methodological and data-related problems, the kind of problems best solved by statisticians, not archaeologists. It was a strong critique that made clustering methods look very bad.

The citation frequency of articles using clustering methods of any kind in classification research declined substantially after these two reviews. The methods were shown to be fragile and rife with unsolvable methodological problems (Aldenderfer and Blashfield 1984). Moreover, they were shown to have little theoretical grounding, and it proved difficult to connect these methods to interesting archaeological theories. This made them all the more unattractive at a time at which archaeologists were demanding that classifications be firmly grounded in theoretical thinking (Whallon and Brown 1982; Aldenderfer 1983). In short, the relevance of the measurement process in classification research using these methods became suspect. Thinking back to the stage definitions presented above, the use of this particular quantitative approach to classification research suffered a loss of definition in its accommodation phase.

While Spaulding's approach to variable clustering has not suffered the same fate, it has not seen the explosion of growth and interest experienced by the object clustering approach. In the context of the relevance of the measures proposed and their theoretical connections, Spaulding's emphasis on the meaning of the types discovered though his procedures—that they reflected emic categories of their prehistoric makers—was always somewhat suspect. While many archaeologists were willing to grant that nonrandom associations of attributes might in some cases represent emic categories, such types were often seen as simply not relevant to the kinds of questions archaeologists were asking of their data. Much archaeological thinking of the 1970s was process-oriented, and the major questions being asked were one of the locus of cultural change, the evolution of cultural systems, and large-scale substantive questions such as origins research into the state and agriculture. The techniques in themselves were not objectionable, but the meaning assigned by Spaulding to types derived through their use did not figure predominantly in the kinds of archaeological research being done at the time. Thus the methods were taught, but they suffered something of a benign neglect.

The interplay of the quantitative idiom and theoretical and epistemological relevance of measurement has played an important role in the course of use and acceptance of quantitative methods in classification research. The idiom must be in place for the methods to enter the discovery phase, but relevance must exist to get the methods into an accommodation phase that does not reflect a loss of definition or other calamity. What is interesting to speculate upon is the thought that classification practice in the 1980s is not all that different from that of the early 1960s before the emplacement of the quantitative idiom and the explosive growth of the discovery phase. This would be a fascinating topic to research.

Classification Research and Methods

Prior to the advent of the quantitative idiom in archaeology, the methods used in classification research were verbal and visual. Comparisons of types, or between areas with different types, were made through examination of trait lists—simple enumerations of objects present or absent from the sites or regions in question. These methods served archaeology well as long as the scope of research was limited to a relatively small region, and the number of archaeologists involved in the classification process was relatively small. The Pecos Conference, for instance, was able to bring together almost all archaeologists involved in southwestern archaeology. These face-to-face meetings allowed all archaeologists to see the types being discussed, and this helped to keep the process of type formation reasonably consistent.

As the discipline grew, however, these routine face-to-face meetings could not be held as frequently, and a major means of dissemination of information that tended to promote typological consistency was lost. Visual comparison and verbal description can be prepared with rigor, but it remains difficult to compare types built solely on these grounds, especially in circumstances in which the basic structures of the typological system are in dispute or are described differently. Berry and Berry (1986) have commented at length about these problems in the context of the classificatory systems of southwestern Archaic projectile points.

With the appearance of the quantitative idiom in classification, these cumbersome methods were fair game for replacement. The traditional process of classification based on trait-list comparison and description was labeled as subjective, and on those grounds, so-called "objective" procedures could be introduced in the classification process. One approach, Spaulding's variable clustering procedure, was already in place and began to see an increased volume of use. But other approaches, such as cluster analysis, had to be borrowed from other disciplines. Although simple matrix ordering methods had once been used extensively in anthropology, this new borrowing of matrix methods came from sources in biology. Numerical taxonomic studies, based on clustering methods, were very popular during this era, and they were perceived as an empirical, objective means of constructing classifications (Sokal and Sneath 1963). Their use in biology had appeared during the late 1950s, but it took the widespread availability of the digital computer to truly popularize these methods. The computer was essentially in place by the time clustering methods were introduced to archaeology. The computer, of course, while not a method, took the sting out of computationally tedious methods like cluster analysis and made them far more attractive.

Serious use of these methods took place in archaeology relatively quickly after their introduction to the discipline. They allowed the evaluation of relatively large data sets on an objective basis, and they promoted a certain degree of rigor in variable and attribute definition. Although the methods in the long run experienced difficulties in the discipline, an unanticipated side benefit of their use was the emphasis placed upon the ways in which variables could be defined and how measurements could be related to archaeological problems on a broader scale.

The Social Context of Classification Research in Archaeology

The social context of the introduction of quantitative methods to classification research in archaeology is truly fascinating. It centers around people, journals, and the timing and place of publication. The most illuminating circumstance in which social factors have played an important role in the evolutionary trajectory of quantitative thinking in archaeology is the way in which cluster analysis techniques were introduced to the discipline.

Cluster analysis methods came to archaeology through biology. Two papers were published in Britain in 1966 by James Doran, F. R. Hodson, and Peter Sneath. One paper was published in *Nature*, while the other came out in *Biometrika*. Both featured the analysis of an assemblage of Paleolithic stone tools, and both discussed hierarchical agglomerative methods of cluster analysis. It is important to note that one of the authors was Peter Sneath, of Sokal and Sneath fame, one of the luminaries of numerical taxonomy in biological classification. Thus, from the outset there was at least some presumed relationship between cluster analysis methods, numerical taxonomy, and archaeological classification. David Clarke, in *Analytical Archaeology* (1968), made a more explicit statement of the "equivalence" of numerical taxonomy with cluster analysis and argued that numerical taxonomy could provide objective, replicable classifications of archaeological data more quickly and more reliably than traditional methods. Hierarchical agglomerative clustering methods were to be used in these efforts. Interestingly, Hodson (1970), one of the original authors of the introductory papers, said relatively little about numerical taxonomy in a major article about the merits of cluster analysis. Of even greater interest was his description of k-means clustering, a method that had not been developed within a numerical taxonomic framework.

But by this time, the association of cluster analysis with numerical taxonomy had been made in the minds of most archaeologists. Thomas (1971) had already described the use of hierarchical agglomerative cluster analysis as numerical taxonomy, a tendency he continued until 1978. In a sense, then, the term "cluster analysis" had been relabeled "numerical taxonomy."

In 1977 Christenson and Read published their critique of numerical taxonomy and r-mode factor analysis. One of their strongest points was that the theoretical underpinnings of numerical taxonomy, primarily the concept of natural taxa and the methodological and theoretical principle of equal character weighting, were inappropriate for archaeological classification on theoretical and methodological grounds. They then proceeded to show how one cluster analysis method failed to recover an intuitive classification of projectile points. Their conclusion was that the cluster analysis of raw data was an inappropriate procedure for archaeologists to follow. Thomas (1978) echoed their concerns and strongly rejected the use of numerical taxonomy in most archaeological situations.

Thomas and Christenson and Read were right, but they were right for the wrong reasons. While there can be no doubt that the assumptions of numerical taxonomy are useless for archaeology (indeed, they have proven useless for biologists as well), they were wrong in assuming that cluster analysis was therefore a suspect procedure. Cluster analysis failed as a quantitative approach to classification not because it was numerical taxonomy, but because the methods as employed failed to be relevant to the kinds of research archaeologists were interested in doing. In part, the methods failed because they were never placed within a theoretically sound framework, but that cannot be considered the fault of the method. As Christenson and Read had pointed out, archaeologists had expected far too much from clustering methods.

Cluster analysis is the generic name for at least seven major families of quasi-statistical methods that place objects or whatever is analyzed into groups. These families include hierarchical agglomerative, hierarchical divisive, iterative partitioning, density searching, factor analytic variants, graph theoretic, and clumping methods. Only one family of these methods—hierarchical agglomerative—has any serious history of use in numerical taxonomic studies. These different families of methods are based on radically different approaches to the formation of clusters, or homogeneous groups, and thus they can and do generate different solutions to the same body of data (Aldenderfer and Blashfield 1984). Cluster analysis is not numerical taxonomy, and one does not have to accept any of the assumptions of numerical taxonomy to use a clustering method.

That hierarchical agglomerative methods have become so widely used in archaeology is in great part a historical accident due to the association of Sneath, the numerical taxonomist, with Hodson the archaeologist and Doran the computer scientist. But it is no accident for archaeologists to continue to associate cluster analysis with numerical taxonomy; it is instead ignorance bordering on willful misunderstanding. Clustering methods have been tarred with the same brush that has blackened numerical taxonomy, and what this has lead to, at least in part, is a premature closure of thought about the value of these procedures in archaeological classification. It is one thing to deny the utility of a method or approach on theoretical grounds, and there is some reason to believe that many studies that have used cluster analysis will fall into this category, but to deny the validity of a technique on the basis of its presumed antecedents without fully understanding its social and historical sources is quite another. This story should serve as a cautionary tale, a warning for archaeologists to become more aware of their borrowings and the potentially diverse contexts of the techniques they do in fact borrow.

Classification and the Intellectual Climate of Archaeology

Each of the examples of the influences on the progress of a quantitative approach to classification in archaeology has made mention of changing paradigms, or intellectual orientations. The most fundamental shift, of course, in the past twenty years has been the development of the so-called "New Archaeology," a theoretical, methodological, political, and social transformation of our discipline. While there is still a debate as to whether or not we really underwent a true paradigm shift, something certainly happened, and the advent of quantification in archaeology, through the establishment of a quantitative idiom, became a part of the transformed theoretical and methodological scene.

The impact the paradigm shift had on classification research centered on the need for classification to become an objective process, freed from the visual and verbal methods of the traditional approach to typology. In essence, classification was asked to become a part of science and thus to move away from a natural historical orientation. As Read (1976: 1042), in a review of Doran and Hodson's (1975) book on quantitative methods in archaeology, described it,

> If archaeology is to become scientific, the archaeologist must first be able to describe accurately and classify objectively the material remains that are his or her primary data. The need for accurate description justifies the emphasis on quantification and the need for objective classification the use of mathematical techniques.

Although the paradigm shift provided a rationale and justification for quantification in classification, it was not enough to guarantee its success. As I have shown above, much of the subsequent use of cluster analysis and other multivariate procedures in classification was done in a theoretical vacuum, and little new or exciting was uncovered by this empirical search for structure in archaeological data. But even the few attempts to move ahead with theoretical thinking with a quantitative idiom in archaeological classification did not fare well either. Read (1974a, 1974b) made two tries at providing a sound mathematical basis for typology in archaeology. The latter of these was an especially ambitious attempt to use set theory to show how categories should be defined and how these categories are to be related to methods that seek to discover structure in archaeological data. While these models are elegant, and are generally cited in an approving manner in the discipline as to how theory, method, and classification should articulate, they are little used to actually build types by archaeologists. The reasons for the failure of these models to transform typological practice in archaeology are numerous, but they can be condensed into two categories: (1) few archaeologists have training in set theory; and although they may be able to appreciate the logic and elegance of the approach as a conceptual matter, it is quite another thing for someone with no background to use these techniques; (2) there is a seldom expressed, but probably very real, current in archaeological thinking that despite the ideology of science, and the lip service paid to the importance of the quantitative idiom in archaeological research, the actual practice of classification is in no need of repair. Traditional methods of type building, especially for morphological types with presumed temporal and cultural meaning, seem to work just fine. Thomas (1978: 236) says it best: "To propose a computer technique for deriving morphological types presumes that traditional methods have failed, and nobody has demonstrated that yet."

What this example shows is that the appearance of a quantitative idiom within a paradigm shift may have taken on an air of ideology, and that far from advancing the cause of "objectivity" in archaeological classification, it may well impede it. The quantitative idiom has taken over a proselytizing role. The "idea" of quantification in classification sounds good, but in practice it seems to be little needed. This does not mean that the great body of archaeologists are right in this opinion, but instead it means that at present, what has passed for quantification in classification research has not proved to be of great practical value. The key to understanding what is going on, however, is to see that there is a strong social and political dimension to this process of acceptance or denial.

Conclusions

The progress of the quantitative idiom in archaeological research is a complex phenomenon, with scientific, sociological, and ideological components. Depending on the mix of these factors, different areas of archaeology will accept or reject a quantitative idiom at different rates, and the ultimate fate (the accommodation phase) of the idiom within any part of archaeology will also depend on these factors as well. This situation is likely to become further confused with the increasing tendency of archaeology to split into relatively small subfields based on area, chronology, and theoretical orientation. In the postpositivist era of the 1980s, new theoretical orientations such as Marxism, structural archaeology, and archaeological interpretation are beginning to be taken more seriously. Someone once said that archaeology lags about twenty years behind major conceptual reorientations in cultural anthropology. If that is the case, we are in for a bout of intense interest in structural arguments; and if this is so, can the idea of archaeological hermeneutics, or the interpretation of meaning of archaeological cultures, be far behind? Each of these new intellectual orientations has a radically different, and generally negative, view of the quantitative idiom. Depending on the degree of acceptance of each of these orientations, the growth of quantitative thinking in all fields of archaeological inquiry will be transformed in a number of ways. By thinking of the evolution of quantitative thinking in archaeological research as a multilineal trajectory that is affected by a scientific, social, and ideological concerns, those archaeologists interested in improving the quality of research in the idiom can look for new ways of defining the "place" of quantitative methods that will have meaning for archaeologists with different intellectual orientations. No one can predict the quality of the use of the quantitative idiom under these changing circumstances; this will ultimately be a judgment of history. What can be done, however, is to foster an awareness of the complexity to the evolutionary process in hopes that the problems seen in the past regarding the use of quantitative methods in archaeological research can be avoided and overcome by future generations of quantitatively and historically aware archaeologists.

References

Aldenderfer, M. 1983. Review of *Essays in Archaeological Typology*, edited by Robert Whallon and James A. Brown. *American Antiquity* 48: 652-654.
Aldenderfer, M. and R. K. Blashfield. 1984. *Cluster Analysis*. Beverly Hills CA: Sage.
Berry, C. and M. Berry. 1986. Chronological and conceptual models of the southwestern Archaic. In *Essays in Honor of Jesse D. Jennings*, eds. D. Fowler and C. Condie. Salt Lake: University of Utah Press.
Binford, L. R. 1965. Archaeological systematics and the study of culture process. *American Antiquity* 31: 203-210.
Binford, L. R. and S. Binford. 1966. A preliminary analysis of functional variability in the Mousterian of Levallois facies. *American Anthropologist* 68: 238-295.
Carr, C. (ed.) 1985 *For Concordance in Archaeological Analysis*. Kansas City: Westport Publishers.
Christenson, A. and D. Read. 1977. Numerical taxonomy, r-mode factor analysis, and archaeological classification. *American Antiquity* 42: 163-179.
Clark, G. and C. R. Stafford. 1982. Quantification in American archaeology: historical perspective. *World Archaeology* 14: 98-119.
Clarke, D. 1968. *Analytical Archaeology*. London: Methuen.
Clarke, D. 1972. Models and paradigms in contemporary archaeology. In *Models in Archaeology*, ed. D. Clarke, pp. 1-60. London: Methuen.
Cowgill, G. 1968. Archaeological applications of factor, cluster, and proximity analysis. *American Antiquity* 33: 367-375.
Doran, J. and F. R. Hodson. 1966. A digital computer analysis of paleolithic flint assemblages. *Nature* 210: 688.
Doran, J. and F. R. Hodson. 1975. *Mathematics and Computers in Archaeology*. Cambridge: Harvard University Press.
Driver, H. E. 1965. Survey of numerical classification in anthropology. In *The Use of Computers in Anthropology*, ed. D. Hymes, pp. 301-344. The Hague: Mouton.
Driver, H. E. and A. L. Kroeber. 1932. Quantitative expression of cultural relationships. *University of California Publications in American Archaeology and Ethnology* 31: 211-256.
Ford, J. 1954. The type concept revisited. *American Anthropologist* 56: 42-54.
Hargrave, L. L. 1932. Guide to forty pottery types from the Hopi country and the San Francisco Mountains, Arizona. *Museum of Northern Arizona. Bulletin 1*.
Hill, J. N. and R. K. Evans. 1972. A model for classification and typology. In *Models in Archaeology*, ed. D. Clarke, pp. 231-271. London: Methuen.
Hodson, F. R. 1970. Cluster analysis and archaeology: some new developments and applications. *World Archaeology* 1: 299-320.
Hodson, F. R., P. Sneath, and J. Doran. 1966. Some experiments in the numerical analysis of archaeological data. *Biometrika* 53: 311-324.
Isbell, W. and K. Schreiber. 1978. Was Huari a state? *American Antiquity* 43: 372-389.
Johnson, L. 1972. Introduction to imaginary models for archaeological scaling and clustering. In *Models in Archaeology*, ed. D. Clarke, pp. 309-379. London: Methuen.
Kaplan, A. 1964. *The Conduct of Inquiry*. San Francisco: Chandler.
Kreiger, A. 1944. The typological concept. *American Antiquity* 9: 271-288.
Kroeber, A. L. 1940. Statistical classification. *American Antiquity* 6: 29-44.
Kroeber, A. L. 1942. Tapajo pottery. *American Antiquity* 7: 403-405.

May, K. O. 1969. The growth and quality of the mathematical literature. *Isis* 59: 363-371.

Nowakowska, M. 1973. Epidemical spread of scientific objects: an empirical approach to some problems of metascience. *Theory and Decision* 3: 262-297.

Price, D. 1963. *Big Science, Little Science*. New York: Columbia University Press.

Read, D. 1974a. Some comments on the use of mathematical models in anthropology. *American Antiquity* 39: 3-15.

Read, D. 1974b. Some comments on typologies in archaeology and an outline of a methodology. *American Antiquity* 39: 216-242.

Read, D. 1976. Review of *Mathematics and Computers in Archaeology*, by J. Doran and F. R. Hodson. *Science* 191: 1041-1042.

Rouse, I. 1939. *Prehistory in Haiti: A Study in Method*. New Haven: Yale University Publications in Anthropology 21.

Rucci, A. J. and R. D. Tweney. 1980. Analysis of variance—the "second discipline" of scientific psychology. *Psychological Bulletin* 87: 166-184.

Scheps, S. 1982. Statistical blight. *American Antiquity* 47: 836-851.

Sokal, R. R. and P. H. A. Sneath. 1963. *Principles of Numerical Taxonomy*. San Francisco: Freeman.

Spaulding, A. C. 1954. Reply to Ford. *American Antiquity* 19: 391-393.

Thomas, D. H. 1971. On the use of cumulative curves and numerical taxonomy. *American Antiquity* 36: 206-209.

Thomas, D. H. 1978. The awful truth about statistics in archaeology. *American Antiquity* 43: 231-244.

Whallon, R. and J. A. Brown (eds.). 1982. *Essays in Archaeological Typology*. Evanston, IL: Center for American Archaeology Press.

Willey, G. and J. Sabloff. 1974. *A History of American Archaeology*. San Francisco: Freeman.

2

Paradigms and Paradoxes in Contemporary Archaeology

G. A. Clark

Preliminary Biases

Several years ago, I wrote an essay that discussed the history of quantification in American archaeology and compared "confirmatory" (hypothesis testing) approaches with those of "exploratory" data analysis (Clark 1982). I showed that quantified approaches could be categorized in several ways, that their "penetrance" in the discipline was longstanding but very partial, and that what I called "statistical reasoning" (thinking about problems in quantitative terms) was becoming increasingly common in many aspects of the archaeological research designs of the 1980s.

I took the position that debates conducted in philosophy of science contexts contributed little or nothing in themselves to the advancement of the "scientific" stature of the discipline, and that archaeology remained broadly anthropological in character. It was my opinion that archaeology would stand or fall as a viable social science not on the basis of how archaeological research is conducted, but rather on its capacity to contribute new and meaningful insights to a general understanding of human social behavior—insights not forthcoming from the other social science disciplines. I noted that archaeology's contribution to an understanding of human social behavior had nevertheless been minimal (cf. Leone 1972: 19), and that the discipline seemed to be operating in the absence of any uniform theoretical orientation apart from that inherited selectively from anthropology.

It also seemed to be true that the polemics of the early/mid-1970s had subsided, and that archaeologists were very much about the business of doing research, in the United States at least, largely in CRM contexts. This seemed paradoxical until it was observed that there might be more held in common by archaeologists with respect to methodological concerns than with respect to overarching, exclusively archaeological theories of human behavior (Meltzer 1979). There did seem to be broad commonalities about how archaeological research was to be conducted, and there was substantial agreement about methodological issues even in the absence of a unifying body of theory.

If it could be shown to exist (or to have existed in the past), a body of archaeological theory would provide the discipline with a cohesiveness, a unity of purpose, the commonly understood "paradigm legitimatized" objectives that supposedly structure scientific research in other fields (Kuhn 1962, 1970). I submit, however, that archaeological theory at the level of paradigm does not exist (indeed, never has existed). What we have now, and have always had, in place of archaeological theory is a partial and eclectic, at times even idiosyncratic dependence upon selected aspects of social anthropology, and other social and natural sciences, that define and validate problems for different segments of the discipline. Adherence to these perspectives is partial at best, and the penetrance of any one of them on the field as a whole is limited. Not everyone agrees with me (cf. Wilcox and Sullivan 1978; Gumerman and Phillips 1978; Fowler 1982).

Thomas Kuhn's (1970) model of rapid change in scientific disciplines by "revolution" and generational replacement has often been invoked to identify those elements of a "new" archaeology (e.g., neoevolutionism, systems perspective, cultural ecology, etc.), which set it apart from an "old" archaeology (concerned with reconstruction of past lifeways, regional culture histories, etc.) in an effort to come to grips with what appears to be a rapidly changing, chaotic, even disintegrating field (e.g., Leone 1972). This point of view is usually juxtaposed with the traditional notion of orderly, regular, cumulative change espoused by Thompson (1972), among others.

The nature of change in American archaeology was the subject of a recent article by Meltzer (1979) who drew the interesting conclusion that while much ink had been split in inconclusive debates and ad hoc assertions as to what form a "new" archaeological paradigm should take, it remained to be demonstrated that we have ever had one in the first place. He goes on to suggest that there has in fact been no change in the underlying archaeological metaphysics, which continues to regard the archaeological record as a special case of anthropological phenomena, to be treated in broadly anthropological terms. In the absence of a competing body of purely archaeological theory, he says, archaeology will continue to derive its concepts of "legitimatized problems" from the parent discipline, and must continue to rely upon anthropology for an overarching theoretical orientation. This issue is explored in greater detail below. However, I am in basic agreement with Meltzer, and regard arguments to the contrary as either limited (although not necessarily misguided or contradictory, as in the case of "middle range theory") or specious and motivated by self-interest (as, for example, the posturings of some CRM archaeologists, anxious to gain credibility in academic circles).

These preliminary remarks should establish in what I hope are unambiguous terms by notions of where archaeology "fits" in the broader contexts of anthropology and the social sciences. Biases about the position and status of archaeology as an intellectual enterprise will inevitably influence the following discussion of creativity in science and in archaeological research. I will return to the question of the nature of the archaeological metaphysic at the end of this chapter.

On Creativity and the Bisociative Act

This is primarily an essay about creativity—what it is and what roles it plays in the research process. In my 1982 paper scant attention was paid to creativity in archaeology because I wanted to emphasize the structural aspects of alternative kinds of quantitative research strategies, proceeding from the supposition that it is the formal evaluation of an idea, and not its conceptualization, that is embodied in common conceptions of research design. The role of creativity in the research process is not one that has attracted the attention of many archaeologists. However, it can be argued that archaeology is no different in any important respect from the other nonexperimental social sciences, and it follows that the role of creativity in the discipline should not be that different either. Here I want to discuss some general characteristics of creativity in science and then talk about it in the more limited contexts of archaeology and "quantitative" archaeology.

One usually initiates the research process already armed with a formidable repertoire of general anthropological knowledge which is augmented and refined by undertaking "background research"— problem and area specific investigations of questions of interest to the investigator and likely to be germane to more tightly focused research objectives. This activity is part of all scientific endeavor. It can culminate in, or indeed originate from, hunches or flashes of insight which the investigator believes likely to express a significant relationship between two or more variables. The perception of relationship is the key that unlocks the door to creativity.

The origins of meaningful insights are obscure, but at a minimum, they appear to involve the capacity to shift habitual formats of reference from one body (or "matrix") of knowledge to another in such a way that new and original relationships become apparent (Koestler 1964). It is in the variable capacity of people to shift referential formats, and to extricate themselves from habitual patterns of thought that differences in creativity lie, with the human tendency for automatized modes of thinking perhaps the single most significant limiting factor. The trick, according to Koestler, is to break the confines of normative thought in such a way that a familiar event, process, concept, or situation is seen in an entirely new light. This is Koestler's "bisociative act" (1964: 35-45), and it has a large subconscious component (cf. below). It is founded on the notion that habitually unrelated matrices of experience can sometimes be conjoined in such a way that a fusion or synthesis emerges, often as a flash of insight, in which a structural analogy is perceived for the first time—a novel relationship that no one had seen before. So compelling is the force of the analogy that when two experiential matrices become integrated in this fashion, they cannot again be torn asunder. "This is why the discoveries of yesterday are the commonplaces of today, and why we always marvel at how stupid we were not to have seen what post factum appears to be so obvious" (Koestler 1964: 105). The bisociative act is represented schematically in Figure 2.1. The interesting planes (M_1, M_2) represent two frames of reference which are not customarily associated with one another. The event L, at the junction of the planes, symbolizes the simultaneous perception of a relationship (situation, concept, idea) in two self-consistent but habitually incompatible frames of reference (Koestler 1964: 35). So long as it lasts, the event L is not linked exclusively with a single associative context, but is rather "bisociated" with two. Although we are concerned with this phenomenon in the sciences, Koestler argues convincingly that bisociation is a common feature of all creative endeavors, and underlies not only the scientist's insight but also the artist's creative act.

Some Examples of Bisociation in Science and Mathematics

The bisociative act is perhaps nowhere more apparent than in the biographical writings of men of genius. The following vignettes illustrate some of the external and internal events and processes surrounding some significant "moments of truth" in the history of western science. Although these are examples of "creativity with a capital C," it is important to keep in mind that the bisociative act appears to be a common feature of creativity in general, and that there is evidence that it operates at all levels of problem solving.

Jules Henri Poincaré (1854-1912), noted for his discovery of the theory of Fuchsian functions and for demonstrating that they were structural analogs to transformations in non-Euclidean geometry, recorded his efforts in some detail over a two-year period. A pattern of conscious struggle, distractedness and (apparently spontaneous) resolution is clearly evident in his autobiography.

> For fifteen days I strove to prove that there could not be any functions like those I have since called Fuchsian functions . . . every day I seated myself at my work table, stayed an hour or two, tried a great number of combinations, and reached no results. One evening . . . I drank black coffee and could not sleep. Ideas rose in crowds; I felt them collide until pairs interlocked . . . making a stable combination. By the next morning I had established the existence of a class of Fuchsian functions, those which come from the hypergeometric series; I had only to write out the results, which took but a few hours.
>
> Just at this time I left Caen . . . to go on a geologic excursion. The travel made me forget my mathematical work. Having reached Coutances, we entered an

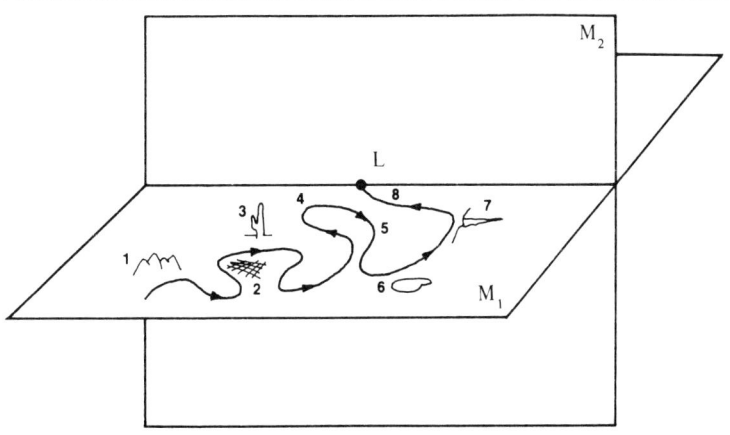

Figure 2.1 Two habitually incompatible frames of reference (M_1, M_2) intersect at event "L," which represents the simultaneous perception of an idea in both referential formats. The meandering line indicates the "blocked" situation typical of stereotyped attempts at problem solving, confined to a single plane (after Koestler, 1964: 35, 36, 106, 107). Some features of the cognitive landscape are indicated: (1) the Melancholy Mountains, (2) Anxietyville, (3) the Desert of Despair, (4) Procrastination Point, (5) Guilty Gulch, (6) Lake Listless, (7) Distraction Draw, and (8) Forgetful Falls. Work avoidance behaviors associated with these features vary with the individual.

omnibus to go someplace or other. At the moment I put my foot on the step the idea came to me, without anything in my former thoughts having paved the way for it, that the transformations I had used to define the Fuchsian functions were identical with those of non-Euclidean geometry. I did not verify the idea . . . but I felt a perfect certainty. On my return to Caen, I verified the result at my leisure.

I then turned my attention to . . . some arithmetical questions apparently without much success and without a suspicion of any connexion with my preceding researches. Disgusted with my failure, I went to spend a few days at the seaside, and thought of something else. One morning, walking on the bluff, the idea came to me with just the same characteristics of brevity, suddenness and immediate certainty, that the arithmetic transformations of indeterminate ternary quadratic forms (on which he had been working) were identical with those of non-Euclidean geometry.

Most striking at first is this appearance of sudden illumination, a manifest sign of long, unconscious prior work. The role of this unconscious work in mathematical invention appears to be incontestable. (from Poincaré [1904] in Ghiselin [1952])

The account of Archimedes' method for determining the volume of complex forms by means of the volume of water displaced is well known to everyone. What are perhaps not so well known are the stages in problem solving by which he arrived at his famous principle. The reader will recall that Hiero, tyrant of Syracuse, had been given a crown, allegedly of pure gold, but he suspected that it had been adulterated with silver. He asked Archimedes' opinion. Archimedes knew the specific weight of gold (its weight per unit volume). If he could measure the volume of the crown, he could determine immediately whether it was pure gold or not, but it was a complex ornament and he could not determine its volume without destroying it.

> We can imagine his thoughts roving round in circles within the frame of his geometrical knowledge and, finding all approaches to the target blocked, returning again and again to the starting point. This frustrating situation is familiar to everyone trying to solve a problem.
>
> One day, while getting into his bath, Archimedes absent-mindedly watched the familiar sight of the water-level rising from one smudge on the basin to the next as a result of the immersion of his body, and it occurred to him in a flash that the volume of water displaced was equal to the volume of the immersed parts of his own (complicated) body—which could simply be measured by the pint. He had melted his body down... without harming it, and he could do the same with the crown. (Koestler 1964: 105, 106)

Évariste Galois (1812-1832), perhaps one of the most original mathematicians of all time, was killed in a duel at the age of 20. On the night before he died, he revised a paper to the French Academy of Sciences, which had previously rejected it as unintelligible, and, in a letter to a friend, outlined a number of other mathematical discoveries which were far in advance of the "normal science" of his time.[1] Only after fifteen years had elapsed did scholars become aware of the significance of the rejected manuscript. It was a complete transformation of the higher algebra and projected from an entirely different perspective what had only been dimly perceived by the greatest mathematical minds of the time (Hadamard 1949: 119). In the letter Galois postulated a theorem which could not have been understood by his contemporaries because it was based on mathematical principles only discovered a quarter-century after his death. Hadamard remarks that:

It must be admitted, first, that Galois must have conceived these principles in some way; second, that they must have been unconscious in his mind since he makes no allusion to them, though they by themselves represent a significant discovery. (1949: 120)

Then there is the dramatic case of Friedrich August von Kekulé, Professor of Chemistry at Ghent, for whom the bisociative act consisted of a dream—a dream that liberated him from the conventional routines of thought that typify and constrain conscious analysis.

> I turned in the chair and dozed... again the atoms were gambolling before my eyes. My mental eye, rendered more acute by repeated visions of this kind, could now distinguish larger structures, of manifold conformation; long rows... all twining and twisting in snakelike motion. But look! What was that? One of the snakes had seized hold of its own tail, and the form whirled mockingly before my eyes. (Findlay 1948: 36-38)

What Kekulé had discovered in 1865 was in fact one of the cornerstones of modern organic chemistry: the then-revolutionary proposal that the molecules of certain important organic compounds are closed chains or rings—like the snake swallowing its tail (Koestler 1964: 118).

There are many other examples. Pasteur, Ampère (after whom the unit of electrical current is named), Gauss, Kepler, Darwin, Wallace, Farraday, Freud, Galileo, Einstein, Bohr, Newton, and some dozens of lesser lights in equally diverse fields recount similar experiences. Kohler's (1957) classic studies of chimpanzee tool use and manufacture suggest that certain fundamental structural similarities in problem perception and resolution probably extend to some of the higher nonhuman primates as well.

Recurrent Features

The recurrent features of the creative process are plain enough upon inspection and admit of some generalization. They appear to take place fairly early on in what we usually think of as the research process. The bisociative act seems always to be preceded by a period of largely unconscious (or subconscious) cerebration, as the scientist first seeks a solution within the familiar confines of an habitual frame of reference. Frustration occurs when the problem involved still resembles in some respects those confronted previously but contains some new elements of complexity which make its solution incompatible with the tenets of an established body of knowledge (e.g., Archimedes could not melt down Hiero's crown and recast it as a rectangular block to facilitate computation of its volume; Kepler could not account for observed deviations in what turned out to be an elliptical orbit of Mars by appealing to the conventional circular orbits of Copernican astronomy, etc.). When this happens, the situation is "blocked," to use Koestler's term, although the realization that this is so might not be immediately forthcoming. (Allegiance to paradigms dies hard, so to speak. Kepler spent six years and produced some 9,000 pages of calculations in a futile attempt to account for the "elliptical discrepancy" in the Martian orbit.) This mental constipation is indicated by the line meandering aimlessly across the horizontal plan in Figure 2.1—a mind running in circles like a rat in a maze. At this juncture stress resultant from frustration often causes temporary abandonment of the problem as other events are allowed to intervene and, on the conscious plane at least, the issue is forgotten. In these intervals of distractedness, subconscious allegiance to the established paradigm weakens or, in some dramatic cases, disappears altogether, and a period of more or less random trial and error ensues which allows for the discovery of hidden analogies between previously unconnected frames of reference. The bisociative act is Poincaré's "manifest sign of long, unconscious prior work" and the creative spark which heralds the emergence of a new synthesis.

Two aspects of this discussion of creativity deserve emphasis. First, although it is perhaps easiest to illustrate these processes by recourse to examples of Kuhn's "scientific revolutions," it is evident that a continuum is involved which is characterized by a constant interplay of conscious reasoning, on the one hand, and sudden flashes of creative insight, on the other. From this perspective the bisociative act is *an integral part of the reasoning process itself*, whether the problem confronted is of "paradigmatic" dimensions (and thus likely to be concerned with broad "theoretical" issues), or whether it is concerned with the relatively circumscribed operational aspects of the research process that we are accustomed to regard as "methodological."

Second, let me underscore the fact that at whatever level and in every case, a *synthesis* of preexisting facts, ideas, and concepts takes place that entails a recombination of these elements rather than an "act of creation" in the biblical sense of the word. Nothing is created ex nihilo, and novelty lies in the restructuring of familiar parts which, once extracted from their habitual contexts, become transformed into a dazzling new whole. As noted above, it is paradoxical that the more familiar the parts, the more obvious the synthesis seems to be after the fact.[2]

Some Observations on Archaeological Research

How well does this discussion of creativity in mathematics, physics and chemistry square with notions of the creative process in archaeology? It must be admitted that only the most optimistic reader would be able to detect in archaeology something akin to the bisociative act at the level of paradigm. On some reflection, most readers could probably come up with examples at lower levels, perhaps in those aspects of the research process which it has become fashionable to call "middle range theory" (Binford 1981).

In thinking about my own research (on Pleistocene hunter-gatherer adaptations in northern Spain), two instances of something akin to the kind of bisociation described by Koestler come to mind. One was at the comparatively low level of ransacking data for pattern, the other was in the context of trying to explain different lines of evidence obtained from a long-term, multidisciplinary, "paleoecological" research project.

An Example of Pattern Recognition

In 1974 I was occupied with writing up my own test excavations and studies of museum collections from several Cantabrian Solutrean and Lower Magdalenian sites. I had been doing this in a conventional "site report" fashion, explaining why a particular site was chosen for testing, describing the environmental setting, discussing the results of prior work, the artifacts and faunal remains recovered, and concluding with inferences about possible relationships among other apparently similar, apparently contemporaneous sites.

I had classified the retouched pieces according to the widely used de Sonneville Bordes-Perrot typology for the Upper Paleolithic, seeking to identify and compare "normatively" defined assemblage types. I noticed by chance that the statistical summaries for some supposedly distinct Solutrean and Lower Magdalenian assemblages were sometimes closely similar to one another, whatever the differences in their archaeological "index fossils" might have meant. To this point I had tended to accept the basic "reality" of the classic culture/stratigraphic designations (e.g., Lower Magdalenian, Solutrean, etc.) as primary analytical units and was attempting to see whether there might be some basis for differentiating *within* them in terms of site function.

The realization that strong patterns *crosscut* these supposedly primary units opened a Pandora's box that ultimately caused me to question their temporal and compositional integrity and to reject them as meaningful analytical units. Subsequent work demonstrated the existence of two major assemblage types which varied completely independently on these and other "classic" culture/stratigraphic units (Clark 1974/5; Clark and Clark 1975).

This work was not conducted in isolation, of course, and it is scarcely coincidental that Lawrence Straus (University of New Mexico) was reaching similar conclusions about similar areas of variability in Cantabrian data, and at about the same time (Straus 1975). Since Straus and I are "products" of a similar intellectual tradition (both University of Chicago Ph.Ds in the early/mid-1970s) and were aware of criticisms beginning to be made of the variety-minimizing phylogenetic approaches then in vogue in French prehistory, only closed-minded adherence to a normative paradigm would have prevented recognition of patterns which were "anomalous" within the context of the normal science of the time.

An Example of the Emergence of an Explanation Candidate

The second example is drawn from the history of the La Riera Paleoecological Project (1976/81). The original research design for the project was developed by me and Straus in 1975 (Clark and Straus 1975, 1977; Straus and Clark 1978). Aware of the prevailing emphasis on "confirmatory" data analysis, we structured the research design in terms of a series of hypotheses, which were "nested" or hierarchical in the sense that they had to be evaluated in order (from simple to complex). The hypotheses expressed relatively deterministic relationships between "primary" variables. Some examples:

Is there a direct relationship between Late Würm climatic oscillations and vectored change in hunting strategies?
Can we detect differences in the intensity of use/occupation of La Riera over either/both the "long" or "short" term?
Are there systematic, covariant relationships between artifact inventories and faunal debris categories?

Over the years, as the results of the various components of the research design became available to us, we tried to make sense out of an increasingly complex mass of ecological information encoded in the abundant La Riera industries, faunas, floras, sediments, etc., and to integrate the La Riera data with those from other Cantabrian Upper Paleolithic and Mesolithic sites. Efforts at reconciling different analyses proved frustrating within the confining frame of the hypotheses, and the relatively simple, deterministic relationships they embodied ultimately had to be discarded as inadequate for describing observed patterns of variability. We were in need of an explanation for the "big picture"—the collectivity of La Riera data and those from other Late Pleistocene Cantabrian sites. The "big picture" showed vectored change in subsistence data, but it could not be correlated with changes in climate nor with the composition of the archaeological industries. The results of earlier work (see above) had caused us to abandon the notion that most behavioral change could be explained by invoking correlations with the allegedly "cultural" entities used to explain pattern in the French Upper Paleolithic. But what could we propose in place of the phylogenetic paradigm?

After considerable soul-searching, we decided to concentrate primarily on explaining pattern in our most abundant, consistent, and reliable data sets, the mammalian and molluscan faunas, which showed increasing diversity over time and indications of intensification in the food quest. As no climate factors could be invoked to account for these patterns, we were led to the conclusion that the inhabitants of the area were moved to increase the diversity of their subsistence base (even to the extent of collecting more labor-intensive, lower-yield, higher-risk foods) by an increasingly dense local population which was fast outstripping its "traditional" resources. The hypothesis of demographic stress was supported by increases in mean site numbers per culture/stratigraphic unit over time, and by other categories of faunal evidence which cannot be explained by recourse to climatic change arguments. The tentative explanation was then tested in a wider temporal and spatial frame (Clark and Yi 1983).

Although we arrived at an explanation very different from that predicted in our original set of hypotheses, in a sense our conclusions were determined beforehand by what were at the time latent (or only partially conscious) preconceptions about what causes change in hunter-gatherer sociocultural systems. We subscribe to the view that sociocultural systems represent ordered, functionally differentiated and integrated adjustments to their natural and cultural environments, and we sought to develop reasonable, defensible monitors of the behavioral variables we wished to examine. While we came to the conclusion, in the absence of evidence to the contrary, that causal priority must be accorded to increasing stress over time on the resources available to the prehistoric Cantabrians, and that a general tendency on the part of human populations to increase might ultimately be responsible for that stress (Dumond 1972; Cohen 1977), it is important to recognize that the orientation of this research determined not only how it was organized, what variables were considered relevant to monitor in the "archaeological context," what hypothetical relationships among variables might have obtained, but also, and most important, the *adequacy* of any proposed explanations (Clark 1982). We did not realize this all at once, "in a flash of insight," nor did we perceive clearly and immediately the relationship between the particulars of the various La Riera data sets and our most general "explanation" for patterns observed in them. This is how archaeological research seems to be conducted, however, and I suspect that the two preceding anecdotes might strike a familiar chord in those who have actually tried to come to grips with large and complex data bases. Hindsight is wonderful stuff in the sloppy, complicated world of "real" archaeology!

We saw that Koestler (1964), Ghiselin (1952), Hadamard (1949), Findlay (1948), and others argue that there are recurrent features in the creative process which admit of some generalization, and that these can be identified by inspection of the self-conscious accounts of the research endeavors of scientists (and the creative efforts of artists) who have recorded their struggles at problem solving for posterity. It seems, though, that there is a discrepancy between notions of creativity in archaeology and anthropology, on the one hand, and the bisociative act in some of the "hard" sciences, on the other. This section addresses three issues related to this observation: (1) What makes archaeology and anthropology different from some other sciences in regard to the relationship between the empirical and the theoretical? (2) Is Meltzer really correct in arguing that archaeology has not witnessed a "scientific revolution"? (3) Is there any indication of the emergence of general archaeological theory?

The Empirical and the Theoretical in Archaeology and Anthropology

In my 1982 paper I made a distinction between disciplines that were primarily "experimental" and those that were primarily "observational" (Clark 1982: 219). I suggested that anthropology was generally an observational science, although there were differences in the extent to which its constituent subdisciplines were experimental. This condition is probably true of all of the social sciences, which tend to cluster at the "observational" end of a continuum between these two polar positions. The carefully controlled laboratory experiments characteristic of some of the natural sciences are usually absent in social science research, as are the exercises in pure logic which are so prominent a feature of theoretical mathematics and physics. Indeed, the essence of a laboratory experiment is to detect the operation of linear causality in an environment in which the effects of all important, relevant variables have been determined beforehand (Blalock 1972: 6).

Causality in anthropology, on the other hand, is generally considered to be multivariate and reticulate, rather than linear, so it is expectable that instances of the "bisociative act" would be much more difficult to detect. Recognizing the impossibility of studying the undifferentiated cultural whole (Binford 1962), what we do in the context of a particular research problem is to break down the system into circumscribed (and therefore manageable) constituent parts. This means that the kinds of relationships that we might expect to "bisociate" would most readily be observed at the level of "middle range theory," where operational definitions of behavioral variables must be made explicit. It is at these "middle" and "lower" levels in the research process that archaeology most closely approximates a laboratory science. If it is granted that archaeology is primarily an observational discipline, that it has for its subject matter past human social behavior, that past social behavior is not directly observable and took place in a complex natural and social setting, and that a host of natural and cultural processes have intervened between the phenomena which are the objects of our investigations (i.e., human social behavior) and the static and partial residues of those phenomena (i.e., the archaeological record), it is not surprising that archaeology appears to be distinct from disciplines characterized by finite, determinate causal relationships.

We would like, of course, to think that archaeological research is all of a piece, guided by "general" theory (which presumably derives from anthropology), and that archaeological theory and archaeological fieldwork should proceed hand in hand. On inspection, however, this turns out not to be the case. "In practice, archaeologists conduct fieldwork or they theorize—rarely both" (Thomas 1983: 8) (or if they do both, they do not do them simultaneously—Flannery [1982]). Why is there such a schism between the "archaeologist as theoretician" and the "archaeologist as practitioner," especially in light of widespread recognition that the challenge of all science is to test our theories against the reality of the empirical world? Thomas (1983: 8, 9) makes the interesting observation that the "new archaeology" of the 1960s began as a theoretical *and* methodological endeavor in which advances in field technique were to generate new and better data, which would in turn be brought to bear on novel theoretical issues. What seems to have happened since then is that emphasis has been placed on innovative methods, but archaeologists have failed to integrate these with theory, old or new.

If Meltzer is correct in saying that the archaeological metaphysic remains that of American anthropology, the reason for the schism between the theoretical and empirical aspects of contemporary archaeology is easily discerned. We have no paradigm "with a capital P" because anthropology itself no longer has a single metaphysic (def.: system of principles underlying the study of a particular discipline). We should be looking to anthropological theory for change at the level of Paradigm, but anthropology is becoming ever more fragmented as witness the proliferation of special interest groups under the aegis of the American Anthropological Association and the defection of some major units, including the Society of American Archaeology, from the AAA following the reorganization of 1983/84. In default of another Darwin, it seems unlikely that "all the king's horses and all the king's men will ever be able to put Humpety Dumpety back together again." Most workers appear to respond to this situation by contenting themselves with paradigms at lower levels—internally consistent sets of concepts and relationships that determine a problem domain within the confines of their own particular set of interests. This, of course, forces them to confront another familiar occupant of the archaeologist's "closet of anxieties"— the Particularist/Generalist Paradox. How does one avoid the Scylla of normative, empirical generalization (which usually explains little observed variability) and the Charybdis of the particular case (which accounts for diversity in a single instance but does not explain it in a theoretically cohesive fashion) (see, e.g., Winterhalder and Smith 1981: 4)? While some might regard the absence of a "paradigm with a capital P" as unfortunate (I think we all tend to imagine a "golden age" of archaeology, when the "big picture" was apparent to everyone), it does little good to turn our backs on the present, less-palatable (although intellectually more stimulating) reality.

Back to the "Revolution"

Part of Meltzer's (1979) argument that archaeology had not undergone a paradigm shift is rooted in criticisms of the paradigm concept itself, as articulated by Kuhn (1962) and criticized by other historians of science. In an early review, Shapere (1964, 1971) pointed out that Kuhn's usage of the term is vague, contradictory, and expresses a range of possible meanings extending from the most inclusive level of the disciplinary metaphysic, to intermediate levels corresponding to somewhat contrastive "approaches" within a discipline, to packages of methodologies and techniques. Masterman (1970) subsequently refined this by identifying paradigms at three levels of scales corresponding to (1) that of the metaphysic, (2) the sociology of a discipline (a set of scientific habits), and (3) artifact or construct paradigms (methodologies, techniques) (1970: 65). She made the point that these are inclusive categories and that the metaphysical paradigm can incorporate more than one sociological, and many construct, paradigms. It thus becomes exceedingly difficult to distinguish change at different paradigm "levels," except perhaps in an impressionistic or conceptual sense (e.g., there is the impression of much methodological change in post-1960s archaeology) (Figures 2.2, 2.3). On the basis of these observations, Meltzer (1979) goes on to examine the extent to which the Kuhn model is an accurate representation of archaeological change. In particular, he notes that

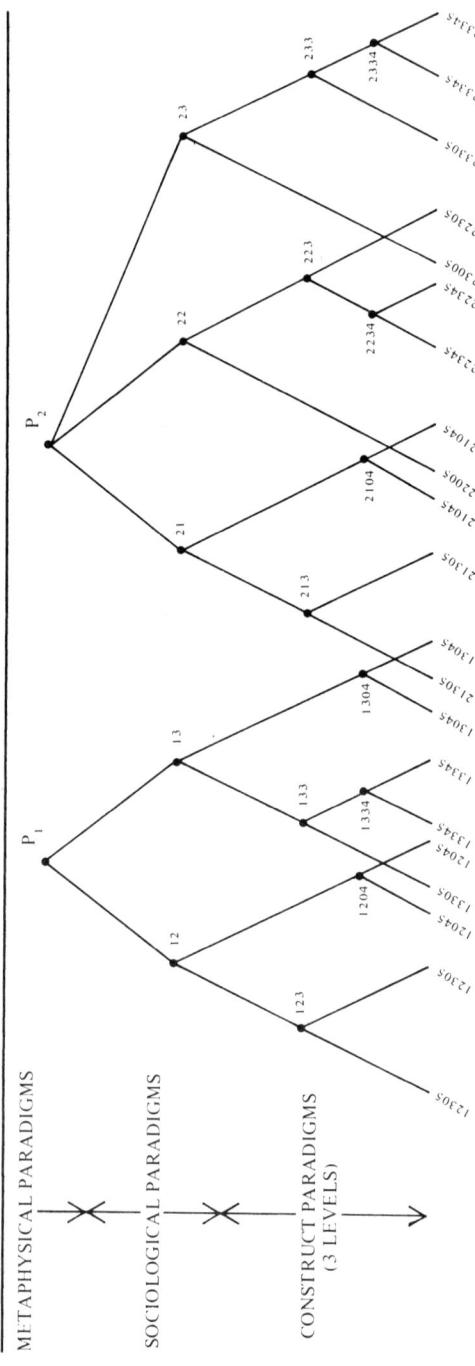

Figure 2.2 A schematic representation of Masterman's (1970) metaphysical, sociological, and construct paradigms. Metaphysical Paradigm P_1 has two and P_2 has three sociological paradigms. Each of these in turn contains a variable number of overlapping construct paradigms, themselves characterized by three levels. Paradigm boundaries below the level of the metaphysic are typically ill-defined. Practically all archaeological applications of quantitative methods are at the level of the construct paradigm.

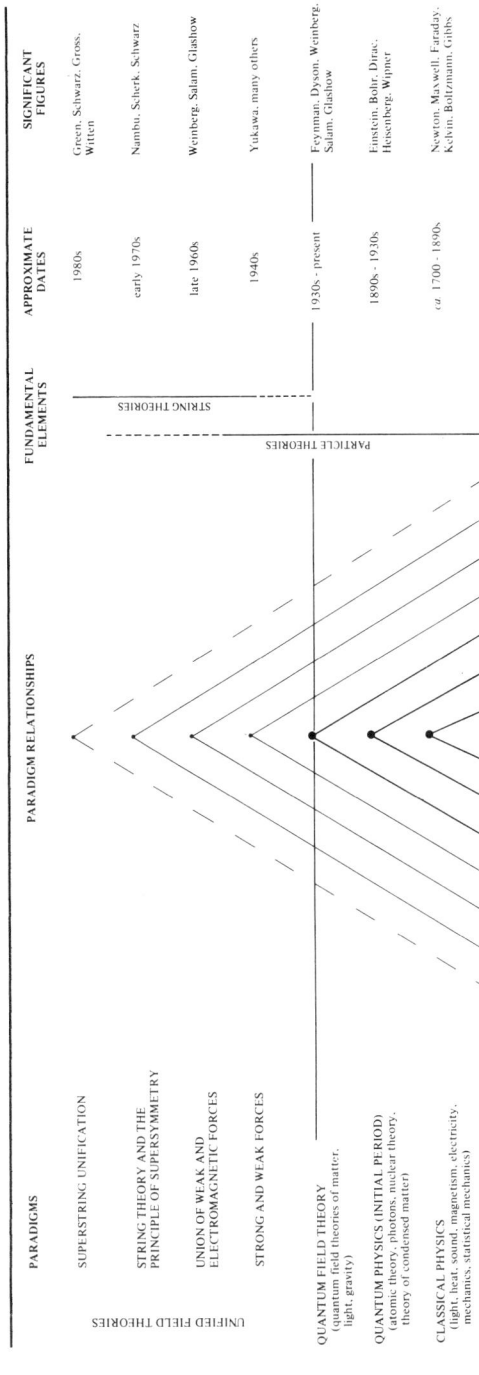

Figure 2.3 A schematic view of metaphysical paradigms in physics research from the 1750s until the present. Physics is the discipline most often modeled by philosophers and historians of science. There are three "epochs" in physics research that correspond to changes at the level of the metaphysic. Notice, however, that the paradigms are more and more comprehensive over time, absorbing and explaining phenomena that defied explanation under earlier models. An approximation of a Kuhnian "revolution" might correspond to the redefinition of fundamental elements from the particles (infinitesimal points) that had been the conventional analytical units through about 1970 to equally tiny, wriggling lines (or "strings"") (Waldrop, 1985).

the near-total incompatibility of successive metaphysical paradigms seems to be absent in the history of American archaeology and offers Thompson's (1972) notion of cumulative, gradual change as more appropriate than the "punctuated equilibrium" model of Kuhn. While much change is acknowledged, most of it is argued to be methodological in nature.[3]

On Change and Laws

The question of change and where it is taking place is closely connected to the issues of "laws" and claims that archaeological theory can be relatively independent of anthropology. Archaeologists have traditionally been relegated to the role of "law consumers" (Reid, Rathje, and Schiffer 1974), who are perhaps capable of testing hypotheses but who apparently are incapable of making independent contributions to the study of human social process on the same order of magnitude as those of social and cultural anthropologists. Meltzer's portrait of post-1960s archaeology raises the interesting question of whether or not independent archaeological theory can be claimed to exist. Put another way, is archaeological theory above the level of methodology wholly dependent on ethnographic data, ethnographic analogy, or other anthropological sources? Are there any indications of the emergence of elements of general archaeological theory, and if so, might the outlines of a new metaphysical paradigm be discernible?

There is no simple or obvious answer to this question. On the level of the metaphysic, as we have seen, the answer presently appears to be "no"—"archaeology is anthropology or it is nothing." However, inspection of the literature reveals the existence of general theory (law candidates with explanatory potential) at or above the level of Masterman's sociological metaphysic. Since archaeologists cannot observe past hominid behavior directly, it is necessary to establish a basis for behaviorally meaningful theoretical statements whose primary referent is the archaeological record itself (Wilcox and Sullivan 1978). We have seen that "middle range" theory operates to accomplish this at intermediate levels, but what about the level of general theory? What do some of these candidates for archaeological theory look like? If they are to have general interest, they must resolve the Particularist-Generalist Paradox, reinterpret previously recognized patterns in new and insightful ways, and synthesize under a common framework phenomena which were previously uncoordinated (Gould and Eldredge 1977). Perhaps the best examples with which I am familiar come from Thomas's initial volume on the structure of the long-term Monitor Valley archaeological project, in central Nevada (Thomas 1983).

Archaeological Theory, Binford, and the Monitor Valley Project: The Particularist-Generalist Paradox Revisited

Cast in a general framework of hunter-gatherer ecology, Thomas begins with a discussion of Steward's (1968) forager-collector continuum, as recently articulated by Binford (1980). The forager-collector dichotomy is presented as a graduated range of organizational strategies along which hunter-gatherer mobility and subsistence practices can be scaled. From one perspective, foragers and collectors are idealized typological constructs characterized by distinct kinds of subsistence-related residential moves (foragers bring customers to resources by "mapping on" in largely undifferentiated environments, collectors use logistical food procurement strategies that move resources to consumers). From another perspective, they identify variables that can be monitored in the archaeological context and that can be operationally defined (although they often are not— e.g., site distributions in geographic space, economic zonation, patterns of faunal transport and discard, etc.). From a third perspective, they represent polar positions on a long-term evolutionary trajectory (i.e., logistical strategies practiced by collectors become more common through time as hominids evolve into the contemporary form). From a fourth perspective, they predict what kinds of strategies would be most prevalent at particular latitudes (e.g., Binford's hypothesized general relationship between storage and effective temperature). All of these perspectives (and there are many others) *constitute expectations about the subsistence behavior of hunter-gatherers that can be tested and that, if supported, are susceptible to generalization* (although it should be noted that empirical support for any of them is presently almost nonexistent).

A reading of Binford (1980) resulted in the following "lawlike" generalizations:

(1) The greater the number of generic functions a site may serve, the greater the number of (activity combinations) and the greater the range of intersite variability (p. 12).
(2) Greater ranges of intersite variability are a function of (bigger) logistical components in the subsistence-settlement system (p. 12).
(3) The greater the seasonal variability in temperature, the greater the importance of logistical mobility in the (site positioning) strategy (p. 15).
(4) (Since storage reduced temporal incongruity in resource phasing), the importance of storage facilities will vary with the length of the growing season (p. 15).
(5) As the length of the growing season decreases, logistical strategies will become more important in the settlement-subsistence system (p. 18).
(6) Other things being equal, we may anticipate regular environmentally correlated patterns of intersite variability deriving from increases in the number and kind of special purpose sites with decreases in the length of the growing season (p. 19).

These lawlike generalizations apply to different levels of analysis (some are "middle range") but all are restatements or corrollaries of the most comprehensive of them—No. 6. They are variously substantiated empirically (Binford sought to support them by reference to data in Murdock's ethnographic atlas [1973]). They are nontrivial and can be tested if operational definitions of basic, relevant variables can be developed. They are, in a sense, "timeless and spaceless." They are, furthermore, not directly dependent on ethnographic information and so could be argued to be components of a quasi-independent archaeological theory of hunter-gatherer adaptation. They may be as close as we are likely to come to law candidates in archaeological theory *at a general level.*

Thomas (1983: 12-15) has pointed out, however, that statements like those above nevertheless remain empirical generalizations and can therefore be criticized from the standpoint of the Particularist-Generalist Paradox. How do we avoid normative descriptions of static, hunter-gatherer ecological relationships while simultaneously explaining both "modal" behavior and anomalies—the particular cases that do not fit the modal pattern (and for that reason are perhaps most informative)? Variability should be of interest and concern to those attempting to explain ecological diversity among hunter-gatherers, and a truly comprehensive approach should be able to take it into account. Ideally we should be able to draw upon hundreds of crosscultural case studies, all meticulously documented and "warranted," in order to be able to extract principles of sufficient generality to have global explanatory potential (Naroll 1973). A moment's reflection, however, shows just how unrealistic this approach would be. At a bare minimum there are insurmountable problems with comparability of data sets linked to different variables chosen for analysis, different operational definitions of those variables, and differences in sampling designs. Another tack would be to hold time (and systemic change) constant and concentrate instead on some kind of absolute standard (e.g., optimal adaptation, as defined by optimal foraging theorists) and then evaluate the particular case in terms of the extent to which it departs from "optimality." However, optimal foraging theory (and optimization models in general) have often been criticized for an inability to deal with systemic change, and there seem to be inherent, probably unresolvable problems with the notion of optimal behavior itself (see Martin 1983 for an extended critique of optimal foraging theory). By holding temporal and regional variability constant, we ignore two of the best sources of input for understanding the dynamics of hunter-gatherer adaptation.

The Particularist-Generalist Paradox is a problem in *any* discipline, but its effects are exacerbated in an eclectic field like archaeology, where there is little agreement even about what to investigate. We are essentially in the predicament of trying to come up with an equivalent to controlled laboratory experimentation in a social science where the unit of analysis is often an entire social system removed from us in time. Naroll (1973) has made the point that "experiments" on societies are impossible on a variety of practical and ethical grounds (e.g., too costly; process is long-term process and change cannot be detected in the short run; the subjects are people, not laboratory animals, etc.). Yet the archaeological record contains the remains of thousands of such experiments. The problem is to be able to monitor them effectively. Thomas (1983: 16, 17) notes (quoting Hill 1977: 91) that in order to be able to test theories regarding system change, we must be in a position to (1) describe the system and its homeostatic processes prior to the suspected change, (2) isolate extrasystemic factors that might promote change and show how preexisting homeostatic mechanisms failed to regulate them, (3) indicate why it would have been adaptive for the system to change, and (4) show how the system would reestablish equilibrium at a new (usually higher) level of integration. Any adequate theory of hunter-gatherer adaptation must be able to accommodate change at both the micro- and macroevolutionary scales, but data pertinent to the former are especially difficult to acquire because of the poor resolution and integrity characteristic of most of the archaeological record. It seems clear that adequate theory must be grounded in a combination of global hologeistic approaches (from which general theory arises) and fine-grained empirically well-founded regional case studies of adaptive change if we are to explain (rather than "explain away") variability in hunter-gatherer adaptive strategies (Thomas 1983: 17). This will require a bigger "middle-range theory" component in most research areas if we are to build convincing links between our ideas about the world of the past and the depauperate physical remains of that world actually available for study.

Quantification and the Research Process

Since this is a book about quantitative approaches in archaeology, the reader might wonder where quantified research designs fit into the research scenarios discussed above. As was the case with laws, I think that we are still pretty much in the position of "consumers" of quantitative methods, albeit increasingly sophisticated consumers—a situation that is unlikely to change in the foreseeable future. While it can be documented that the *amount* of quantification is increasing dramatically in various aspects of the discipline (see, e.g., Clark and Stafford 1982), the *contribution* of extensively quantified research designs has been, and is likely to continue to be, somewhat limited. I think there are two reasons for this.

First, although archaeologists are becoming more sophisticated in their appreciation of the descriptive potential of (especially multivariate) quantitative approaches, it is quite simply a fact that inquiry at the ordinal or even nominal level is usually more appropriate for most archaeological data sets. This is because of the poor resolution (coarse "grain," weak integrity, incomplete data matrices, high probability of sampling error) characteristic of most of the archaeological record. While we might be able to create sophisticated mathematical approximations of human systems of various kinds, we usually are in no position to evaluate their credibility very effectively. In fact Perlman (1977: 326) has remarked that "some archaeologists may find that the real challenge at the present time, lies, paradoxically, in the use of *qualitative* models." There is a growing malaise about overquantification (see, e.g., Thomas 1978), and at some point those of us *who actually do field research* must ask ourselves whether the formal elegance of sophisticated mathematical models has not blinded us to the eventual necessity of comparing them to the ugly reality of actual data. Since such a comparison is ultimately required if we are serious about the research endeavor, it could be argued that an untestable model, no matter how intuitively appealing it might be, is ultimately a useless model, constituting no more than a disingenuous form of speculation, cloaked in the garb of "real science." These considerations suggest to me that we will increasingly seek to develop explanations based on evaluations of ordinal or qualitative data (see, e.g., Clark and Straus 1983). This means greater use of relatively assumption free, robust, data-ransacking, pattern-search techniques (e.g., exploratory data analysis [Tukey 1977, 1979, 1980; Hartwig and Dearing 1979]), models based on ordinally scaled variables, rank-order statistical evaluations of goodness of fit, and a comparative deemphasis on standard multivariate numerical summaries and the "confirmatory" modes of data analysis that have dominated the field since the statistical revolution of the mid-1970s. Most of this will take place in the context of "middle-range theory"; ordinal scale analysis is all that is usually warranted for such applications.

A second reason for taking a cautious view of archaeological quantification is that sophisticated model-building is at best an elaborate *description* of a phenomenon of interest. In and of itself, it does not (indeed, cannot) provide an *explanation* of that phenomenon. That must come from the researcher and is ultimately a subjective process inextricably linked to and conditioned by a multiplicity of factors that cannot be disentangled, controlled, or even appreciated directly. I tend to think of this dilemma mainly in terms of systems theory, but it is a problem with many sophisticated forms of mathematical modeling. Where does explanation of the characteristics of a particular system trajectory lie? Mathematical systems theory has developed to the point where it consists of a series of conventions that are probably largely unrealistic whenever they are applied to a "real" problem (I might add that this observation is probably true for all but the simplest systems, whether physical, chemical, biological, social etc.). At what point does an exhaustive description of a phenomenon of interest become an explanation of that phenomenon? In my opinion, the answer is probably "never."

And yet these conventions, which are most problematical when applied to complex phenomena, are an integral part of *any* potential explanation. The "explanation" is really integral to the mathematics of systems theory itself, rather than constituting an explanation of a particular system of archaeological interest. The same might be said of much mathematical modeling.

Concordance in Data Structure and Analysis

The major implication of these observations is not, of course, that archaeologists should eschew quantitative approaches, but rather that they should pay more attention to the extent to which methods are appropriate to the data to be analyzed. It is often assumed that logically coherent relationships obtain between theoretical populations, analytical methods and the data samples to which they are applied, but in fact this is an area where archaeologists have been notably remiss (see Carr [1985a] for a book-length treatment of concordance among theory, methods, and data). We sometimes forget that data are characterized by many and various structures, only some of which are relevant to a particular phenomenon of interest. Moreover, we bring with us *expectations* about what data structures are present in a given data base. We typically proceed by choosing variables intuitively in terms of their potential relevance to a broad problem domain that comprises not one but many phenomena of interest (Clark 1982: 232-235). We also typically choose analytical techniques on the basis of a supposed concordance between their constraining assumptions, expectations about the structure of the phenomenon of interest, and expectations about how those phenomena might be reflected in actual data sets (Carr 1985: 8-10). In fact, however, we are not usually in a position to know with certainty whether those assumptions of concordance are realistic or not. At this juncture, researchers either ignore these issues of agreement altogether (especially in regard to concordance between the theoretical population about which we wish to make references and the sample actually evaluated), or they begin with a number of possibly relevant variables, ransack them for pattern, and decide after the fact which ones show some sort of structure which is meaningful in behavioral terms (Cowgill 1982: 39). These problems result in two kinds of discordance between actual data structures and our assumptions about them (Carr 1985: 8-10):

(1) Since variables are chosen in relation to a broad problem domain, they reflect multiple processes that determine multiple (theoretical) populations. However, most analytical techniques either use statistical models that assume that a *single* process accounts for observed variability or they use models that specify multiple but parallel and coterminous processes, again resulting in the definition of a single population. Analytical results will therefore be "discordant" since they confound several kinds of relationships between multiple populations of observations (see also Christenson and Read 1977; Read 1985).

(2) Since any data set will have multiple structures (many different kinds of relationships between variables and observations), only some will directly indicate a phenomenon of interest. Analytical results will be discordant if the structure of the phenomenon of interest in the actual data set is different from the structure that the investigator expects to be expressed in that data set. Expectations about structure typically determine choice of an analytical technique. Therefore a discrepancy between the actual nature of the phenomenon of interest, its expression in the data, and its supposed structure can lead to quantitative results that are meaningless or uninterpretable (Carr 1985c).

Carr (1985b: 10) remarks that these major kinds of discordance are usually features of the early stages of an analysis when the researcher might know relatively little about the nature of data structures and the extent to which they are likely to be expressed in a sample (also see Clark [1982: 232-234] for a discussion of the mental gymnastics that surround generation of what I refer to as a "behavioral hypothesis"). These discordances can also recur in the later stages of an analysis if the investigator has not been relatively successful in isolating the kinds and probable causes of variability in a data set.

The obvious general solution to the problem of understanding data structures is to try to learn as much as possible about them *before* they are used in any formalized evaluation of hypothesized relationships (Clark 1982: 250). In commonsense terms, this means as much "data snooping" as possible and relegation of "confirmatory" hypothesis testing to the final stages in an analysis.[4] I think that the by now traditional concern with confirmatory modes of analysis in archaeology has led to a misplaced emphasis on hypothesis testing that is inappropriate given the incomplete data sets and the complex, multivariate causal relationships that are a feature of all social (and much natural) science research. It has also tended to delay archaeological recognition and use of recently developed alternative approaches to quantification that circumvent the relatively simple, linear, deterministic causal models that underlie most applications of classic Neymann-Pearson statistics (e.g., Tukey 1977; McNeil 1977; Hartwig and Dearing 1979; Leinhardt and Wasserman 1979).

Conclusions

In this essay I offer what is admittedly a personal view of the research endeavor in archaeology, but one founded on the commonly held notions that past human behavior is knowable, that propositions about the past are testable, and that there are valid scientific criteria for evaluating the credibility of statements about the past (Binford 1968; Watson et al. 1971). At the most basic level, it is assumed that there is a real, knowable, empirically observable, orderly world out there, and that a portion of it comprising aspects of past human behavior can be isolated for study. Information about the world can be subdivided into phenomena of interest, data collected in the context of a problem domain that includes phenomena of interest (Carr's "total data structure"), aspects of data that are relevant to a particular phenomenon of interest (Carr's "relevant data structure"), and aspects of data that are expected to be relevant to a particular phenomenon of interest (Carr 1985b: 12, 13). These categories of information stand in an increasingly specific relationship to one another and serve to progressively isolate portions of the "real" world (Figure 2.4). Most readers will probably share this basic metaphysical perspective; however, we might differ among ourselves regarding lower-level paradigms. These simple statements about concepts that bear on the research endeavor belie an enormous amount of complexity, of course, and it is tempting to treat them as if we really knew what they meant in detail. Such things are enormously difficult for us to understand, and yet all of them are intrinsic features of the "doing" of archaeological research.

Beginning with a statement of biases about aspects of the recent history of American archaeology, I proceeded to examine different notions of change in the discipline in an effort to show where archaeology "fits" in the broader context of anthropology. I then outlined some general characteristics of the creative process at different levels in science and mathematics and tried to compare these notions with examples of creativity in archaeology using prehistoric hunter-gatherer research projects in Spain in which I had participated. It was determined that "fit" was poor at the highest levels because of the fragmentation of anthropology itself and because the classic Kuhnian notion of revolutionary change works best in disciplines characterized by cohesive, well-established metaphysical paradigms (and that often have a major experimental component or

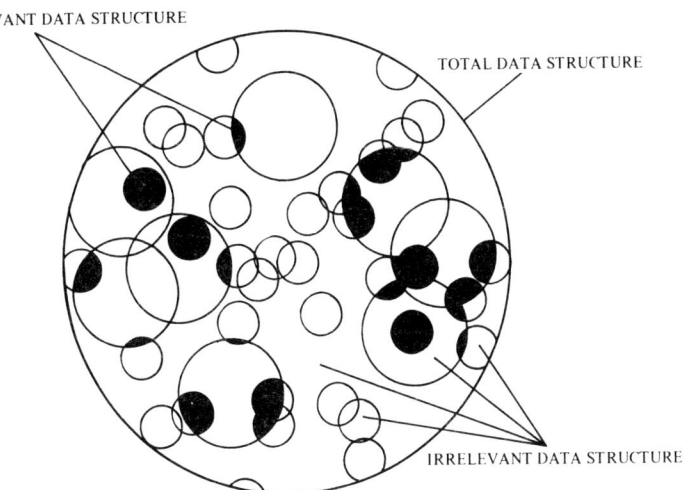

Figure 2.4 A schematic representation of Carr's (1985c) categories of information about the real world. Expected data structure (not shown) may correspond poorly, well, or not at all to relevant data structure.

are exercises in pure logic). This led to a discussion of the empirical and theoretical in archaeology and anthropology and to the *bête noire* of all scientific endeavor—the Particularist-Generalist Paradox. While it can be shown that there are "lawlike" theoretical propositions in archaeology that have the characteristics of empirical generalizations, the challenge of future work will be to make these more credible through "middle-range" research. The essay finished with a brief assessment of the contribution of quantified research designs in archaeology and appeals for more extensive pattern searching to elucidate data structures, greater use of nominal and rank-order statistical models, and greater concordance between archaeological data and the methods used to analyze them.

Notes

1. Galois's activities on the night before his death must stand as a monument to consummate professionalism!

2. The impact of creative endeavors on a discipline is of course very variable depending on the "scale" of the creative act, but also on the extent to which it is publicized. In addition to "originality" (independent, flexible ways of solving problems), the persistence of the "creator" in promoting novel ideas plays a major role in their eventual acceptance.

3. For a view of revolution in science that emphasizes the intellectual history of the concept of "revolution" itself, and the nature of change associated with great leaders and movements, see Cohen (1985). For a discussion of the organizational structure of "big science" and its impact on university-based control of scientific work in the archetypal "big science" (physics) and in other fields, see Whitley (1985).

4. I refer to this as "pattern searching without guilt," an allusion to the "wine without guilt" slogan of the Bully Hill Vineyards in up-state New York!

Acknowledgments

I thank Chris Carr (Department of Anthropology) for bringing his recently published book to my attention, and Robert Marzke and Richard Jacob (Department of Physics) for valuable advice in the preparation of Figure 2.3.

References

Binford, L. 1962. Archaeology as anthropology. *American Antiquity* 28(2): 217-225.
Binford, L. 1968. Archaeological perspectives. In *New Perspectives in Archaeology*, eds. S. R. Binford and L. R. Binford, pp. 5-32. Chicago: Aldine.
Binford, L. 1980. Willow smoke and dogs' tails: hunter-gatherer settlement systems and archaeological site formation. *American Antiquity* 45(1): 4-20.
Binford, L. 1981. *Bones: Ancient Men and Modern Myths*. New York: Academic Press.
Blalock, H. 1972. *Social Statistics* (2nd ed.). New York: McGraw Hill.
Carr, C. 1985a. (Ed.) *For Concordance in Archaeological Analysis*. Kansas City: Westport Publishers.
Carr, C. 1985b. Perspective and basic definitions. In *For Concordance in Archaeological Analysis*, pp. 1-17.
Carr, C. 1985c. Getting into data: philosophy and tactics for the analysis of complex data structures. In *For Concordance in Archaeological Analysis*, pp. 18-44.
Clark, G. 1974/5. Excavations in the late Pleistocene cave site of Balmori, Asturias (Spain). *Quaternaria* 18: 383-426.
Clark, G. 1982. Quantifying archaeological research. In *Advances in Archaeological Method and Theory*, ed. M. Schiffer, pp. 217-273. New York: Academic Press.
Clark, G. and V. Clark. 1975. La cueva de Balmori (Asturias, Espana). *Trabajos de Prehistoria* 32: 35-77.
Clark, G. and C. R. Stafford. 1982. Quantification in American archaeology: an historical perspective. *World Archaeology* 14(1): 98-119.

Clark, G. and L. Straus. 1975. Paleoecology at La Riera: late Pleistocene hunter-gatherer adaptations in Cantabrian Spain. Proposal submitted to the National Science Foundation, Washington, D.C.

Clark, G. and L. Straus. 1977. Cueva de La Riera: objetivo del "Proyecto Paleoecológico" e informe preliminar de la campana de 1976. *Boletin del Instituto de Estudios Asturianos* 91: 489-505.

Clark, G. and L. Straus. 1983. Late Pleistocene hunter-gatherer adaptations in Cantabrian Spain. In *Hunter-Gatherer Economy in Prehistory: a European Perspective*, ed. G. Bailey, pp. 131-148. Cambridge: Cambridge University Press.

Clark, G. and S. Yi. 1983. Niche width variation in Cantabrian archaeofaunas: a diachronic study. In *Animals and Archaeology I: Hunters and Their Prey*, eds. J. Clutton-Brock and Caroline Grigson, pp. 183-208. Oxford: British Archaeological Reports No. 163.

Cohen, I. B. 1985. *Revolution in Science*. Cambridge: Harvard University Press.

Cohen, M. 1977. *The Food Crisis in Prehistory*. New Haven: Yale University Press.

Cowgill, G. 1982. Clusters of objects and associations between variables: two approaches to archaeological classification. In *Essays on Archaeological Typology*, eds. R. Whallon and J. Brown, pp. 30-55. Evanston: Center for American Archaeology Press.

Dumond, D. 1972. Prehistoric population growth and subsistence change in Eskimo Alaska. In *Population Growth: Anthropological Implications*, ed. B. Spooner, pp. 311-328. Cambridge: MIT Press.

Findlay, A. 1948. *A Hundred Years of Chemistry* (2nd edition). London: Duckworth.

Flannery, K. 1982. The golden Marshalltown: a parable for the archaeology of the 1980s. *American Anthropologist* 84(2): 265-278.

Fowler, D. 1982. Cultural resources management. In *Advances in Archaeological Method and Theory*, ed. M. Schiffer, pp. 1-50. New York: Academic Press.

Ghiselin, B. (Ed.) 1952. *The Creative Process*. Berkeley: University of California Press.

Gould, S. and N. Eldredge. 1977. Punctuated equilibria: the tempo and mode of evolution reconsidered. *Paleobiology* 3: 115-151.

Gumerman, G. and D. Phillips. 1978. Archaeology beyond anthropology. *American Antiquity* 43(2): 184-191.

Hadamard, J. 1949. *The Psychology of Invention in the Mathematical Field*. Princeton: Princeton University Press.

Hartwig, F. and B. Dearing. 1979. *Exploratory Data Analysis*. Beverly Hills: Sage.

Hill, J. 1977. Systems theory and the explanation of change. In *Explanation of Prehistoric Change*, ed. J. Hill, pp. 59-104. Albuquerque: University of New Mexico Press.

Koestler, A. 1964. *The Act of Creation*. New York: Dell.

Kohler, W. 1957. *The Mentality of Apes*. London: Pelican Books.

Kuhn, T. 1962. *The Structure of Scientific Revolutions*. Chicago: University of Chicago Press.

Kuhn, T. 1970. Reflections on my critics. In *Criticism and the Growth of Knowledge*, eds. I. Lakatos and A. Musgrave, pp. 231-278. London: Cambridge University Press.

Kuhn, T. 1974. Second thoughts on paradigms. In *The Structure of Scientific Theories*, ed. F. Suppe, pp. 459-482. Urbana: University of Illinois Press.

Leinhardt, S. and S. Wasserman. 1979. Exploratory data analysis: an introduction to selected methods. In *Sociological Methodology 1979*, ed. K. Schuessler, pp. 311-372. San Francisco: Jossey-Bass.

Leone, M. 1972. Issues in anthropological archaeology. In *Contemporary Archaeology*, ed. M. Leone, pp. 14-27. Carbondale: Southern Illinois University Press.

Martin, J. 1983. Optimal foraging theory: a review of some models and their applications. *American Anthropologist* 85(3): 612-629.

Masterman, M. 1970. The nature of the paradigm. In *Criticism and the Growth of Knowledge*, eds. I. Lakatos and A. Musgrave, pp. 59-90. London: Cambridge University Press.

McNeil, D. 1977. *Interactive Data Analysis: a Practical Primer*. New York: Wiley.

Meltzer, D. 1979. Paradigms and the nature of change in American archaeology. *American Antiquity* 44(4): 644-657.

Murdock, G. 1967. The ethnographic atlas: a summary. *Ethnology* 6(2): 109-236.

Naroll, R. 1973a. Holocultural theory tests. In *Main Currents in Cultural Anthropology*, eds. R. Naroll and F. Naroll, pp. 309-384. New York: Appleton-Century-Crofts.

Naroll, R. 1973b. Cross-cultural sampling. In *A Handbook of Method in Cultural Anthropology*, eds. R. Naroll and R. Cohen, pp. 889-926. New York: Columbia University Press.

Perlman, M. 1977. Comments on explanation, and on stability and change. In *Explanation of Prehistoric Change*, ed. J. Hill, pp. 319-333. Albuquerque: University of New Mexico Press.

Reid, J., W. Ralthje, and M. Schiffer. 1974. Expanding archaeology. *American Antiquity* 39(1): 125,126.

Shapere, D. 1964. The structure of scientific revolutions. *The Philosophical Review* 73(2): 383-394.

Shapere, D. 1971. The paradigm concept. *Science* 172: 706-709.

Steward, J. 1968. Causal factors and processes in the evolution of pre-farming societies. In *Man the Hunter*, eds. R. Lee and I. DeVore, pp. 321-334. Chicago: Aldine.

Straus, L. 1975. ¿Solutrense o Magdaleniense inferior cantabrico?—significado de las "diferencias." *Boletin del Instituto de Estudios Asturianos* 86: 781-790.

Straus, L. 1976. A new interpretation of the Cantabrian Solutrean. *Current Anthropology* 17(2): 342,343.

Straus, L., and G. Clark. 1978. Prehistoric investigations in Cantabrian Spain. *Journal of Field Archaeology* 5(3): 287-317.

Thomas, D. H. 1978. The awful truth about statistics in archaeology. *American Antiquity* 43(2): 231-244.

Thomas, D. H. 1983. The archaeology of Monitor Valley I: Epistemology. *Anthropological Papers of the American Museum of Natural History* 58(1): 1-194.

Thompson, R. 1972. Interpretive trends and linear models in American archaeology. In *Contemporary Archaeology*, ed. M. Leone, pp. 34-38. Carbondale: Southern Illinois University Press.

Tukey, J. 1977. *Exploratory Data Analysis*. Reading: Addison-Wesley.

Tukey, J. 1979. Comment on "Non-parametric statistical data modeling." *Journal of the American Statistical Association* 74(1): 121, 122.

Tukey, J. 1980. We need both exploratory and confirmatory. *American Statistician* 34(1): 23-25.

Waldrop, M. 1985. String as a theory of everything. *Science* 229: 1251-1253.

Watson, P., S. LeBlanc, and C. Redman. 1971. *Explanation in Archaeology: an Explicitly Scientific Approach*. New York: Columbia University Press.

Whitley, R. 1985. *The Intellectual and Social Organization of the Sciences*. New York: Clarendon.

Wilcox, D. and A. Sullivan. 1978. Toward independent archaeological theory. Manuscript in possession of authors.

Winterhalder, B. and E. Smith. (Eds.) 1981. *Hunter-Gatherer Foraging Strategies: Ethnographic and Archaeological Analyses*. Chicago: University of Chicago Press.

3

Formal and Statistical Models in Archaeology

A. Voorrips

> ... was there anything down deep inside?
> —Dory Previn

Introduction

A discussion of formal and statistical models in archaeology must begin with a definition of the position occupied by models in archaeological thinking as a whole. They stand somewhere between a theory about the world-out-there and the world-out-there reality itself. They are partial representations of a theory and are formulated in a manner which enables the archaeologist to test the theory by means of empirical data (Orton 1980:20). A model therefore must be expressed in terms of the theory under which and for which it has been built.

It is necessary to know the form of a theory to understand which parts are represented by a model of some kind, to define the characteristics of the reflection, and to outline expectations about the usefulness of the reflection.

The forms taken by archaeological theories are heavily influenced by ideas about the aims and the subject matter of archaeology. A basic idea is, however, that a theory in some way expresses and organizes our knowledge about the world-out-there. Therefore we must begin with posing the question what is meant by the word "knowledge": We must look into epistemology.

In this chapter first an epistemological viewpoint will be established. Next, the structure of scientific knowledge will be discussed in terms of the selected epistemology. Finally, an approach to the construction of formal and statistical models will be presented.

Epistemology

An epistemology cannot be proven. It is a basic belief system about ourselves and about the way in which we interact with all that is not ourselves. Terms used in the description and defense of an epistemology have meaning, or their "right" meaning, only inside that epistemology. Thus an epistemology cannot be fruitfully discussed unless it is to some extent shared. Epistemologies have been and are discussed, and this "matter of fact" (in the sense of Hume 1748) leads to the conclusion that basic beliefs exist about what knowledge is.

In the following, the term "knowledge" will be used in a restricted sense. It will stand for knowledge about the world-out-there and the way in which we interact with that world. Questions such as: How do we know that we know—the problem of the criteria (Chisholm 1966: Chapter 5)—will not be addressed here.

Two approaches can be distinguished in an inquiry about knowledge in this restricted sense. The first approach deals with the manner in which knowledge becomes available to the mind: How do we learn to know? The second approach concentrates on the role that knowledge has in the existence of the human species: Why do we want to know?

To answer each of these questions separately will provide a partial insight only. The first approach is ahistorical and individualistic and, to that extent, context-free. The second approach is causative, if not teleological, and holistic and seeks an acceptable reason for the existence of knowledge altogether. In combination, however, the two approaches may allow us to state a satisfactory epistemological viewpoint.

The first problem to be considered when dealing with the *how* of knowledge is in which manner the "world-out-there" gets known to us. Reality is experienced through sense impressions. The inbuilt constraints of the observational apparatus imply that reality, whatever it might be, is only impressed on us: we are only able to experience a partial representation. A sense impression will not be recognized as such unless it is processed by the brain (Russell 1927: Chapter 5). The combination of sense impressions and their processing then is the *perception* of the world-out-there. The "lower" processes of the perception, the actual manner in which the senses together with the rest of the neural system pick up, recode, transport, recode, and deliver an impression to the processing units in the brain, are among the fascinating subjects of biology and information theory (Miller 1978: Chapter 8) but will not be discussed here. The focus will be on what happens at the more or less conscious level of perception. The processes at this level can be described as the registration of a finite number of properties, the latter being the characteristics of the piece of reality that is observed. From a combination of properties the observer defines what the piece of reality "is," and this definition is a conceptual category (for a more detailed discussion see Voorrips [1982]).

The second problem is that the epistemological link between the conceptual categories and reality needs to be established. "Genetic epistemology," also called "constructivism," which was developed by Jean Piaget and his co-workers, will be adopted here (e.g. Piaget 1970). Two assumptions underlie this epistemology. The first one is that reality has no properties which can be known in a manner which is independent of the observer. The second one is that the human brain has a genetically determined capacity for the making of abstract structures. The differentiation between "me" and the world-out-there, between the conceptual categories and reality, develops as a product of the interaction between "me" and reality. Conceptual categories get constructed because of and by means of stimuli from reality, and at the same time reality is perceived and, in turn, constructed in terms of those conceptual categories. The process of learning-to-know not only consists of the building of more and more complex and refined abstract structures but it also entails "jumps": Sets of already existing conceptual categories are compiled and transformed into qualitatively different, incommensurable, new categories at a more general level of abstraction. The less general categories and their accompanying perceived reality are consequently understood and reconstructed in terms of the more general categories. Linking the concept of the latter to the former, however, again implies "jumps" because of the qualitative differences between the levels.

In summary, according to Piaget, the world-out-there as perceived does not exist independently from the "me," but neither does the "me" exist independently from the "real" world-out-there. Perceived reality, however, is the only reality for the "me," and "me" and perceived reality develop together. A major attraction of this viewpoint is that it neither assumes that reality is knowable directly nor postulates inform categories, at which fundamental level there is indeed a genetically determined common way in which our species thinks.

A general epistemology based on the outcomes of the two approaches now can be defined as follows:

(1) The basic characteristic of human thinking is its ability to make abstract generalizations. Abstract generalizations are constructed on different and incommensurable levels. In combination with the transformations that link them together, these constructs are called knowledge.
(2) Only knowledge about a perceived reality can be developed. Perceived reality and knowledge develop together, subject to evolutionary processes.
(3) Knowledge is a tool to manipulate reality in order to increase the intake of energy and information, which means to increase survival potential in space/time.
(4) The recognition of evolutionary processes is in itself an abstract generalization about perceived reality. Thus the disposition ("nature") of knowledge is dependent on culture, that is, on the perception of the overall structure about perceived reality. Thus the disposition ("nature") of knowledge about the world-out there, and vice versa.

Theory

In this section the structure of theories in empirical science will be discussed in accordance with the epistemology outlined above. In contrast to the previous paragraph the terms "reality," "world-out-there," etc., will stand for their perceived forms, unless explicitly stated otherwise.

Following Nagel (1961) a distinction can be made between "common-sense" knowledge, "formal" knowledge, and "scientific" knowledge. Common-sense knowledge is knowledge by experience and expresses the connections between events in causal chains of reasoning. The causal organization enables decision making and action: Implications when dealing with reality are clear and no intermediate levels of abstract generalizations are needed. Linked with this aspect, however, is a lack of generalization power because this type of knowledge structure is implicitly based on the assumption that connections between events will not undergo major change, both in space and in time.

The "highest" form in which common-sense knowledge can be said to describe reality is the empirical generalization (Hempel 1966). While events may be abstracted in the sense that their connections can be described in the form of lawlike statements (Nagel 1961: 48), such statements still are based on experience only. The importance of common-sense knowledge must be understood. The assumption of irreversible connections in time (causality) enables us to deal with reality because causality is "built into" our perceived world-out-there.

The subsuming of particular events and their connections under an empirical generalization is a first jump from one level of abstraction to another; but the next jump, from empirical generalization to formal structure, is even a greater one because the statements of common knowledge are transformed into formal relations, which in turn, constitute the content of knowledge at the formal level. A common-sense knowledge statement such as "All ravens are black" refers to the experience that every bird that has been identified as a raven also has been black and that this is expected to be the case in the future as well. This statement becomes a particular instance of a formal knowledge statement of the form "For all A, A implies B." This latter statement has been lifted out of reality in the sense that the actual relationships between events which can be substituted for A and B, the causal and time-bound conditions of reality, are ignored. The gain of constructing formal knowledge is a gain in generalization power: The conscious simplification of reality enables subsuming its different aspects under a form which can provide more prediction and manipulation power.

But there is a snake in this paradise. Before predictions obtained from formal knowledge can be used, another transformation is necessary. The link with reality has to be reestablished by reentering the assumptions of causality and irreversibility in time. This step cannot be justified in any formal way, precisely because of the characteristics of formal knowledge. There is a basic incongruity here that led Hume (1748: section 4) to conclude the impossibility of a formal definition of causality and Wittgenstein (1921: proposition 6.3 and comments) to conclude the impossibility of a causal explanation of formal thinking. Paraphrasing with Godel's theorem (Nagel and Newmand 1958), it is impossible to map reality into the formal domain without losing decidability.

Scientific knowledge tries to bridge the gap between formal knowledge and reality by constructing theories. Again following Nagel (1961), we can distinguish three qualitatively different parts or aspects of a theory. First there is the *calculus*, the purely formal expression of the theory. Second we have the *model*, a "causal narrative," whose task it is to make the theory "visible" and discussible by means of a free use of analogies. Third there is the *bridging argument* in which the links between the calculus and that part of reality which the theory has been built to cover are located.

It should be noted that the meaning of the term "model," as used in this context by Nagel, is rather different from the meaning the term commonly has in archaeology (e.g., the next section of this paper). An example of the model of a theory in Nagel's sense is Spencer's "organic analogy" for the development of society that aids discussion about the theory of social evolution but does not contribute to the understanding of how the formal statements of that theory are linked to empirical reality.

The transformations from calculus to reality occur somewhere in the bridging argument. The transformations are analogies; but unlike those used in Nagel's models analogies that cannot be selected freely, they have to relate calculus and reality as directly and unambiguously as is possible.

Transformations occur in satisfactory bridging arguments between general anthropological theory and the empirical evidence of archaeology at two levels minimally. The lower level, which in current archaeology is labeled "middle-range theory" (e.g., Binford 1977), comprises the construction of dynamic processes out of static material remains and the explanation of these processes in terms of "special" theories which cover restricted aspects of the cultural system under study (Raab and Goodyear 1984). The constructed processes and their lower-level explanations are the data for the higher-level argument where they are explained in the framework of a general anthropological theory. At both levels the necessary analogical steps often stay implicit, either because they are not recognized as a valid part of an explanation, or because they are so deeply hidden in a chain of bridging arguments that they go unnoticed. In my opinion the actual transformations are to be found where a bridging argument contains probability statements and quotations of probability laws. Probability is brought into a bridging argument when the calculus is operationalized into a form which enables comparisons of the formal predictions of the calculus with empirical outcomes.

There are different concepts of probability. Boldrini (1980: Section 42), following Carnap (1950), recognizes five different approaches, two of which are of importance here:

(1) ... The classical conception ... here probability is defined as the ratio of the number of favourable cases of an event to the number of all possible cases, provided that they are equally possible. This is a definition axiomatically assumed for analytical purposes and therefore unexceptionable in itself.
(2) The conception of probability as the relative occurence of a particular modality of an event with respect to the occurrence of all the modalities (Boldrini 1980: 24).

Both concepts give rise to statements that have the same form but are based on entirely different axioms or assumptions. In the classical approach the probability of an event is defined as a formal "property" of that event. In the frequency approach the probability of an event is defined as the conclusion of an—infinite—series of trials which occurs, or which at least can be thought to occur, in reality (Boldrini 1980: section 434). In the calculus of a theory the first concept of probability is used, and in the description of reality, the second one. In the interpretation of probability statements we recognize and use the analogy between these two approaches, switching back and forth between them and thus linking the calculus of the theory to the empirical reality.

Therefore, the crucial part of a bridging argument is the development and definition of *formal-statistical models*, which will be discussed in the next section.

Model

The term "model" is vague, as has been emphasized by various authors (e.g., Bertels and Nauta 1974). The common denominator for all definitions is that a model is a partial and/or simplified representation of something else. Making the distinction between "empirical" and "formal," we obtain four possible combinations.

(a) an empirical model of an empirical reality (a scale model of an engine);
(b) an empirical model of a formal abstraction (the realization of a stratified society as a little wooden pyramid);
(c) a formal model of an empirical reality (the "rank-size model" as a representation of Sumerian site sizes and site numbers in the Susiana Plain [Johnson 1981]);
(d) a formal model of a formal abstraction (the geometric representation of an algebraic equation, as well as the algebraic equation for a geometric figure).

In archaeology, field drawings and artifact drawings belong to category a. They attempt to represent what is observable, and they highlight those aspects of reality which at the time and place of production of the drawing are considered important. The jump in abstraction level is present, even though there is usually no explicit formalization of the implicit notions which determine what is drawn and how it is drawn. The lack of explicitness makes it often difficult to interpret old field drawings. One has to understand the general climate of thought at the time the drawing was done before valid inferences can be made.

Reconstructions of prehistoric houses, to be found in museums and exhibitions, belong to category b: empirical models of the abstract notions of what a house in a specific space/time locus may have looked like. The "model of a theory" *sensu* Nagel also can be considered to belong to this category. For example, picturing an atom as a planetary system is one out of many possible empirical realizations of a formal theory selected to convey the general "message" of the theory. For the history of science these models preserve the general attitudes prevailing at the time of their construction. One can compare, for example, the different ways in which the appearance of Neanderthal man has been reconstructed since its first discovery (e.g., Vandermeersch 1982).

Most models that apply mathematics and statistics to archaeological problems belong to category c: a formal representation of a piece of empirical reality. These models belong to the "lower level" of archaeological theory and are initially descriptive. The latter does not concern similarity between the elements of reality and the elements of the model, but rather analogy between the *relationships* among the modelled entities and the *relationships* among the formal entities in the model. When, for example, Johnson (1981) discusses Sumerian sites of different sizes in the Susiana Plain, he shows that there is a certain quantitative relationship between a number of empirical entities and then draws an analogy between the relationships observed and a formal relationship which is given by the mathematically defined log-normal distribution. Voorrips et al. (1978), a simulation of stratified sampling, and Voorrips and O'Shea (in press), a discussion and application of conditional spatial analysis, are examples of models of category c as well.

In the sampling simulation the performances in estimating the densities of material remains in an archaeological site of a number of different sampling strategies are compared. The strategies are defined in terms of probabilistic sampling theory and presume a formal representation of the dispersion of materials in the site. Therefore, the actual archaeological remains are transformed into formal entities such as counts and proportions. In theoretical terms the exercise is on a low level—the models, while using the patterning that exists in the data to obtain precise estimates, do not try to explain that patterning in terms of processes. The sampling simulation is a study of the applicability of a measuring device; it is not a study in which the measurements made by means of that device reinvestigated themselves.

In Voorrips and O'Shea (in press), the spatial relationships among the graves in a Mesolithic cemetary are studied. The graves are first classified into subsets based on the presence or absence of a selected characteristic. Next the members of the subsets are considered as point in a two-dimensional space. Then, using appropriate formal-statistical techniques, decisions are made about whether or not there is statistically significant spatial patterning of the subsets in relation to each other. Such patterning is thought relevant for the understanding of aspects of the cultural system that produced the cemetery.

In this case the first transformation is the classification of the graves. Following lines of thought developed in the previous section of this chapter and in Voorrips (1982), variables are constructed on the basis of a "special" theory of mortuary symbolism, and the description of the graves in terms of such variables—the possession or nonpossession of a selected attribute—is considered adequate for the research goals. Next, the classified graves are transformed into points in a two-dimensional space. After the two transformations the graves have become formal entities in a formal structure, and their relationships are then defined and described in statistical terms. These spatial relationships are subsequently discussed in terms of the theory selected, which relates mortuary symbolism to cultural processes. The conditional spatial analysis thus is an example of the construction of a descriptive formal model under a "middle-range" archaeological theory.

In archaeology, formal models of formal abstractions (category d) attempt to subsume the "outcomes," the formal descriptions, provided by models of category c within a more general framework. A case in point is G. Johnson's rank-size model. In a simple descriptive fashion it shows that settlement sizes in the Susiana Plain around 3400 B.C., conforming to the "rank-size rule," can be modeled as a sample from a log-normal distribution (a category c model). Then Johnson argues that a mathematical manipulation which produces a log-normal distribution (the multiplication of random variates) is a formal model for the formal abstraction "compound influence of sociopolitical processes at spatial loci in a cultural system," an abstraction which is derived from a "special" theory on social organization. Under this model, distributions of settlement sizes describe the amount of investigation of a sociopolitical system (Johnson 1981).

In summary, formal models in archaeology fall within the realm of "middle-range theory" and generally entail a transformation of empirical reality into a formal abstraction. The link between abstraction and reality is the analogy between the "classical" and the "frequency" approach to probability. The transformation, while being descriptive, represents at the same time a jump in abstraction level by declaring that an aspect of reality can be expressed or be modeled in terms of a formal construction. At this level of abstraction there is an attempt to extend the applicability of the model to other empirical situations, that is to define the model in a way that it can describe as many real-world relationship-structures of a given kind as possible. A formal model that cannot be extended should be discarded because of its lack of applicability.

Furthermore, statements other than those related to the original research purposes which can be derived from the definition of a formal model must have counterparts in reality as well. If not, then it must be concluded that the model constructed is not the most complete formal representation of a selected aspect of empirical reality. Whether or not that conclusion invalidates the model depends on which observable empirical relationships are considered relevant for inclusion in the model. In the "normal science" (Kuhn 1970) that decision will be governed by the theory from which most research problems are derived, and whose calculus provides formal conclusions used to test the validity of the theory with empirical analogues.

In the case of nonformalized or partially developed theory—as in archaeology—the selection of research problems and formal models is more haphazard. Choices are primarily determined by the prevailing attitudes and interests in specific communication networks or archaeologists, or "pre-paradigmatic schools" in Thomas Kuhn's (1970) sense. Thus different groups of scientists emphasize different kinds of research problems and construct different types of models accordingly. Whatever the particular "school" may be, in all cases a main purpose of the scientific effort must be to move toward a formalized theory that is as general as possible. In today's archaeology this may well mean a "middle-range theory" which: "explain(s) not merely the archaeological record, but the cultural dynamism responsible for that record" (Raab and Goodyear 1984: 226).

Fulfillment of this goal would constitute the next phase for using formal models in archaeology. Once there is a "promising"—that is, a reasonably well tested—formal model, there is another jump in abstraction level in which the model is no longer considered descriptive but becomes part of the calculus of a theory, and in which the initially described aspects of reality serve as the empirical model of that theory.

References

Bertels, K., and D. Nauta. 1974. *Inleiding tot het Modelbegrip*. Amsterdam: Wetenschappelijke Uitgeverij.
Binford, L. R. 1977. Introduction. In *For Theory Building in Archaeology*, ed. L. R. Binford, pp. 1-10. New York: Academic Press.
Boldrini, M. 1980. *Scientific Truth and Statistical Method*. London: Griffin.
Carnap, R. 1950. *Logical Foundations of Probability*. Chicago: University of Chicago Press.
Chisholm, R. M. 1966. *Theory of Knowledge*. Englewood Cliffs, (N.J.): Prentice-Hall.
Hempel, C. G. 1966. *Philosophy of Natural Science*. Englewood Cliffs, (N.J.): Prentice-Hall.
Hume, D. 1965. *An Enquiry Concerning Human Understanding*. Reprinted. Chicago: Henry Regnery. Originally published 1748.

Johnson, G. A. 1981. Monitoring complex system integration and boundary phenomena with settlement size data. In *Archaeological Approaches to the Study of Complexity*, ed. S. E. van der Leeuw, pp. 143-88. Amsterdam: Institute for Pre- and Protohistory, University of Amersterdam, Cingula VI.

Kuhn, T. S. 1970. *The Structure of Scientific Revolutions*, 2nd ed. Chicago: University of Chicago Press.

Miller, J. G. 1978. *Living Systems*. New York: MacGraw-Hill.

Nagel, E. 1961. *The Structure of Science*. London: Routledge and Kegan Paul.

Nagel, E., and J. R. Newman. 1958. *Godel's Proof*. New York: New York University Press.

Orton, C. 1980. *Mathematics in Archaeology*. Cambridge: Cambridge University Press.

Piaget, J. 1970. *Genetic Epistemology*. New York: Columbia University Press.

Raab, L. M., and A. C. Goodyear. 1984. Middle range theory and archaeology: a critical review. *American Antiquity* 49: 255-68.

Russell, B. 1927. *An Outline of Philosophy*. London: Allen and Unwin.

Vandermeersch, B. 1982. De huidige mens. In *De Evolutie van de Mens*, ed. Th. J. M. Mertens, pp. 292-309. Maastricht: Natuur en Techniek.

Voorrips, A. 1982. Mambrino's helmet: a framework for structuring archaeological data. In *Essays on Archaeological Typology*, ed. R. Whallon, and J. A. Brown, pp. 93-126. Center for American Archaeology Press.

Voorrips, A., D. P. Gifford, and A. J. Ammerman. 1978. Toward an evaluation of sampling strategies: simulated excavations using stratified sampling designs. In *Sampling in Contemporary British Archaeology*, ed. J. F. Cherry, C. Gamble, and S. Shennan, pp. 227-261. British Archaeological Reports, British Series 50.

Voorrips, A., and J. M. O'Shea. 1986. Conditional spatial patterning: beyond the nearest neighbour. *American Antiquity*, in press.

Wittgenstein, L. 1961. *Tractatus logico-philosophicus*. Trans. D. F. Pears and B. F. McGuiness. Reprinted. London: Routledge and Kegan Paul. Originally published 1921, Annalen der Naturphilosophie.

4

Anthropological Archaeology, Computational Modeling, and Expert Systems

Jim Doran

Introduction

Whallon (1982) has defined anthropological archaeology as the attempt to explain the organization, operation, and evolution of human cultural systems. I shall call the body of theory emerging as a result of this attempt "sociocultural theory." Unfortunately it is clear from reviews such as those of Wenke (1981) and of Carneiro (1981) that, insofar as it exists at all, sociocultural theory is currently nonrigorous, controversial, and insufficient to do the tasks required of it. If anthropological archaeology is to achieve scientific status, this must change; and in this paper I shall suggest ways in which a change for the better may perhaps be brought about.

This weakness of sociocultural theory underlies, I believe, the disappointing performance of formal techniques as they have been applied over the last two decades. A diversity of particular techniques has been applied to a range of problems. Those deployed include univariate and multivariate statistical analysis, seriation techniques, linear programming, catastrophe theory, and computer simulation techniques. Although often associated with theoretical positions, these applications have in practice tended to be experimental in nature and relatively peripheral. The results rarely seem to have genuinely advanced archaeological insight. The impression is of a diversity of techniques being applied without a great deal of theoretical or methodological consistency. What have not emerged (except at the most elementary level) are standard methods in standard use.

While I agree with those who argue that there has all too often been a mismatch, a discordance, between the precise structure of the data and the theoretical preconditions of the techniques which have been applied, the heart of the matter, I repeat, is the lack of a developed and sound theoretical context within which to deploy our formal tools. Little can be done to interpret the archaeological record without going beyond our common-sense everyday knowledge to some theory of the social events which gave rise to it. Unavoidably, archaeological theory is ultimately social theory.

It is natural, therefore, to turn to general social theory for guidance. Unfortunately, this natural strategy encounters major difficulty. Current social theory, of whatever variety, is itself contentious and inadequate to support rigorous inference. We can therefore only seek to develop sociocultural theory starting from the distinctive problems of anthropological archaeology. But we can hope thereby to make a contribution to wider social science. The remainder of this chapter should be read in this light.

My particular argument here will be that those logical, computational, and mathematical techniques which are (mis)named artificial intelligence techniques can help with the central theoretical and practical problems of anthropological archaeology. Specifically I shall argue that artificial intelligence techniques:

(a) provide potentially powerful means of experimenting with and therefore developing and testing sociocultural theory by way of computational modeling,
(b) provide a conceptual repertoire within which to embed sociocultural theory,
(c) clarify the role and potential of multivariate statistical analysis within archaeological data interpretation,
(d) provide practical tools to aid data interpretation.

Each of these claims is controversial. The reader may need to be reassured that my emphasis on artificial intelligence is more than just an attempt to start another briefly rolling bandwagon and more than arbitrary pounding with my favorite hammer (Moore and Keene 1983). Artificial intelligence has, I hope to show, important contributions to make to anthropological archaeology very much as it is already making important contributions to a wide range of applications areas (Hayes-Roth et al. 1983). It is this applications potential which underlies the major expansion in the effort and funding devoted to AI research and development (including expert systems) over the past few years by scientists, industrialists, and governments alike.

Artificial Intelligence Studies

Artificial intelligence (henceforth AI) arguably represents the next stage in the evolution of computer systems (e.g., Winston 1984; Charniak and McDermott 1985). Although the origins of AI lie in sometimes naive attempts to make machines intelligent, the field now comprises a wealth of concepts and techniques overlapping with the domains of computer science, engineering, logic, and cognitive psychology.

The terminology of the subject can be confusing. To a first approximation artificial intelligence studies and the study of intelligent knowledge-based systems (IKBS) are equivalent. Cognitive science is the application of AI concepts and techniques specifically to the understanding of human cognition (especially in the area of natural language). Expert systems are utility programs very much at the practical applications end of the subject.

Major topic areas within AI are automated knowledge representation and reasoning, planning and problem solving, natural language processing, visual data interpretation, and learning techniques. AI scientists employ both experimental and formal research techniques. In the experimental approach computer programs are written which are intended to embody good design principles. These principles are then refined or discarded in the light of the programs' performance in practice. This experimental technique ensures that AI has intimate links with computer science, which has to provide the tools needed for AI experimentation, and also that it has something of an engineering flavor. At the same time, however, substantial progress is being made in the task of describing reasoning processes within formal logical frameworks so that their implications and validity can be rigorously explored. Although the experimental approach is more immediately accessible to the outsider, that via suitably tailored formal logics is equally important.

Aspects of AI particular relevance here are:

knowledge and its representation. To be capable of substantial problem-solving behavior in the practical world, programs need to use specialist knowledge about the problem domains in which they operate. Typically this knowledge cannot be expressed in numerical terms. Hence much effort has been devoted to nonnumerical ways of representing and automatically using domain specific knowledge within a computer and to the development of computer programming languages which facilitate knowledge representation.

distributed planning and sensing. A branch of AI which is rapidly growing in importance concerns collections of essentially independent information-processing systems which cooperate on the interpretation of environmental data or on some kind of problem solving (see, for example, Smith and Davis 1981; Yang et al. 1985). These systems could, but need not necessarily, be spatially distributed computing systems. This branch of AI, which I shall illustrate in a little more detail in the next section, has important links to traditional systems theory and also to brain studies.

expert systems work. This concerns the development of design principles for computer programs capable of performing usefully in task domains normally requiring human expertise. A number of different systems architectures have been explored (Hayes-Roth et al. 1983), notably the MYCIN rule-based diagnosis architecture whose significance for archaeological work I shall consider later in this paper.

The Teamwork Project

A directly relevant example of an AI distributed problem-solving system is provided by the TEAMWORK project (Doran 1985; Doran et al. 1985), which is a computer-based investigation of how effective communication and cooperation can be established between semi-autonomous programmed actors for the solution of practical tasks.

In this project we are writing programs (in the language Prolog) which simulate, on a single processor, two or more actors cooperating on some simple assembly task. This implies simulation of the common task environment with individual actors "cloned" so that, while they have individual knowledge bases, they employ common plan generation and plan execution mechanisms.

The type of behavior which interests us is illustrated by the following imagined scenario:

> Annie, Fred, and Bill are working on a car. Annie is pondering how best to dismantle and overhaul the engine. At the same time Fred is thinking about how best to tighten a screw on the dashboard. Bill is drinking coffee. Fred comes to a conclusion and asks Annie to pass a screwdriver. She interrupts her thinking to do this. While Annie is passing the screwdriver to Fred, he asks Bill exactly how you go about tightening a screw with a screwdriver. Bill realizes he doesn't know the entire answer to this and therefore asks Annie which way you turn a screw to tighten it. Annie answers Bill's question, who then answers Fred. Annie resumes thinking about engine overhaul, Fred successfully tightens the screw, and Bill continues drinking coffee. Annie then asks Bill to fetch the hoist and herself begins to unscrew the airfilter bolts....

A number of basic features of cooperative multiactor systems are illustrated by this scenario:

> Independent goal setting, plan generation, and plan execution by several actors sharing a common task environment
> Concurrency among the actors: different actors are doing different things at the same time
> Requests for action by one actor to another
> Requests for information by one actor to another
> Successive delegation

Although communication acts are central to any such scenario, we have no direct interest in natural language (compare Appelt 1985). Our interest in communication is limited to understanding and modeling the essential content and the genesis of communications between actors, irrespective of any particular surface form that they may take.

Other relevant aspects of planning and cooperation include broadcast requests, actions by different actors which conflict perhaps due to unintended side effects, and unexpected spontaneous events.

All these requirements make demands upon the design of the actor embodied in the simulation program, especially its planning system. And the simulation of the task domain must be sufficiently rich to support the phenomena we wish to explore. Much of our experimental work is to find principled ways of meeting these requirements at the computational level.

Of particular importance in the TEAMWORK project is belief, notably one programmed actor's belief about the capabilities of another. In order to achieve their goals by cooperation, the actors need models of one another, and these actor models can vary in complexity and accuracy. The exact form that the models take and the ways in which they evolve during actors' "lifetimes" are major technical issues. Part of the motivation for the project is to explore the relationship between belief, individual behavior, and group behavior in this computational setting.

The TEAMWORK project is a long-term one, and as yet the programs we have written demonstrate only relatively simple forms of the mechanisms and behavior I have mentioned. There are many substantial conceptual and systems design problems to be overcome before behavior comparable in complexity to that of humans can be demonstrated. But progress is being made, and there seem to be no insurmountable problems. Work continues.

Theories and Models

The TEAMWORK program is not conceived as a model of human social behavior. It is intended to explore mechanisms of action, planning, communication, and cooperation and to demonstrate how they can be programmed. But can it, or something like it, seriously be used as a model of human social systems?

To answer this question requires some consideration of theories and models. From the AI viewpoint a theory is an encompassing web of abstractions and generalizations which seeks to explain observations in terms of underlying real or virtual entities, and of the causal processes operating upon them. It thereby imposes constraints so that gaps in observation may be filled by reference to the theory. Preferably, of course, a theory is rigorous so that inferences which it engenders are objective, repeatable, and reliably sound.

A theory is also a generator of models, that is, of more specific structures which are built from the computer elements of the theory and which may be put into explanatory or predictive relationship with more specific observations. For a model to be explanatory it must demonstrate how the phenomena of interest may be derived from more fundamental theoretical assumptions which are themselves inherently plausible or demonstrable.

Computational models, that is, models which are either programmed for a computer or are formulated in computational terms, enable a much greater complexity of experimentation and theory testing than those of the more traditional mathematical or statistical variety. It is a common error to assume that a computer can serve only as a subordinate tool to ascertain the consequences of a mathematical or statistical model. In fact, models expressed directly in computational terms are often possible where a mathematical or statistical formulation is unnecessary and unduly limiting.

When a model is constructed, it is formed not only from certain theoretical elements, but also at a certain level of abstraction and from a certain perspective. Models are intended to capture and work with only relevant essentials. It may therefore be quite appropriate to employ models of differing degrees of abstraction in one and the same context. I shall illustrate this point later in the paper.

From this AI viewpoint the TEAMWORK program, or something like it, can prove a useful model of a human group provided that the conceptions which underlie TEAMWORK (e.g., the kinds of problem solving and communication acts incorporated) do constitute, however imperfectly, a theory of the essentials of human social behavior. This is to make only the obvious association, that between programmed actor and human being. But both in social science and in AI work, the concept of an actor is defined merely by the ability to act in a purposeful manner. This prompts using programmed multiactor systems to model sociocultural systems in which the actors are some type of social component. To this possibility I now turn.

Modeling a Sociocultural System with a Programmed Multiactor System

As an example of modeling a sociocultural system using these AI techniques, I shall briefly describe more of my own work again with a colleague.

Wright and Zeder (1977) have published a simulation study of dynamics in a linear settlement exchange system in which the rates of exchange of goods are related to their annual levels of production. Gary Corcoran and I (Doran and Corcoran, 1985) have extended this work from an AI perspective by modeling a network of settlements with a programmed multiactor system, here called EXCHANGE. Each actor (i.e., settlement) in the model possesses 'technological' knowledge of how to form desirable compound products by combining basic products obtained directly from the environment. The products manipulated by the actors are entirely abstract in the sense that they have no properties except their distribution and rules of combination which they obey. Since the availability of basic products is uneven in the network, an individual actor is motivated to engage in reciprocal exchange to obtain the constituents it needs to generate its requirements of compound products.

It follows that the pattern of production and exchange in the network as a whole derives from the distribution of basic products, the knowledge of the actors and its distribution, the way in which exchange is structured, and the actors' individual production goals. Within this framework can be explored patterns of trade, of innovation, and the spread of knowledge.

The existing Prolog program models each settlement as an actor with its own knowledge and capable of setting certain goals, formulating simple plans to achieve them by suitable acts of exchange and production, and then attempting (not necessarily successfully) to carry out its plans. A particular experiment involves specification of the products at issue and their properties and of the network of settlements and their initial knowledge and then "letting it run" and observing the resulting behavior.

Experimentation with the EXCHANGE model has so far concentrated on the processes underlying long-distance trade and the adaptivity of the network to changing circumstances. No attempt has been made to model a specific exchange system in a specific locality and time: at this stage the objective is to model general mechanisms of exchange with some realism.

The Contract Model

Earlier I mentioned that for any given system to be modeled there was a multiplicity of models available and that these models would themselves often be abstractions of one another. In any given context this invites the question: Which model is the right one? There can be no general answer. The level of abstraction that a model is pitched at must depend, for example, on the specific questions that it is intended to answer and the data that are available. In the case of the EXCHANGE model, the amount of detail incorporated seems unnecessarily great if attention is restricted to broad questions of sociocultural system dynamics. This prompts the question: What *are* the central elements in the EXCHANGE model? The following seem fundamental:

> A number of actors exists each of which has its own behavioral repertoire and goals in a common environment
> Contact and communication between actors are limited
> Actors must cooperate to achieve their individual objectives
> There are particular possible forms of cooperation between actors whose effectiveness depends upon the current properties of the environment
> Cooperation is cumulative; complex forms of cooperation can be built upon simple forms

This list is as important for what it omits as for what it includes. For example, the EXCHANGE model includes representation of knowledge about specific products and their specific properties (e.g., to make a box you need wood, nails, tools). Further, it represents a settlement's specific goals and models the actual planning process by which a settlement decides how best to achieve its goals. In the attempt to achieve an effective level of abstraction, I have entirely discarded this level of detail in the foregoing list of essentials.

A new model, CONTRACT, is a natural outcome of this process of abstraction. It is very different from EXCHANGE, and I shall describe it only very briefly here (for details, see Doran 1986). CONTRACT represents a sociocultural system as structured by contracts between its component actors. These contracts correspond to the exchange agreements reached between settlements in EXCHANGE. Unlike exchange agreements, however, contracts have no detailed structure but merely a fluctuating value to the particular actors involved in them. Further, contracts can be formed out of existing contracts enabling the formation of a multiple hierarchy. The value of a particular contract is determined partly by the state of the actors' common environment at that point in time and partly by the contract's role in underpinning other higher level contracts.

The heart of the model is made up of the rules that specify the circumstances in which particular contracts are added to or deleted from the contract hierarchies. These rules, which are probabilistic, refer only to the state of the system at the point at which the contract is to be added or deleted. The global dynamics of the system are therefore ultimately determined by a combination of local considerations.

What this model offers is the chance to focus in a relatively abstract way upon the cooperative structure of a sociocultural system and to relate its variation over time to environmental variation and the characteristics of a multitude of local decisions. A further interesting property of CONTRACT is that the notion of a contract which it embodies is similar both to the concept of an abstract data type in computer science theory and also to that of a frame in AI knowledge representation theory. The implications of these similarities have yet to be determined but look to merit investigation in some detail.

Computer Experimentation and the Development of Sociocultural Theory

As stated above, a version of the TEAMWORK program exists and is being further developed. Experimentation with the EXCHANGE model has concentrated on the processes underlying long-distance trade and the adaptivity of the network to changing circumstances. The results obtained so far are merely preliminary. The CONTRACT model has not yet been implemented as a computer program and initial experiments performed (Doran 1986).

My purpose here is to focus attention not on any particular piece of this ongoing work but on the potential these modeling techniques offer for the investigation of basic sociocultural mechanisms. If one accepts at all the relevance of computational models to sociocultural theory, then many of the current debates can be addressed by these techniques. Using these methods one could, for example, set out to investigate the significance or otherwise of (a) redistribution, (b) warfare, and (c) new social concepts in the emergence of chiefdoms. I do not suggest that computational modeling makes the development of sociocultural theory easy, merely that it is a powerful and available tool. As stressed earlier, to be useful the models must not be merely descriptive. They must demonstrate how structures and properties can emerge from lower level assumptions.

Computational Models and Theoretical Presuppositions

How far does AI based computational modeling imply a particular theoretical position? In my presentation here I have made a number of general assumptions about sociocultural systems (compare Doran 1982). Thus I have taken it for granted that they are structured and processual, that they are appropriately seen as computational and distributed, that they are both locally and globally goal achieving, and that much of their behavior can be understood in terms of the technological knowledge and cultural beliefs which they contain.

These characteristics are assumed whether the components of a sociocultural system are taken to be, for example, individual human beings, nuclear families, classes, or settlements units. I have also assumed that there do exist mechanisms which are of ubiquitous significance in human society and that these focus on the relationship between individual cognition and the properties of sociocultural systems. But this is certainly not to imply that all mechanisms are uniform over space and time.

These assumptions may seem rather restrictive. Apart from being in some sense mechanistic, they seem to relate strongly to ecological, evolutionary, and functionalist ideas. But it is important to realize that computational models can encompass language and belief and ideology. In principle, cultural belief systems are as open to computational experimentation as are trade networks or aspects of population dynamics. The correct view, I suggest, is that any theory, even one labeled Marxist or structuralist or historicist, can be given computational life once it is precisely formulated, and that even the attempt to do so will enrich the theory concerned.

Relating Theory to Data

At the outset I suggested that AI could impact upon anthropological archaeology in four ways: by enabling useful computer experimentation, by enriching the conceptual repertoire for sociocultural theory, by helping relate archaeological data to sociocultural theory, and by the provision of practical tools for data interpretation. In this section I shall turn to the third and fourth of these claims, those concerning archaeological data interpretation.

The techniques of formal multivariate data analysis which have been deployed in archaeological work (e.g., cluster analysis, correspondence analysis) are essentially methods for seeking structure in large data sets in the absence of detailed domain knowledge. The structure they identify (in some cases define) is itself very abstract. Unfortunately, the recognition of the mere existence of an abstract cluster, for example, may say very little about the interpretation of it. A cluster of stone tools in multidimensional space identified by some formal technique may well mean something, but what? The task of interpreting abstract structure can be so difficult and uncertain that it is natural to question (e.g., Voorrips, 1982) the usefulness of exploratory studies, especially those which pay relatively little attention to the descriptive variables employed. However, these studies do seem to be useful if only to prompt further investigation in a particular direction and may be the only option given a large body of relatively homogeneous data divorced from interpretive context.

The difficulties that have been experienced with these techniques in practical archaeological work reflect not so much the inadequacy of the techniques themselves as the frustrating limitations of the data sets to which they are typically applied. Strong conclusions cannot be derived from inadequate evidence however hard one may try and whatever the sophistication of the mathematical and statistical tools deployed. The answer is not to refine the techniques but to stand back and then proceed in a slightly different direction. The promising road ahead, I suggest, is that which takes us in the direction of AI expert systems and their interaction with the standard multivariate statistical methods.

This needs elaboration. When interpreting archaeological data, there is usually a quite rich context of common-sense and anthropological knowledge. For example, given a camp site the data can immediately be placed in a substantial interpretive framework however unsophisticated and liable to error it may be. The reason why such situations have not been handled by formal methods in the past is partly because they are to some degree immediately tractable by subjective reasoning and partly because the necessary computational machinery has not existed. The latter objection is rapidly losing force. It is now quite feasible (ignoring issues of resource availability) to create AI expert systems capable of assisting the interpretation of archaeological data in limited specialist domains.

A typical expert system is a program which can consider imperfect nonnumerical data and draw interpretive conclusions from them. The classic example is medical diagnosis: given the symptoms, the program infers the disease the patient is suffering from and possibly goes on to suggest treatment. But there are many other actual and potential application domains. The typical expert system can reason allowing for uncertainty and can give some explanation to the user of how its conclusions have been reached. Indeed, it is a defining characteristic of an expert system that there is an interaction with the user in which the machine takes the initiative in collecting and interpreting the available evidence.

None of this can be done by magic. An expert system must be provided with the specialist knowledge to do its job, typically provided by a human expert in the form of condition-conclusion rules with associated uncertainties (i.e., rules of the form: if X is the case then Y is the case with certainty C). Further, an expert system can only be expected to show competence in a narrow, well-defined task domain where human expertise is well established. Thus there are no general medical diagnosis systems. There are, however, systems for very special and specific areas of medical expertise.

Expert systems make economic sense not because they enable human expertise to be surpassed or even simulated, but because they enable its effective content to be duplicated and reduplicated. They also aid the systematization of knowledge. They are, in a way, intelligent handhooks. They have potential in an archaeological context wherever the demand for a particular interpretive expertise outstrips supply. Thus it seems realistic to think of expert systems to interpret particular kinds of artifact (bone combs, bronze axes), for example, or particular types of settlement site.

Statistical Analysis and Expert Systems

At a sufficient level of abstraction, methods of statistical analysis and AI expert systems are doing the same job. Both are working from incomplete and unreliable evidence to uncertain conclusions. The major difference is that the statistical methods are trying to do the job without using domain knowledge—they are abstract general purpose methods—while the expert system is explicitly designed to deploy as much domain knowledge as may be acquired and embodied in the system. But it is clear that there are intermediate possibilities.

Consider the task of interpreting spatial distributions of postholes. This is a task which invites both general purpose techniques of spatial analysis and also the use of domain specific knowledge about, for example, typical house structures for the period and area in question. As yet little is known about how to relate in theory or to combine in practice these two kinds of interpretive tool. It is clear, however, that they are complementary rather than in conflict.

Important also is the complexity of the conclusions which these tools are designed to reach. The conclusion of a cluster analysis will typically be a small number of clusters which the archaeologist must then interpret. An expert system will itself reach a relatively detailed and meaningful interpretation of the evidence. And, further, this interpretation may be the time trajectory of the system under study. For example, the expert system CASNET (Weiss et al. 1978) infers the time trajectory of a disease state (in the eyeball) using a stochastic model to relate the disease progression to the symptoms observed.

At this point it begins to appear how expert systems theory can be used to relate archaeological data to computational process models of sociocultural change of the type discussed earlier. If sociocultural theory can be expressed in computational terms, then expert systems of the CASNET variety, which interpret data in terms of process models incorporating stochastic variables, and which therefore necessarily employ statistical techniques, look capable in the long term of providing both bridging theory linking sociocultural theory to the archaeological record and the practical tools needed to implement it.

Practical Implications

Anthropological archaeology needs good fieldwork. No mathematical or computational sophistication can ever remove that need. But in this paper I have argued that AI techniques of computational modeling and expert system design have much to contribute to the development of sound sociocultural theory within the limits of the evidence provided by fieldwork. If accepted, these arguments have certain immediate practical implications.

More experiments in computational modeling are needed. This is not a new suggestion (see, for example, the proposals of Flannery 1972, and of Plog 1977), but the time is now ripe. Similarly, the existing pilot expert system studies (Lagrange and Renaud 1983; Reynolds 1985; Ennals 1985) need to be followed up by more substantial work. Given the availability of expert system shells, this will not be as difficult to achieve within existing archaeological computing resources as might at first appear.

Within archaeological training there is needed some shift of attention away from relatively sophisticated multivariate statistical methods toward computational and AI techniques. No archaeological student should be left unaware of the potentialities of information science in general, and of computer modelling and AI expert systems in particular. This is not an extreme suggestion. Such a shift would merely reflect broader trends in the education of scientists across the world.

Acknowledgements

The TEAMWORK project is funded by the UK Science and Engineering Research Council under grant number GR/C/44938.

References

Appelt, D. E. 1985. Planning English Referring Expressions. *Artificial Intelligence* 26: 1-33.
Carneiro, R. L. 1981. The chiefdom: precursor of the state. In *The Transition to Statehood in the New World*, eds. G. D. Jones and R. R. Kautz, pp. 37-79. Cambridge: Cambridge University Press.
Charniak, E., and D. McDermott. 1985. *Introduction to Artificial Intelligence*. Reading, MA: Addison-Wesley.
Doran, J. 1982. A computational model of sociocultural systems and their dynamics. In *Theory and Explanation in Archaeology*, eds. A. C. Renfrew, M. J. Rowlands, and B. Seagraves-Whallon, pp. 375-388. New York: Academic Press.
Doran, J. 1985. The computational approach to knowledge, communication and structure in multi-actor systems. In *Social Action and Artificial Intelligence*, eds. G. N. Gilbert and C. Heath, pp. 160-171. Aldershot. Gower.
Doran, J. 1986. A contract-structure model of sociocultural change. In *Computer Applications in Archaeology* 1986, ed. S. Laflin, pp. 171-178, University of Birmingham Computer Centre.
Doran, J., and G. Corcoran. 1985. A computational model of production exchange and trade. In *To Pattern the Past*, eds. A. Voorrips and S. H. Loving, pp. 349-359. Journal of the European Study Group on Physical, Chemical and Mathematical Techniques Applied to Archaeology, 11.
Doran, J., S. Steel, and C. Trayner. 1985. The TEAMWORK project: a progress report. Ms. on file. Department of Computer Science, University of Essex.
Ennals, R. 1985. *Artificial Intelligence: Applications to Logical Reasoning and Historical Research*. Chichester: Wiley.
Flannery, K. V. 1972. The cultural evolution of civilisations. *Annual Review of Ecology and Systematics* 3: 399-426.
Hayes-Roth, F., D. A. Waterman, and D. B. Lenat. 1983. *Building Expert Systems*. Reading, MA: Addison-Wesley.

Lagrange, M-S. and M. Renaud. 1983. La representation des connaissances dans le cadre d'un systeme expert: SNARK et l'iconographie Seldjoukide et Grecque. *Document de travail no. 5* (roneotype). Paris: CNRS.

Moore, J. A. and A. S. Keene. 1983. Archaeology and the law of the hammer. In *Archaeological Hammers and Theories*, eds. J. A. Moore and A. S. Keene, pp. 3-13. New York: Academic Press.

Plog, F. 1977. Systems theory and simulation: the case of Hawaiian warfare and redistribution. In *Explanation of Prehistoric Change*, ed. J. N. Hill, pp. 259-270. Albuquerque: University of New Mexico Press.

Reynolds, R. G. 1985. The application of expert rule-based systems. Paper presented at International Union of Pre- and Protohistoric Sciences (Commission 4: Data Management and Mathematical Methods in Archaeology) Symposium, Denver.

Smith, R. G. and R. Davis. 1981. Frameworks for cooperation in distributed problem solving, *IEEE Transactions on Systems, Man, and Cybernetics*, SMC-11(1): 61-70.

Voorrips, A. 1982. Mambrino's helmet: a framework for structuring archaeological data. In *Essays on Archaeological Typology*, eds. R. Whallon and J. A. Brown, pp. 93-124. Centre for American Archaeology Press.

Weiss, S., C. Kulikowski, S. Amarel, and A. Safir. 1978. A model-based method for computer-aided decision-making. *Artificial Intelligence* 11(1,2): 145-172.

Wenke, R. J. 1981. Explaining the evolution of cultural complexity: a review. In *Advances in Archaeological Method and Theory*, vol. 4, ed. Michael B. Schiffer, pp. 79-127. New York: Academic Press.

Whallon, R. 1982. Editorial introduction. *Journal of Anthropological Archaeology* 1(1): 1-4.

Winston, P. 1984. *Artificial Intelligence*, 2nd ed. Reading MA: Addison-Wesley.

Wright, H. and M. Zeder. 1977. The simulation of a linear exchange system under equilibrium conditions. In *Exchange Systems in Prehistory*, eds. T. K. Earle and J. E. Ericson, pp. 233-253. New York: Academic Press.

Yang, J-Y. D., M. N. Huhns, and L. M. Stephens. 1985. An architecture for control and distribution in artificial intelligence systems. *IEEE Transactions on Systems, Man, and Cybernetics*, SMC-15(3): 316-326.

5

On the Structure of Archaeological Data

Mark S. Aldenderfer

Introduction

When we think of the structure of archaeological data, most of us consider the sets of cases and observations on the cases we may have collected from a site or series of sites. Data in this sense are "things," or objects and their attendant descriptors. We can easily think of other structural attributes of data, such as the three "dimensions" of archaeological data postulated by Spaulding—time, space, and culture—or of somewhat less general categories of data such as "settlement" data or "spatial" data. Those of us with some mathematical or statistical training may think of data in reference to some scale of measurement, such as the now-familiar quartet of nominal, ordinal, interval, and ratio data. Still others may think of data as swarms of points in Euclidean hyperspace and be concerned with the degree to which these point swarms resemble standard models of statistical distributions.

Thinking of the term "data" in these ways suggests that it would be foolish, and probably of little value, to attempt to construct a definition of the term that would prove satisfactory to most archaeologists. In part, this belief stems from the intuitive way in which archaeologists use the idea of data. We all "know" what data are appropriate for the study of our problems, so a definition of the term is simply not necessary. Even if we are unsure of what precisely constitutes data for any particular problem, to proceed with the analysis we must still make some choices about just what it is we need. We are routinely instructed to insure that are our data are appropriate for the solution or exploration of the problem, but detailed explanations of this prescription are hard to find. For most of us, data are simply the givens of the research process.

Most archaeologists, however, are aware that there is danger in the intuitive concept of data that most of us use. Taking data for granted permits us to focus more of our attention on methods, or ways to manipulate data. The danger with taking our data for granted, however, is not that we move to the analysis of our data but that most of our creative energies focus on the search for methods that will allow us to make maximum use of our data. Again, in itself, this is no bad thing, but the modern history of archaeological research has shown that up until very recently, archaeologists have been content to ransack other disciplines for methods, looking for technological "quick fixes," rather than thinking hard about just what data are and how one creates them effectively for the solution of archaeological problems. This tendency is best illustrated by the field of quantitative archaeology. Although simple quantitative and statistical procedures have had a long history of use in archaeology, the decades of the 1960s and 1970s witnessed the "Great Borrowing," in which archaeologists searched through all sorts of sciences, ranging from physics to ecology, in an effort to find methods to help make sense of archaeological data (Aldenderfer n.d.; Clark and Stafford 1982). While some real advances have been made in understanding the past and building more effective and reliable uses of statistical and quantitative methods through this borrowing (Carr 1985), there has been much misuse of methods and a fragmentation of effort. There have been frequent expressions of dissatisfaction with the use of quantitative methods in archaeological research; and while most of us may have our favorite studies, I would nevertheless wager that most of us would agree that quantitative methods have yet to fulfill the promise we thought they offered.

Our attention to methods at the expense of real or perceived progress in understanding the past is a complex phenomenon

(Aldenderfer, Chapter 1). Although there are sociological and evolutionary sources, much of the problem can be traced to a real failure to think long and hard about the idea of data. By this I mean that archaeologists, because of their straightforward, intuitive appreciation of data, really do not understand the complexity of the idea of data and the ways in which data are structured. Some, upon reading this, will suggest that I am referring to "middle-range" theory or operational principles; others may identify the idea of bridging arguments or warranting arguments; still others may point out that I am really talking about empirical generalizations. None of these guesses is correct; although each deals with some aspect of theoretical thinking or philosophical considerations regarding the construction of a valid argument, I am asking archaeologists to look at a deeper level; the role of numbers and the concept of structure of archaeological data. I want to explore how archaeologists give meaning to their data: the use of numbers and the perception of structure are fundamental to this task.

Why numbers and structure? Numbers are basic. Through the use of numbers, we can measure or more precisely define things we think are of importance to the solution of our problems. Numbers are proxy measures of things: counts of objects, sites, or attributes; densities of habitation, scales of intensity, and more complex statements of multivariate relationships. Most of us believe that by the proper manipulation of numbers, we can obtain significant insight into the past. Measurement, the logical extension of numbers, must be regarded as a methodological presupposition. We can measure until it is demonstrated that in a specific context that measurements are not feasible or are meaningless (Kaplan 1964: 176).

Likewise, structure is a basic idea. The Random House dictionary definition of structure is simply "the manner in which the elements of anything are organized or interrelated." This definition, while necessarily general, nevertheless points out the key features of the concept: relationships and the definition of the relationships. But structure is a trendy concept, and if not made more specific and useful, my use of the term would be yet another flashy borrowing of clearly limited value. What is needed is an operational language of structure, something that can take the fuzzy, intuitive concept of structure we all possess and transform it into a powerful tool we can use in everyday research. Such a language of structure exists in polyhedral dynamics, or Q-analysis (Atkin 1974; Gould 1980).

Simply put, Q-analysis is an algebraic, nonquantitative language that operates on relationships between sets. It is not a method but more an approach, or a metatheory, on how to express the concept of structure in a parsimonious but powerful fashion (Gould 1984: 542). It is multidimensional in the sense that relations between sets can be made across a number of definitional levels. This differs from the traditional Euclidean definition of multidimensional or multivariate space, which is based upon a mathematical extension of our familiar three-dimensional thinking. Although this chapter is not the best place for an extended description of Q-analysis, some of the most important concepts will be illustrated through examples.

Thus the concepts of numbers and structure can be used in a creative synthesis to show just how it is, or perhaps, how we should learn, to create our data so that they can be used to answer questions we have about the past. Understanding the role of numbers and structures in the process of data creation can serve as a very important stimulus to the poorly understood "logic of discovery," the nonlogical, intuitive way in which ideas and observations may be transformed into scientific statements (Kaplan 1964: 15-16; Clark, Chapter 2). Understanding numbers and structure cannot develop rules for implementing the logic-of-discovery, but it can certainly help to cultivate it.

Looking at the structure of archaeological data through numbers and structure can also help us better understand the relationship between "data," "theory," and "method." In traditional archaeological thinking about the research process, "method" has always been kept at some distance from "theory," implying that there is no necessary relationship between these two aspects of the research process. "Theory" in the form of hypothesis initiates the research process; the hypothesis is confirmed or rejected through analysis of "data." This has had a number of unfortunate effects; "theory" has been developed with little regard to how the implications of the "theory" might be tested in the empirical world of archaeological observations via the medium of "methods." Likewise, "method" has often been developed in a world of its own, and any consideration about the meaning those methods might have for solving problems about the past either has been ignored or paid lip service only. As Doran (Chapter 4, p. 74) has put it, "these applications have been experimental and relatively peripheral." Another version of this kind of thinking is that methods are perceived as "tools," to be drawn from the tool kit and used whenever necessary. This separation of "theory" and "method" is easily seen in the application of quantitative methods to archaeological problems. Most specialists in the field suggest that quantitative methods will have a greater impact on the field when archaeologists become better statisticians. While no one wants archaeologists to become statisticians, the implication is that once we have better training and learn how to appreciate quantitative methods for what they are, we will then be in a more secure position to study the past. The tools can then be put to proper use. Although important advances in integrating statistical or quantitative methods into the archaeological research process are being made by some (Carr 1985; Read, Chapter 9; Carr, Chapter 10), the idea of "data" is still waiting to be led back into the fold.

I would like to reverse the traditional wisdom regarding this view of "data" in general and in quantitative wisdom in specific by arguing that archaeologists will become better statisticians if they instead become better archaeologists. Here, I mean "better" in the sense of being in a stronger position to solve problems about the past if we recognize that "theory," "method," and "data" are highly interconnected, and that until we understand just how it is we create our "data," we can never confidently apply "methods" to the study of "theory." In short, we must look more deeply into the creative act of how we assign meaning to data.

A Theory of Data

One way to better understand this aspect of the creative process is to place the act of data construction into a reconstructed logic of the research process (Figure 5.1). In a real sense, this reconstructed logic

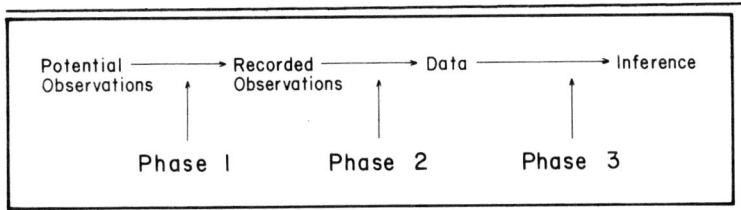

Figure 5.1 A theory of data and its creation (after Coombs, 1964: Fig. 1.1).

is no more than a hypothesis on how to think about data. Following Coombs (1964), three phases of data creation can be identified. Phase 1 of the process is the act of deciding which observations of a potentially large universe of observations are to be taken. This phase is intimately identified with the recognition and definition of a problem within the broader context of the research process and with the subsequent selection of observations said to be relevant to the solution of the problem. In Phase 2, the observations are transformed into data by assigning meaning to them. This is done by clarifying the expected relationships that are expected to hold between the observations; and in effect, we attempt to anticipate the types, range, and content of the patterns we expect to discover when we finally begin to analyze our data. This step is crucial and clearly depends on both the state of knowledge we possess (or think we possess) about the phenomena under study and the quality of the thought or expressed in the definition of expected relationships between observations. Clarity and sharpness of thought are the keys to this phase of the data definition process, although we must recognize that in most cases, we will be unable to anticipate all of the potential relationships among our observations. Finally, Phase 3 involves the analysis of the newly created data by whatever methods are deemed appropriate. As Coombs (1964: 5) puts it, "phase 3 involves the detection of relations, order, and structure which follow as logical consequences of the data." There is no requirement that the methods to be used must be quantitative in nature or anything else, for that matter. What is important, however, is that the choice of methods is guided by how we have created our data, and not the reverse.

In short, the process of creating data is perhaps best described as the way in which we assign meaning to what we find in and on our sites. Phrased in this manner, this question becomes one of epistemology, or of how we know what we know. If we at least tentatively accept the hypothesis of data creation described above, then we must also recognize that the success of our inferences in understanding the past depends not so much on method but on the building of realistic relationships among those things we have defined as data. The successful combination of numbers and structures is an essential aspect of the process of assigning meaning.

Assemblages, Numbers, and Structure

To explore these ideas more fully, I will use the concept of the "assemblage." The idea of an assemblage of artifacts has played a special role in the evolution of archaeological thinking during the past 20 years. It has served as a vehicle for the introduction of sophisticated quantitative methods to the discipline, and perhaps more importantly, it has served as a forum for debates concerning the epistemology of the archaeological record. Modern interest in assemblages, of course, began with the postulation of the famous "Mousterian problem" first articulated by Binford and Binford (1966) and subsequently refined through further debate and analysis as the "functional argument." Although the problem as originally articulated centered on the debate between partisans of "ethnicity" versus "differential site function," in more recent times the focus has shifted toward an interest in how to use collections of stone, bone, and other objects found at sites to make sense of human land use and adaptation through time. This shift in emphasis can be labeled a concern for assemblage formation dynamics and the search for "archaeological signatures," which are unambiguous indicators of a behavioral process or a type of site within a settlement system. Whatever we wish to call it, however, the problem of how to interpret collections of objects found at sites is still with us.

It is instructive to examine how numbers and structures are used to characterize archaeological assemblages by three different archaeologists: Francois Bordes, Lewis Binford, and David Hurst Thomas. Bordes and Binford, of course, crystallized the assemblage variability debate during the late 1960s and early 1970s. Thomas has extended the "functional argument" as proposed by Binford, and has attempted to study hunter-gatherer settlement systems "in the field." I think the following exposition will establish two important points: (1) numbers have been integrated more easily into assemblage arguments, and this has tended to emphasize the role of method, and (2) until recently, the notion of structure has remained either implicit or at the level of assumption in most assemblage models. This, combined with the postulated emphasis on method, has resulted in the development of few "practical" models of assemblage formation processes and dynamics. By "practical," I mean more or less comprehensive models of assemblages that can realistically be used in archaeological analysis. Table 5.1 summarizes that most important features of the three

TABLE 5.1
Data Structures of Assemblages

	Phase 1 Choosing Observations	Phase 2 Assigning Meaning	Phase 3 Searching for Structure
Ethnicity	Tool forms and classes based on morphological similarity/dissimilarity	Counts of tool classes transformed into percentages; significant differences in percentages monitor cultural differences	Visual comparison of ordered profile data
Functional model	Tool forms and classes with inferred functional interpretations; some classes collapsed on assumption of presumed functional redundancy	Count data of tool classes used to form correlation matrices between tool/artifact classes; covariation structure of these matrices contain toolkits	Factor analysis to discover dimensions (toolkits) in covariation structure
Extended functional model	Wide range of material culture, including tool forms, bones, other types of observations used to postulate tool use, dietary habits, site structure, and use	Count data of material culture types; transformation of count data into indices, especially for unused bone. Other transformations of count data to examine size effect	Simple statistics; bivariate correlation; verbal presentation of argument using numbers and measurements as a basis for discussion. Discussion operates within expectations of a model of site use and land use

approaches to the problem of assemblage variability in terms of the theory of data presented in this paper.

The ethnicity model assumes that assemblage variability represents different cultural traditions. Although most North American archaeologists are familiar with Bordes's argument for Mousterian assemblage variability, this approach to understanding the assemblage has also been advocated by Mellars (1970), David (1985), and David and Bricker (1985), among others. For instance, David (1985) claims that differences in tool design, especially in burin forms, monitor the appearance of the Noaillan "people" in the Perigordian region of southwestern France. Despite the emphasis on certain tool forms, however, all ethnicity arguments acknowledge that the assemblage is the proper unit of analysis, and the assemblage is the collection of tool forms within a homogeneous stratigraphic unit. Tool types or classes are assumed to monitor ethnicity; that is, tool designs and their varying combinations are unambiguous markers of "peoples." Therefore, counts of different tool forms, expressed as percentages of their contribution to assemblage, are proxy measures of culture. Variation in assemblage content is detected from the analysis of cumulative graphs, which are simply ordered profile data. Visual comparison of profiles is deemed sufficient to distinguish between different types or assemblages; these, of course, translate as cultures or "peoples."

The functional model of Binford and Binford (1966) postulated that assemblage variability is affected primarily by organizational and distributional variability in the ways in which people perform activities. Although the concept of an assemblage is still retained (the collection of tool forms within a homogeneous stratigraphic unit), a new unit of analysis is defined: the toolkit. The toolkit is simply a collection of tools used to perform an activity (Binford 1983:147). Note that this definition of the toolkit is not observational in the traditional sense; toolkits are contained within assemblages. The relationship between toolkits and assemblages is said to be complex: identical toolkits may be used for different activities, or different activities may require multiple toolkits. Because of these complex behavioral relationships, toolkits crosscut traditional assemblage definitions and have thus been labeled "multidimensional" (Binford 1972: 131-32). Tool forms are assigned functional meaning, and in some cases, categories are collapsed. Pattern recognition is accomplished through factor analysis, a multivariate statistical method first developed by psychologists interested in investigating human intelligence. Counts of tool forms no longer have the same meaning in this model, and thus they are not data as I have defined it. Data are now the complex relationships of different tool forms across traditional expressed as the mutual covariation of these tool classes. Factor analysis is ideally suited to discover the underlying structure of covariance data. Extracted factors are the toolkits, which require interpretation depending on the set of tool classes possessed by each.

Thomas's (1983) conception of the assemblage is complex and is firmly rooted in modern thinking about how assemblages must be seen as both the products of human behavior and postdepositional forces that have modified the structure and content of assemblages to an unknown degree. Assemblages, however, are not simply collections of objects found in stratigraphic levels at sites but are instead the material remnants of different scales of human activity. The contents of assemblages, in terms of the kinds of evidence now included, has expanded considerably; bone, including a variety of inferences about just how that bone was used, plant remains, and microwear analysis of stone tools, not simply the counts of different tool forms. Lithic debitage also has a role in the interpretation of activity at the site. These objects are then lumped into seven functional assemblage categories: general utility tools, weapons, harvesting equipment, fabricating equipment, domestic equipment, recreational equipment, and ceremonial equipment (Thomas 1983: 511). These assemblage categories, combined with data on the structure of individual sites, and the movement of populations across the landscape in response to seasonal variation in food resources, are used to identify different types of sites that once existed within a regional-scale settlement system. Under ideal conditions, the objects found at sites with different structural characteristics in different locations should provide archaeological "signatures," or in this case, site types as embedded in a mobility strategy. Toolkits, in the sense defined in the original functional argument, are no longer sought. Patterns in this complex body of data are recognized by pattern matching, or the assessment of the degree to which assemblages match the expectations of a formal model of the presumed archaeological signatures of different mobility strategies. No complex statistical methods are either advocated or used; instead, the relationships of important model features are carefully explored and described in an expository manner. Statistics are kept at the simple level; nothing more complex than bivariate correlation is used in the analysis.

Assemblages and Numbers

Numbers play a very great role in the definition of assemblages and ways in which patterns of similarity or difference are recognized in all three assemblage models. However, the specific roles that numbers play and the ways in which meanings are assigned differ considerably. Note that both the Bordes and Binford approaches use the same observations (i.e., tool classes and assemblages) but assign radically different meanings to them, thus creating different data sets. One lesson to be learned from this is that there is no single statistical method that is more appropriate for the study of the problem of assemblage variation than any other. The choice of method (pattern recognition procedure) depends on how we frame our questions and how we give meaning to our data. Thus there is no "ideal" quantitative structure of archaeological data, and debates such as those between Hodson (1982) and Spaulding (1982) over the superiority of cluster analysis over contingency table analysis are really more debates about theories of data and what meanings are assigned to data than they are debates about statistical methodology, which is often how the debate is cast.

It is also important to recognize that the numbers used in the Bordes and Binford arguments are given meaning through assumption. Both models assume that numbers and measurements on them in and of themselves can be directly translated into either ethnicity or function (Kimball, Chapter 6). This mistaken notion can be described as the mystique of quantity, "an exaggerated regard for the significance of measurement, just because it is quantitative, without regard to either what has been measured or to what can subsequently be done with the measure" (Kaplan 1964: 172). Except for Binford himself, who eventually eschewed the numbers game, this mystique has led to a rather large cottage industry of methodological specialists who introduced new methods for searching for toolkits in tool count data or criticized previous approaches. The emphasis on numbers is aided and abetted by the law of the instrument: the belief that since we have at our disposal powerful statistical or quantitative methods, then their use should necessarily produce worthwhile results (Kaplan 1964: 172).

I should emphasize that I am not taking the naive and rather ridiculous position that numbers are not useful or important in archaeological research; instead, I am arguing that we have failed to assign valid meaning to our numbers, and that in these circumstances, the use of any statistical method, simple or complex, is a potentially meaningless exercise unlikely to advance our understanding of the past.

Under what circumstances, then, do numbers become meaningful? This is not a trivial question; it is essentially the question we have been asking ourselves about the functional argument when some began to realize that number crunching in and of itself was not improving our understanding of what we have been seeing when we study assemblages. Numbers take on meaning within the context of concept formation. Concepts serve to "mark the categories which will tell us more about our subject matter than any other categorical sets" (Kaplan 1964: 52). The content of a concept ranges across a continuum of the empirical or observational to the theoretical. The former are simple, direct statements or descriptions of what can actually be seen or observed. "Stone artifact" is an empirical concept; "Noaille burin" is another with a more specific meaning: a certain type of burin form found in specific cultural contexts with a specific technology. Indirect observables are concepts in which inference plays a role; many of the things we "observe" as archaeologists are this type of concept. Activity areas are good examples of indirect observables. Constructs are neither empirical or indirectly observable, but they can be defined on the basis of observables (Kaplan 1964: 55). Toolkits certainly cannot be observed but are instead inferred through the covariation of artifact types as found in archaeological assemblages. Finally, there are theoretical terms, for which definition by observables is not possible. A theoretical term has meaning only within the context of some theory; as such, it has systemic meaning (Kaplan 1964: 57). Curation is a theoretical term that is embedded in a theory about tool use and tool making. It cannot be observed in the archaeological record, but instead, it is concept that is invoked to describe how and why certain tool forms do or do not make their way into the archaeological record. Understanding the different kinds of concepts can help to clarify exactly what we can expect to measure and how we can go about doing it.

Concept formation thus represents the interplay of both empirical observation and theoretical speculation. What should be clear from this is that measurements are best assigned meaning at the empirical end of the continuum. That is why count data of stone tools appears to be so basic to the research process: it can be done easily. However, simply being able to make measurements like counts hardly insures a meaning has been assigned to that count. The relevance of the count depends on the nature of the linkage between the empirical observation and the way in which the theoretical term has been defined (the range of the term). There is nothing intrinsic in the count or its numerical quality that makes it meaningful. Although a number of technical procedures have been developed to help specify meaning in this context, such as definition and indication (Kaplan 1964: 71-78), there can be no question that the successful specification of meaning comes from a strongly developed theoretical context; theory, then, *guides* the specification of empirical terms that can infact be successfully measured. The better the theory, the more likely it is we can develop useful concepts; the better the concepts, the better the theory. In archaeology, we often find ourselves in the *paradox of conceptualization*: We need strong concepts to build our theories, but at the same time we need good theories to tell us what kinds of concepts we need (Kaplan 1964: 53). Under this catch-22, it is often easy to do what can be done; numbers of a variety of kinds are there, and they are easily manipulated. Concepts remain at an implicit level, and much of what is measured cannot really be justified simply because the linkages between the empirical observation (the numbers and measurement) and the theoretical terms have never been systematically explored or stated.

Understanding the role of concepts also helps to place "middle-range" theory into proper perspective in the context of how we create data and assign meaning to our observations. Middle-range theory, of course, has been viewed as the way to get ourselves out of the paradox of conceptualization, or the way in which the statics of the archaeological record can be translated into the dynamics of past human behavior. Binford saw this as one powerful way to help solve the "Mousterian problem." There can be no question that middle-range theory is of signal importance to archaeology; it has helped to identify the range of processes that may have been responsible for creating archaeological sites as we find them. However, it is not a substitute for our concepts and the ways in which we combine our concepts to build models of the past. Consider this example. Archaeologists frequently use the term "intensity of occupation" to describe the use of their sites. In many research settings, this term would be a construct, certainly not directly measurable in the archaeological record. The empirical observations that may reflect the intensity of occupation are large numbers of artifacts found at sites, thick middens, and a high density of artifacts per occupation (an indirect observable in this context). The question that then must be asked is how confident are we that the empirical observations we have made necessarily linked to "intensity of occupation." The answer, of course, depends on how we have defined the construct: If we have chosen a narrow meaning, one that implies sedentism (a theoretical view), middle-range theory informs us that there are other factors that could lead to large numbers of artifacts being deposited at sites: a large number of people using the site for a short period of time, or thick middens could be accumulated by a series of cleanings of the site. Thus middle-range theory only informs us of what could happen, but it is up to us to specify our terms, both empirical and theoretical, as clearly as possible.

Assemblages and Structure

Until very recently, the concept of structure has not been of great importance in the study of archaeological assemblages. In a real sense, structure was what we got out of data, what we attempted to interpret, instead of being the basis for our investigation into the processes of assemblage formation. For instance, factor analysis was seen as a method that sought structure in highly complex, multidimensional data, and the hoped-for structures, of course, were toolkits. On a simpler level, ordered profile data were searched for structure, and in this case, structure was represented by "ethnic" groups. Emphasis was placed on the detection of relationships (phase 3 of the theory of data), and we were essentially forced into that position by a lack of agreement on the kinds and content of concepts deemed necessary to solve the "functional argument." It is difficult to characterize the conceptual basis of assemblages under either the Bordes or Binford models simply because structure was assumed to exist in principle. Although both models had expectations presumably derived a priori, these cannot serve the role of the conceptual foundation of the models. Numbers, then, filled the conceptual vacuum.

Even with the assemblage model of Thomas, structure, while more apparent and important than ever before, often remains difficult to interpret. Unlike the Bordes and Binford models, Thomas's model embodies a healthy respect for concept formation. In arguments like these, we may not like what we see, but at least we can argue about our disagreements on the basis of definition and content rather than assumption. Even though Thomas's model represents a significant advance in looking at assemblages, at least from the conceptual level, there are nevertheless important drawbacks with it, the most prominent being the nature of the argument. Although Thomas devotes one whole volume to the question of epistemology in the study of Gatecliff Shelter and its environs, the manner of exposition and of model construction is a combination of academic and eristic styles. The academic style is one that essentially tells a plausible story; there is an emphasis on verbal definition, the development of a jargon, and the use of principles to buttress argument. In the eristic style there is a strong interest in proof. Mathematical and statistical data become important, and logical connections between propositions, principles, and expectations are spelled out as clearly as possible (Kaplan 1964: 259-260). While each of these styles of model building is respectable, they have been combined in such a way to make it difficult to see exactly how data have been constructed, how empirical concepts have been related to higher-level constructs, and how the constructs and theoretical terms employed are connected. In short, the pieces are present but the puzzle remains.

An example of this tendency is the way in which sample size is shown to be a potentially damaging factor in making interpretations of site use at Gatecliff Shelter. Thomas (1983: 425) discusses the sample size effect as an outgrowth of middle-range theory. Simply stated, as the size of the assemblage increases, the diversity of tools also increases. If we are interested in defining site types, as Thomas is, then we must ask ourselves the question "Is what I find at this site simply a reflection of the size of the assemblage, or is it a true reflection of activity or behavior?" Thomas (Fig. 217) develops an "ideal" mathematical model of what the sample size effect should look like. While the sample size effect is said to condition the nature of interpretation of activity at the site, it is difficult to see how the concept is integrated into the discussion of the activities performed (Thomas 1983: 446-486). The academic style in this case makes it hard to see exactly how the concept is used to influence the interpretations made.

No matter what style of model building is used, there is a great need for an understanding of the different kinds of structure that can be encountered in archaeological data. As I have shown above, much of our use of numbers is closely tied to the way in which we form concepts, and this is also true for understanding structure. To create data, and to build solid arguments, and knowledge of the types of structure likely to be encountered in archaeological data is essential, as is the development of a language that can powerfully express relationships. Since structure is such an open term, it is likely that any number of definitions of it can be offered. Some definitions are likely to be more useful than others, and to that end I propose four types of structure with which archaeologists must become familiar: statistical, analytical, inferential, and relational.

Statistical structure is the degree to which the observations at hand, once transformed into data, can be said to be representative of some phenomenon of archaeological interest. Such concepts as population, universe, and sample are familiar here. As Read (Chapter 9) has observed, many archaeological data sets seldom meet the requirements demanded by inferential statistics, and therefore there is a discordance between the archaeological materials and the statistical methods used to analyze them. This limits the efficacy of inferential statistics considerably.

Analytical structure is the dimensional structure of data once it is defined. For instance, the frequency of occurrence of artifact types in burials often is said to be described by a Poisson distribution: There are high frequencies of no occurrence, with lower frequencies of counts greater than one. Other analytical structures of interest are the degree to which archaeological data match other well-known statistical distributions, such as the normal, geometric, or multidimensional normal. Many powerful statistical procedures require that certain assumptions of data structure be met; the degree to which these assumptions are violated and the robustness of the procedure to this violation condition the validity of these results. Another aspect of analytical structure is the degree to which the dimensional structure of the data is compatible with the types of statistical or quantitative procedures used to examine that data. Almost all statistical methods have certain expectations of data structure; many procedures will in fact impose structures on data regardless of the dimensional structure of the data. All of us are aware that factor analysis will create factors in random data; other methods impose structure as well. The question during analysis then becomes "Is this structure inherent in the data, or has it been imposed by the procedure?" One way to minimize the possibility of an unwarranted imposition is to match dimensional structure to technique. While this sounds good in theory, in practice, it is difficult, and there are few helpful rules available for guidance.

Inferential structure is concerned with the linkage of method, technique, and the processes thought to be responsible for the formation of the archaeological record. Inferential structure is the set of linkages that exist between the expectations we have of a behavioral or natural process and the kinds of methods we deem relevant to the solution of the problem. In one sense, the idea of inferential structure is related to the process of model building and subsequent data analysis. Carr (Chapter 10) discusses this aspect of data structure at some length, although primarily from a statistical and analytical perspective. He is concerned with the removal of another kind of discordance from data: the failure to think about the necessity to match the inferential structure of data to the methods that are to be used to detect structure and pattern. Read (Chapter 9) discusses an idea similar to this as well.

Finally, relational structure is the relationship between data as created and the concepts used to link data together to create arguments and models. There is some overlap with this concept and inferential structure, although there are some important differences as well. The idea of inferential structure is more concerned with how we relate substantive issues to analytical and statistical questions; relational structure is concerned primarily with the definition of observations relevant to the study of the problem at hand, the definition of data (how we give meaning to data), the linkage between concept and data, and the linkage between concepts to form models. In essence, it is the archaeological end of the model building: the creation and subsequent linkage of concepts in a logical and meaningful fashion for the study of the problem. Relational structure is also concerned with the language of structure and the ways in which structural relationships can be defined and portrayed.

I have already briefly discussed the role of concepts and the identification of different kinds of concepts in the discussion of numbers and assemblages. The same basic arguments about concepts and numbers hold for the idea of concepts and structure. We are now in a position, however, to briefly explore the implications of the language of structure for the creation of data and the construction of models and arguments. Q-analysis is the language of structure developed by Ronald Atkin, a British mathematician. This language is an algebraic topology used to describe and explore the relationships among sets of objects, concepts, or whatever subject matter is desired. The basis of the language is the definition of the sets that form the structural features of the problem. As Gould (1984: 543) puts it, "The definitional task always contains a deep obligation to think about and sort the data before a structural analysis ever begins." This is the point made earlier in the chapter: We must form our concepts and define our data before we can begin to sort them out. This obligation suggests why Q-analysis should not be seen as another panacea or borrowed technique that will solve our problems for us, but as a tool that can be used to force us to be the better archaeologists we must become. In Q-analysis, the definitional task is hierarchical in form, and the goal of the task is to create sets at more inclusive levels. Cover sets simply subsume concepts, constructs, or empirical observations at lower levels of the hierarchy. Note the overlap between the idea of a cover set and the idea of the continuum of empirical and theoretical terms as defined above. The continuum defines what should be considered at any level of the hierarchy, and the cover sets link the different levels of the hierarchy together. The hierarchy employed in Q-analysis is not a partition, as in more familiar tree diagrams, but instead a true cover. Partitions are one-to-one identifications; an entity at some level of the hierarchy can only be in one partition; a cover implies that an entity can be in more than one set in that level of the hierarchy. Thus while all covers are partitions, not all partitions are covers (Gould 1980: 174). The idea of a cover imparts considerable flexibility to the hierarchy, in that it allows for multiple relationships between things that would be forbidden by traditional partitions. Figure 5.2 presents an example of a cover set as applied to assemblage data. Even in this simple example, the flexibility of the hierarchical cover set idea is obvious. Long ago, Binford made a distinction between three contexts in which artifacts could operate: the utilitarian, sociotechnic, and

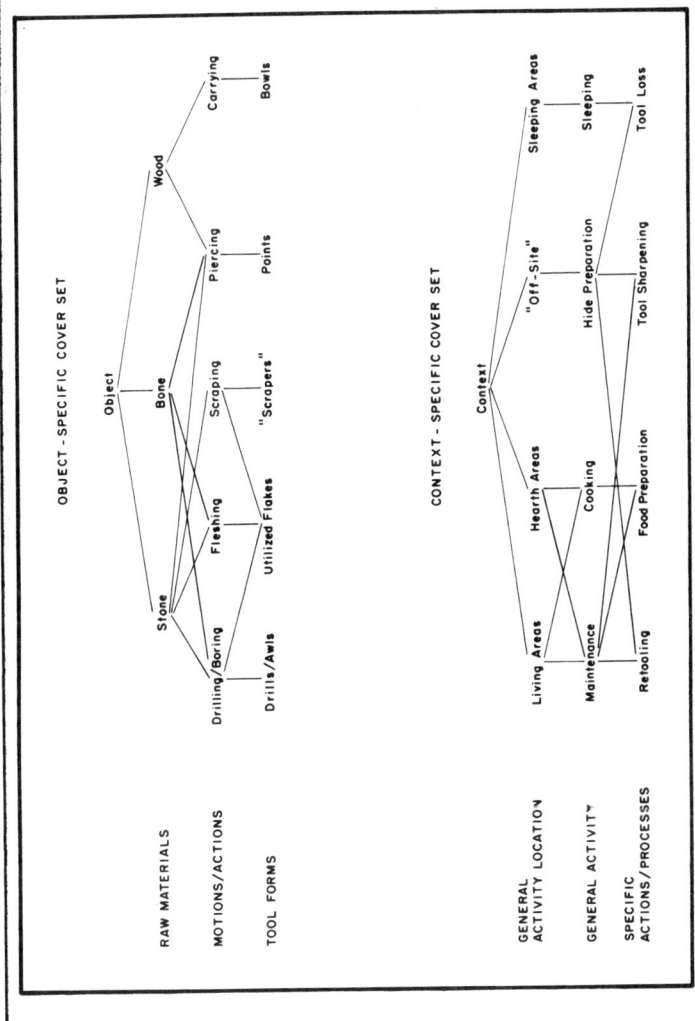

Figure 5.2 Possible cover sets of assemblage data.

idiotechnic. A single artifact could operate one within a single level or any combination of levels. Hierarchically arranged cover sets allow us to "see" these relationships more clearly.

The concept of a relation is fundamental to Q-analysis. Gould (1980: 176-177) makes the point that much of thinking in the human sciences has been functional; that is, we assume that relations between things are naturally represented by such basic functional equations as $Y = f(x)$. We tend to think this way, at least in part, because we have used tools, such as regression analysis or various forms of multivariate analysis, that require us to think of the relations between things in this form. Thus we case our data in a functional framework. However, from the perspective of Q-analysis, this kind of functional thinking is probably the most restrictive way to form a relation between things. But there are other, less restrictive ways to form relations, and Q-analysis provides the framework to explore these possibilities (Gould 1980: 177).

Q-analysis begins with the idea of binary relations. Given well-defined sets (through the definitional task of forming cover sets), relationships between pairs of objects can be represented by (0,1) mappings. This kind of mapping is not necessarily the familiar presence-absence dichotomy (although it could be) but instead simply a rule that establishes a relation. For example, values that fall above a certain figure could be labeled 1; those below the value, 0. This value is the slicing parameter, some number deemed appropriate to form the basis of a rule. Relationships between the sets can then be represented by an incidence matrix or graphical procedures in the case of four-dimensional relationships or lower. For example, the relationships between five archaeological assemblages, using Thomas's (1983) seven different types, can be represented as simplices, or geometrical figures (Figure 5.3). Each of the assemblage types in this sample represents a dimension, and the simplicial complex defines the connections between archaeological assemblages. The dimensionality of the simplicial complex depends on the number of members of the set used to form the relationships. Higher-dimensional structures are obtained by computers through combinatorial searches of incidence matrices.

The power of Q-analysis lies in its ability to "let the data speak for itself." This is not the old notion archaeologists once had regarding the "natural" basis of types, or the naive hopes we as a discipline had in the accumulation of data as a means to solve a problem. What

	General Utility Tools	Weapons	Harvesting Equipment	Fabricating Equipment	Domestic Equipment	Recreational Equipment	Ceremonial Equipment
	1	2	3	4	5	6	7
A	1	0	0	1	0	0	0
B	0	1	0	1	0	0	0
Sites C	1	1	1	0	0	0	0
D	1	0	0	0	0	0	0
E	0	0	1	0	1	0	0

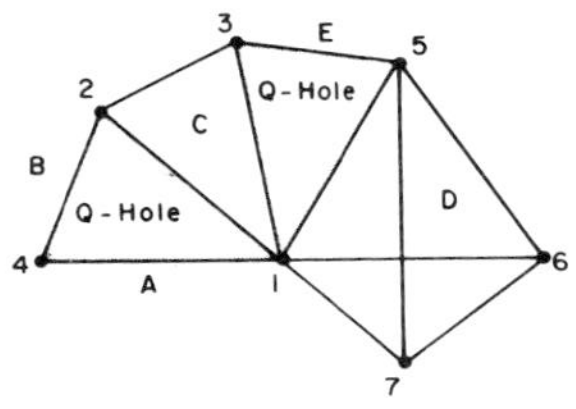

Figure 5.3 Incidence matrix and simplicial complex of assemblage data.

Q-analysis does is to express the relationships between our concepts *in terms of those concepts*. The archaeologist defines them as well as possible; Q-analysis permits us to look at those relationships with as few assumptions as possible. If done with care (proper regard to the definitional task), we can avoid the imposition of potentially inappropriate structures on our data. Therefore, thinking of data as being created in this framework is a powerful practical tool for understanding the relationship between archaeological things.

As an approach to understanding structure, Thomas's model begins to approximate what we need in order to understand the processes that lead to the formation of archaeological assemblages and the ways in which we can begin to unravel their complex structures. I think the addition of Q-analysis to the modeling procedure could go far to systematize and strengthen the model and to extend it into unexplored areas. In some ways, Thomas's model represents a sort of backlash to the use of quantitative procedures in the analysis of archaeological assemblages. So many well-meaning abuses have been proffered as substantive advances that such a backlash was inevitable. What the multivariate models did for us, however, is present us with some structure, albeit inappropriate and misleading. Q-analysis, in the context of concept formation and data definition, can bring us back to an appropriate means of defining structure.

Conclusions

Thinking hard about numbers and structures forces us to reconsider our notions about the linkages between "data," "method," and "theory." "Data" are not merely givens, and "methods" are not just tools. In effect, "methods" are languages, ways of thinking about relationships; and in the context of Q-analysis, it should be clear that many quantitative and statistical procedures that are based upon functional thinking place substantial restrictions on the kinds of things that can be thought about and expressed. Such techniques, of course, emphasize numbers, and until recently this emphasis has been at the expense of a full understanding of structure and the structural relationships between the things we think we are looking at in archaeological assemblages or in other archaeological problems, for that matter. Furthermore, the techniques have been used in place of concept building; and under these circumstances, it should be no surprise that the post hoc interpretations of "structure" in assemblage data generated by factor analysis, cluster analysis, or correspondence analysis have been so unsatisfactory. Without some understanding of the structure of archaeological data, in all of its forms, we cannot hope to make sound inferences about the questions that interest us about the past. This suggests that we must devote more attention to the business of building our concepts and relating our concepts to one another in the process of model building. Languages of structure such as Q-analysis can help us both create concepts and then link concepts together to build models.

Thinking about the kinds of structure in archaeological data can help us remember the "place" of methods in the research process. Inferential methods, or those that seek structure, must not be allowed to influence the analysis and creation of relational structure. In effect, this says "Archaeology first!" The concepts, from empirical to theoretical, have logical priority. It is at this point that we decide whether or not numbers have meaning or not and whether they are appropriate to the study of the problem at hand. This does not mean we cannot use simple statistics to help us in our search for meaning at the empirical end of the continuum, or elsewhere if appropriate. It is an acknowledgment, however, that we allow the structural relations to speak for themselves in the context of the theory, and that these relationships must not be constrained by a priori notions of data structure based on *method*. Method is pulled into the research process when we wish to obtain inferential structure.

In archaeology, it is inevitable that in many instances, despite our best efforts, we will create poorly structured data (i.e., data with unexpected or unanticipated relationships). In many archaeological situations, we often simply cannot define our concepts as clearly as we might like due to the paucity of middle-range theory, lack of observations in sound archaeological context, or in situations that are truly exploratory. How can we proceed from here? Once we have defined relational structure, we can then chose those methods that when applied to the data will result in the violation of the fewest assumptions that form the basis of the procedure. This is good statistical sense, but it also makes good practical sense within the context of research. If we can keep our methods simple and under control, we can feel more confident in the results obtained from their use. If the data are already poorly structured, it makes no sense to use a sophisticated multivariate procedure to impose yet another poorly defined structure on them. But does this mean we cannot explore our data except under the best circumstances? Obviously not; but you shouldn't play unless you think very hard about what it is you are playing with. You should only tinker with those methods you understand. We don't permit our children to play with matches because we think they are not mature enough to deal with the unforeseen consequences of their actions; likewise, we should not permit archaeologists to play with their data unless we are convinced that they are aware that they could well burn down their interpretative frameworks.

An understanding of the structure of archaeological data will not solve all our problems, but it is a good place to start. We will obviously have to become more sophisticated in our understanding of statistical and quantitative methods. But by thinking hard about meaning, how we give meaning to our concepts, how we create data, and how we perceive structural relationships within our data, we can feel more confident that we are truly studying the past and not some artifact of our ignorance.

Acknowledgments

I would like to thank my wife, Karen Aldenderfer, for her encouragement and for her efforts in drafting the figures for this paper. Larry Kimball of Northwestern University has been a source of information as well as critical thinking about archaeological assemblages. Discussions with Larry have always resulted in new insights into the problem.

References

Aldenderfer, M. n.d. The analytical engine: computer simulation and archaeological research. *Advances in Archaeological Method and Theory*.
Atkin, R. 1974. *Mathematical Structure in Human Affairs*. London: Heinemann Educational Books.
Binford, L. R. 1972. Contemporary model building: paradigms and the current state of Paleolithic research. In *Models in Archaeology*, ed. D. L. Clarke, pp. 109-166. London: Methuen.
Binford, L. R. 1983. *In Pursuit of the Past*. London: Thames and Hudson.
Binford, L. R. and S. Binford. 1966. A preliminary analysis of functional variability in the Mousterian of Levallois facies. *American Anthropologist* 68(2): 238-295.
Carr, C. (ed.) 1985. *For Concordance in Archaeological Analysis*. Kansas City: Westport Publishers.
Clark, G. and R. Stafford. 1982. Quantification in American archaeology: a historical perspective. *World Archaeology* 14(1): 98-119.
Coombs, C. H. 1964. *A Theory of Data*. New York: John Wiley.

David, N. 1985. The Noaillan (Level 4) assemblages and the Noaillan Culture in Western Europe. *American School of Prehistoric Research, Bulletin 37*. Cambridge, MA: Peabody Museum, Harvard University.

David, N. and H. Bricker. 1985. Perigordian and Noaillan in the greater Perigord. Paper presented at the Fiftieth Annual Meeting, Society for American Archaeology, Denver.

Gould, P. 1980. Q-analysis, or a language of structure: an introduction for social scientists, geographers, and planners. *International Journal of Man-Machine Studies* 13: 169-199.

Gould, P. 1984. Destructive retrieval in the realm of three-mode thinking. In *Research Methods for Multimode Data Analysis*, eds. H. Law, C. Snyder, J. Hattie, and R. McDonald, pp. 536-554.

Hodson, F. R. 1982. Some aspects of archaeological classification. In *Essays in Archaeological Typology*, eds. R. Whallon and J. Brown, pp. 21-29. Evanston, IL: Center for American Archaeology Press.

Kaplan, A. 1964. *The Conduct of Inquiry*. San Francisco: Chandler.

Mellers, P. 1970. Some comments on the notion of "functional variability" in stone tool assemblages. *World Archaeology* 2: 74-89.

Spaulding, A. 1982. Structure in archaeological data: nominal variables. In *Essays on Archaeological Typology*, eds. R. Whallon and J. Brown, pp. 1-20. Evanston, IL: Center for American Archaeology Press.

Thomas, D. H. 1983. The archaeology of Monitor Valley. 2. Gatecliff Shelter. *Anthropological Papers of the American Museum of Natural History*, 59, part 1.

6

A Consideration of the Role of Quantitative Archaeology in Theory Construction

Larry R. Kimball

Introduction

One of the less discussed aspects of quantitative archaeology is its relation to theory. It appears that higher priority is given to the selection of the "best solution" to a problem. Consequently, the anthropological relevance of the linkage among problem definition, its arguable resolution, and the method chosen to measure relationships in the empirical domain is reduced to secondary importance. Certainly there are those who give primacy to the discussion of the theoretical ramifications of using quantitative methods (either general or specific) or the relevance of assumptions held in the selection of one technique over another. I am not going to discuss either of these positions. What I refer to in my title is the move from *theory* (assumed independent of the chosen statistical procedure) to selection of a quantitative technique in testing a hypothesis *or* the move from empirical evidence discovered via quantitative methods to the creation of theory.

It seems evident to me that there are relatively few formal theories chasing quantitative techniques in contemporary archaeology. This is true for two reasons:

(1) There are relatively few well-constructed theories explicit enough to generate numerous implications for testing with archaeological data.
(2) The major investment by quantitative archaeologists has been to borrow, revise, abuse, and occasionally create quantitative methods that best extract the "true" patterning of the archaeological record.

This second situation is most clearly exemplified by the following kinds of problems for which "best solutions" have, and continue to be, advanced: (1) typology, (2) spatial patterning (inter- and intra-site), (3) intersite assemblage variability, and (4) probabilistic estimations of land use.

Best Solutions and Pattern Recognition

A "best solution" proceeds by the criticism of old techniques to the replacement of old with new techniques, usually argued to be better on statistical grounds. In this regard, best solutions are reactions to existing or traditional methods of classifying artifacts, detecting site structure, etc. The obvious examples are selection of the "best" clustering algorithm, numerous techniques of grouping piece-plotted artifacts, and various attempts to classify artifacts into statistical types with discrete variables.

Pattern recognition approaches differ, for the emphasis is placed upon the patterns themselves, and, I argue, hold the implicit assumption that patterns are out there for us to detect if we are armed with the appropriate software to "do the job right." More often, I think, pattern recognition approaches are "problem specific" in archaeology. The problems of decoding the assemblage variability of the Mousterian and site structure are clear examples. Although one might argue that this is not true in the case of typological studies (often touted as pattern recognition analyses), they do relate to the problem of formal variation through time (establishment of temporal markers) and space (cultural markers). Still a problem is clearly implied.

Exactly what is pattern recognition and what is its relation to theory? Duda (1970: 4) defined *pattern recognition* as "the extraction of significant characterizing features followed by classification on the basis of the values of the features." Examples beyond archaeology include: fingerprint identification, electrocardiogram analysis, cloud pattern recognition, and blood cell classification. The method requires only two things: (1) the design of a pattern extractor, and (2) the design of a pattern classifier. The only problem left is the determination of how well the pattern recognition system works. Its performance "often depends crucially on the performance of the feature extractor" (Duda 1970: 23). In other words, you make sure that attributes are measuring values relative to the question and the degree of sensitivity necessary to solve problems.

What Duda suggests here is that pattern recognition is not theory-dependent but it is concerned with "fit." For example, meteorologists have created a reliable system of discriminating types of clouds. But the pattern recognition system does not explain why clouds vary in their formal characteristics or in terms of the evapotranspiration process that causes clouds. This is true despite the fact that correlations between cloud morphology and future weather conditions are known and that predictive statements can be generated from the sequence of cloud morphogenesis. I think that most of our quantitative pattern recognition systems in archaeology exhibit a similar structure and weakness—a lack of explanatory power.

Perhaps it is also important to believe that quantitative methods should not only facilitate theory-testing but also theory-construction. In this sense, the pattern recognition school seems bankrupt. For by what method, argument, or logic do they give *meaning* to the "recognized" patterns? I have been told that it is possible to find patterns without theory or in the absence of a model. I wonder how even variable definition, attribute measurement, and sample selection are possible under such a perspective! I think that we are dealing with a discipline so shell-shocked by the overemphasis of theory-building in the last decade that no one wishes to admit the answer—that is, implicitly (and perhaps individually) held theories are more common than formal ones.

The problem with the pattern recognition approach is the method by which *verification* or technique evaluation is made. This is usually by comparison to the established or "known" pattern. Examples include Whallon's (1984: Fig. 32) comparison of the results of his unconstrained clustering procedure to the known pattern of site structure as presented by Binford (1978) at the Mask site. The fallacy here is that the pattern is *known*. This is not true unless: (1) Binford had a motion picture camera running for the entire duration of the Mask site inhabitation, and (2) spatial patterning was evaluated with such temporal control. Binford's model of Mask site structure is *already* an abstraction. However, Whallon's analysis is a significant step forward over previous attempts at spatial analysis, because *assumptions* inherent in the modeling of site structure, à la Binford, are taken into account by the specific quantitative technique employed (Ward's hierarchical grouping procedure of two-dimensionally smoothed data). There is a good "fit" between model and pattern extractor in terms of the logic behind Binford's theory of site formation processes.

Another example is the way several archaeologists (Simek and Larick 1983; Simek 1984; Johnson 1984) evaluate their spatial analytic techniques in the detection of site structure at Pincevent, a late Magdalenian site in the Paris Basin (Leroi-Gourhan and Brezillon 1972). In these cases, a good "fit" of pattern extractor to pattern is determined by how well the method finds the site structure as defined by Leroi-Gourhan. One problem here is that Leroi-Gourhan's model of site structure may be "wrong." Certainly, there is an alternative interpretation of this pattern by Binford (1983, Fig. 93). This further complicates the evaluation of fit between model accuracy and the "true" pattern.

In both examples, a best solution to the general problem of objectively detecting site structure is forwarded. The veracity of pattern detected is determined subjectively by appeal to authority, both of whom (Binford 1978; Leroi-Gourhan and Brezillon 1972) employed spatial analytic techniques no more complicated than the visual inspection of density and item plotted maps. One wonders how much labor is actually saved or objectivity employed, which are two of several rationales for these quantitative procedures. It is indeed ironic that the objective search techniques need the human calculator (*analyse cérébrale* of Bordes et al. 1972: 23) to establish the "expected pattern" to test the "fit" of the new method.

Pattern Recognition as Model: Model as Theory

An interesting example of the pattern recognition approach taken as theory is the use of factor analysis in the functional variability argument of Binford. This example is important for several reasons:

(1) This was the first use of quantitative methods to solve an archaeological problem which affected the discipline at large in the use of quantitative methods.
(2) This began the factor analysis bandwagon.
(3) The search for "toolkits" in lithic assemblages became synonymous with the use of factor analysis.

In short, the relevance of this example to the question "What is the role of quantitative methods in theory-building?" is that the theory behind the functional variability model becomes reduced to the recognition of lithic toolkits via factor analysis.

As we all know the functional model was first presented by Lewis and Sally Binford in 1966. The general model is that the structure and content of Mousterian assemblages are determined by: (1) seasonally regulated phenomena, (2) environmental conditions, (3) ethnic composition of the group, (4) group size, (5) group structure, (6) food needs, (7) shelter, and (8) tool supply (Binford and Binford 1966: 241). Unfortunately, most of these factors cannot be directly or reliably measured in Paleolithic contexts despite their relevance to the modeling of hunter-gatherer systems. In hindsight, one wonders why we have held so tenaciously to the functional model given the nature of these causal factors. Perhaps one answer is to be found in the applicability of the concept of toolkit, as well as the lure of multivariate statistical pattern recognition using factor analysis.

The toolkit concept is unquestionably one of those ideas which is rapidly adopted by a discipline. I think that almost every archaeologist has an implicit understanding or folk definition of the term. However, Binford's (1983: 239) recent statement that everyone has misinterpreted his use of toolkit comes as a surprise! He claims that the functional variability model does not concern tool use as most archaeologists who have employed the concept have assumed (Freeman 1964; Cahen et al. 1979; Anderson-Gerfaud 1981 among others). An inspection of Table 1 in Binford and Binford (1966) leaves little doubt in one's mind what Binford *originally* perceived to be the basis of Mousterian tool design differentiation. Is this where the discipline got the "wrong" idea about what Binford meant by toolkit? Perhaps the only problem was that Binford forgot to define toolkit; for a definition of the concept is not found in the 1966, 1972, or 1973 functional papers. As the word toolkit was used in the 1966 paper I think it can be defined as follows: "A *toolkit* is a factor of linear combination of tool types weighted according to their common variance employing a principal components technique." (While Binford and Binford [1966: 242] would have probably viewed this as perfectly congruent with the notion of assemblage composition, I suggest assemblage structure is a more appropriate analogue because the individual factor scores of an assemblage [the case] represent its composition in terms of the structure.)

This definition of toolkit points up the importance of a quantitative technique to the development of a model of more general importance. Since 1966, the detection of toolkits in lithic research has been synonymous with the extraction of a varimax-rotated principal components structure using SPSS run on the local university mainframe (Freeman 1964: Binford and Binford 1966; Binford 1972; Schiffer 1975; Vierra 1975; Aldenderfer 1977; Harrole 1978; Mueller-Wille 1983; and others). The only exceptions to this are the spatial analytic approaches of Whallon (1973, 1974) and the refitting approaches of several European archaeologists (Leroi-Gourhan and Brezillon 1972; Cahen et al. 1979; Audouze et al. 1981; and Marks 1983).

This linkage between toolkit recognition and use of factor analytic methods is a particularly troubling one. Problems of inadequate sample size, an absence of sampling design, use of more variables than cases, inclusion of cases from very disparate regions, and the use of "closed array" data (percentages) aside (see Cowgill 1968; Speth and Johnson 1976; and Aldenderfer 1977 for reviews); there is an even bigger problem! That is, there is the *lack of similarity* among extracted factor structures for the Mousterian technologies in France and Spain (cf. Binford and Binford 1966; Freeman 1964; and Mueller-Wille 1983). Furthermore, the method by which *meaning* is attributed to these structures is totally ex post facto. A functional interpretation of any factor structure of Mousterian data will always follow because the analyst *believes* all factors are toolkits and logically proceeds to create a "functional" rationalization for the observed pattern. I claim this is true despite the Binfords' (1966: Fig. 1) models of expected bivariate plots of factor loadings. However, these models of expected factor loading patterns for the Mousterian data are interesting for several reasons:

(1) "*The diagonal,*" which Binford argues represent "two factors that are similarly determined and therefore inferred as being functionally equivalent" (1966: 246) is somewhat difficult to understand. Clearly, an analogy is made to bivariate

correlation, for an inspection of the two factor analysis texts cited by the Binfords (Fruchter 1954 and Harmann 1961) does not reveal the basis for such an interpretation of relationships between two factors. In fact, factors should be as uncorrelated as possible according to the extraction procedures. However, we might expect some degree of correlation between factors in random data.
(2) Pattern A is about what we expect for a factor structure when the data structure is random.
(3) Only two of these patterns were observed and presented in the study (Binford and Binford 1966, Figs. 3-4)—for Factors I and III (which are similar to Model Pattern A) and Factors II and V (which are like Model Pattern C). Functional interpretations for both of these bivariate factor patterns are presented in the study. However, there can be no functional interpretations of a variable loading if the variables are not supposed to have a functional basis, as Binford now purports.

I took the liberty to inspect all of the bivariate plots for this analysis (Figure 6.1). Clearly, most of the loadings are concentrated around the origins of the axes. This suggests that very little structure is measured by these variables; and perhaps, as Cowgill (1970) has pointed out with small samples that include many zero values, there is little to explain in such when manipulated using techniques based on correlations. Perhaps this inspection of the study reveals that tighter arguments are necessary in order to avoid problems faced after new solutions have been evaluated in terms of the linkage between theory, model, and method.

Possible Solutions

Part of the current problem in quantitative archaeology is due to a blind acceptance that the deductive side of the scientific cycle (Figures 6.2-6.3) is the only place to be, and that inductive or creative thoughts are to be avoided at all costs. In this regard, it is interesting to contrast the models of the scientific process of David Thomas (Figure 6.2) with that of Stanley South (Figure 6.3). Both archaeologists derive their model from Kemeny (1959), so any differences are theirs alone.

The model of Thomas portrays quantitative methods (or mathematics) as the means by which we move away from mere fact-finding (fieldwork) through inductive theory-building and theory verification through hypothesis testing. South is less emphatic about the nonfieldwork domain. In his Nomothetic Atmosphere, induction

Larry R. Kimball 121

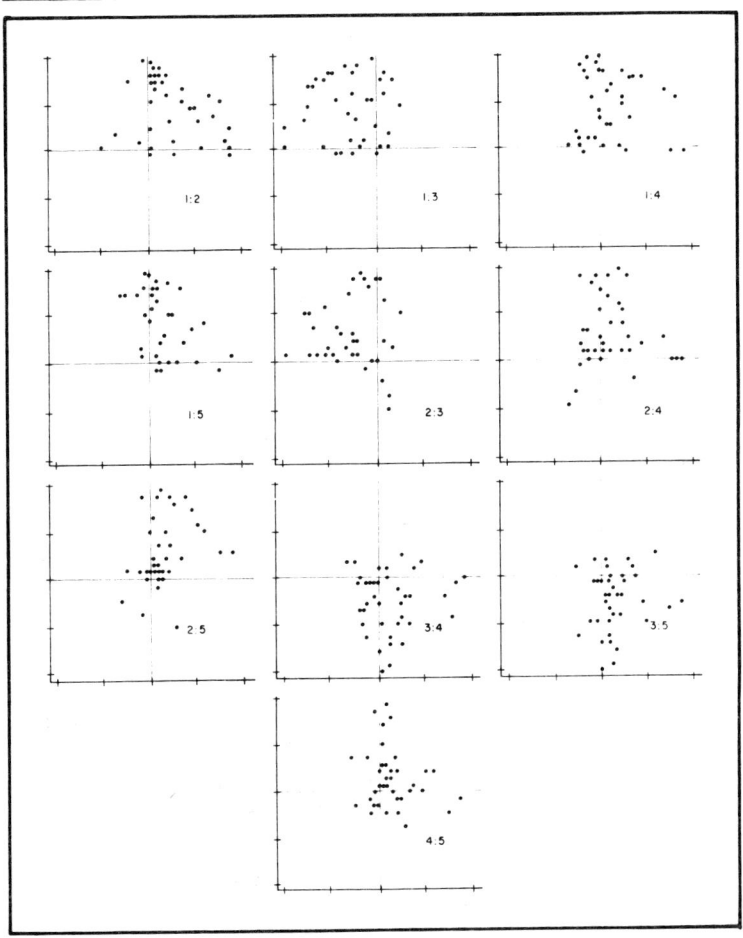

Figure 6.1 Bivariate plots of the factor loadings from the Binford and Binford (1966: Tables 2-6) analysis.

(exemplified by the pattern recognition dolphin) and verification (the testing dolphin) move us from the nomothetic domain into the empirical domain. Herein I see a distinction. For South, the linkage between theory and evidence is facilitated by quantitative methods— hypothesis testing is the deductive dive down from theory, and pattern recognition is the inductive leap up toward theory. As I read Thomas's flowchart, quantitative concerns are privy to the analytic

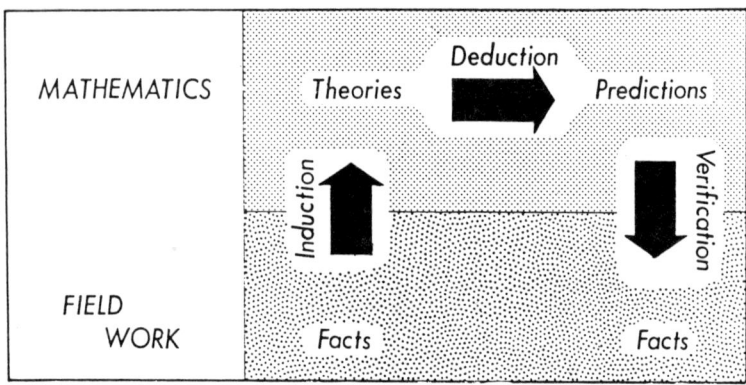

Figure 6.2 David Thomas's flowchart of the scientific cycle. Reproduced by permission of the Society for American Archaeology from D. H. Thomas (1973) "An empirical test of Steward's model of Great Basin settlement patterns." *American Antiquity* 38: 155-176.

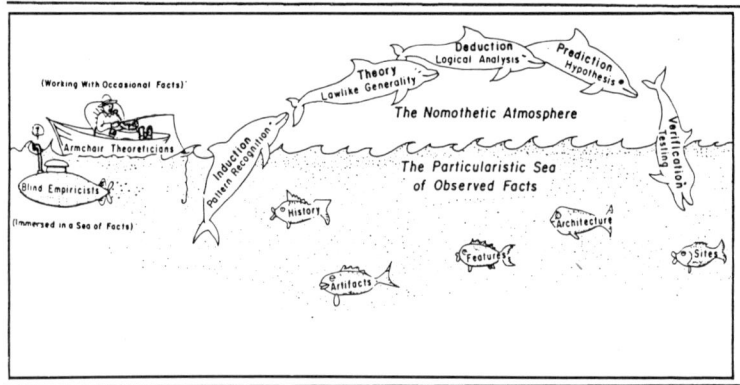

Figure 6.3 Stanley South's flowchart of the scientific cycle (1977: Fig. 2). Reproduced, with permission, from *Method and Theory in Historical Archaeology*, published by Academic Press, Inc., Orlando, FL.

domain and not the facilitator for the move from the empirical and theoretical domains. Perhaps this is reading too much from their diagrams. Certainly Thomas (1979: Figure 2-3) now refers to the theoretical domain as the "World of Generalizations." But I maintain that the role of quantitative methods in theory construction is somewhat different between these two archaeologists, who would otherwise agree on a number of conceptual issues.

I contend that one solution to the confusion over the role of quantitative methods in archaeological theory is to admit that most of what we have been doing is on the inductive data-dredging side of theory construction. However, we should admit that this is perfectly acceptable given that theory-building is a creative process, which is not necessarily deductive. Unfortunately, because we have associated theory-building with deductive processes (which most pattern recognition work is not), we fail to see the vast wealth of data and ideas available for synthesis. The status of theory in contemporary archaeology, as reviewed by Renfrew (1982) and Binford (1982) (both of whom bemoan a lack of formal theory or a specific road to theory-building), might be altered by a more explicit statement of our theoretic investments and ambitions as quantitative archaeologists, while we continue to crank out the patterns. We could fall back to building middle-range theory or finding new quantitative solutions; but I doubt these strategies will solve the more general problem, at least as it relates to the role of quantitative methods in theory creation. That is, we cannot move toward theory construction until we admit that quantitative methods and traditional quantitative archaeology have remained to date merely method.

On the positive side, one area of fruitful investment may be *causal modeling*. The use of path analysis or structural equation modeling has demonstrated power in social science research (Duncan 1966; Hadden and DeWalt 1974; Goody and Buckley 1980). Yet archaeology has lagged behind in exploring this method. Causal modeling virtually assures a good fit between theory and technique—for it is impossible to define a causal model in the absence of a theory. In my opinion, one compelling reason to adopt causal modeling is that the researcher is forced to demonstrate explicitly the linkages among all variables in the model. In addition, now that structural equations have been worked out for discrete variables (Winship and Mare 1983), I see only one reason why archaeologists would not want to adopt such a method—the lack of formalized theories. Finally, these causal models for discrete data solve another problem in quantitative archaeology—that is, the cumbersome evaluation of log-linear or cross-categorical models, which presently appear to be the only way to deal with multivariate discrete data. Much is possible, when the researcher lets the reader know which dolphin he is riding—are we moving toward theory or diving into the data from the theory springboard? I contend that both are possible and necessary in modern quantitative archaeology.

Acknowledgments

I wish to thank Mark Aldenderfer for encouraging me to write this paper. Malcolm Dow has been most influential during my "retooling" at Northwestern. I extend my heartfelt gratitude to Kerry Knox (Northwestern) and William Autry (University of Chicago) who read and criticized this paper.

References

Aldenderfer, M. S. 1977. *The Computer Simulation of Assemblage Formation Processes: The Evaluation of Multivariate Statistical Methods in Archaeological Research.* Ph.D. dissertation. Department of Anthropology. Pennsylvania State University.
Anderson-Gerfaud, P. 1981. *Contribution Methodologique a l'Analyse des Microtraces d'Utilisation sur les Outils Prehistoriques.* These de 3e Cycle, Talence: Universite de Bordeaux I.
Audouse, F., D. Cahen, L. H. Keeley, and B. Schmider. 1981. Le site magdalenien du buisson campin a Veberie (Oise). *Gallia Prehistoire* 24(1): 99-143.
Binford, L. R. 1972. Contemporary model building: paradigms and the current state of Paleolithic research. In *Models in Archaeology*, ed. D. L. Clarke, pp. 109-66. London: Methuen.
Binford, L. R. 1973. Interassemblage variability—the Mousterian and the "functional argument." In *The Explanation of Culture Change*, ed. C. Renfrew, pp. 227-254. London: Duckworth.
Binford, L. R. 1978. Dimensional analysis of behavior and site structure: learning from an Eskimo hunting stand. *American Antiquity* 43: 330-61.
Binford, L. R. 1982. Objectivity, explanation, and archaeology 1980. In *Theory and Explanation in Archaeology*, eds. C. Renfrew, M. J. Rowland, and B. Segraves, pp. 125-138. New York: Academic Press.
Binford, L. R. 1983. *In Pursuit of the Past: Decoding the Archaeological Record.* New York: Thames and Hudson.
Binford, L. R. and S. R. Binford. 1966. A preliminary analysis of functional variability in the Mousterian of Levallois facies. *American Anthropologist.* 68(2): 238-295.
Bordes, F., J. P. Rigaud, and D. de Sonneville-Bordes. 1972. Des buts, problemes et limites de l'archéologie paleolithique. *Quaternaria* 16(1): 15-34.
Cahen, D., L. H. Keeley, and F. L. Van Noten. 1979. Stone tools, toolkits and human behavior in prehistory. *Current Anthropology* 20(4): 661-83.
Cowgill, G. L. 1968. Archaeological applications of factor, cluster, and proximity analysis. *American Antiquity* 33: 367-75.
Cowgill, G. L. 1970. Some sampling and reliability problems in archaeology. In *Archeologie et calculateurs: problemes semilogiques et mathematiques*, ed. J.-C. Gardin and M. Borillo, pp. 161-76. Paris: CNRS.
Duda, R. C. 1970. Elements of pattern recognition. In *Adaptive, Learning, and Pattern Recognition Systems*, ed. J. M. Mendel and K. S. Fu, pp. 3-33. New York: Academic Press.
Duncan, O. D. 1966. Path analysis: sociological examples. *American Journal of Sociology* 72: 1-16.
Freeman, L. 1964. *Mousterian Developments in Cantabrian Spain.* Ph.D. dissertation. Department of Anthropology. University of Chicago.
Goody, J. and J. Buckley. 1980. Implications of the sexual division of labor in agriculture. In *Numerical Techniques in Social Anthropology*, ed. J. C. Mitchel, pp. 33-47. Philadelphia: Institute for the Study of Human Issues.
Hadden, K. and B. DeWalt. 1974. Path analysis: some anthropological examples. *Ethnology* 13(1): 105-28.

Harrold, F. B. 1978. *A Study of the Chatelperronian.* Ph.D. dissertation. Department of Anthropology. University of Chicago.
Johnson, I. 1984. Cell frequency recording and analysis of artifact distributions. In *Intrasite Spatial Analysis in Archaeology*, ed. H. J. Hietala, pp. 75-96. Cambridge: Cambridge University Press.
Kerrich, J. E. and D. L. Clarke. 1966. Notes on the possible misuse and errors of cumulative percentage frequency graphs for the comparison of prehistoric artefact assemblages. *Proceedings of the Prehistoric Society* 32: 57-69.
Kemeny, J. G. 1959. *A Philosopher Looks at Science.* New York: Van Nostrand Reinhold.
Leroi-Gourhan, A. and M. Brezillon. 1972. *Fouilles de Pincevent, Essai d'Analyse Ethnographique d'un Habitat Magdalenien.* Paris: CNRS.
Marks, A. E. 1983. The middle to upper Paleolithic transition in the Levant. In *Advances in World Archaeology*, ed. F. Wendorf and A. E. Close, Vol. 2: 51-98. New York: Academic Press.
Mueller-Wille, M. 1983. *Analysis of Variability among Mousterian Industries in Eastern and Northern Spain.* Ph.D. dissertation. Department of Anthropology. University of Chicago.
Renfrew, C. 1982. Explanation revisited. In *Theory and Explanation in Archaeology*, ed. C. Renfrew, M. J. Rowlands, and B. Segraves, pp. 5-24. New York: Academic Press.
Schiffer, M. B. 1975. Factors and "toolkits": evaluating multivariate analyses in archaeology. *Plains Anthropology* 20(67): 61-70.
Simek, J. 1984. A K-means approach to the analysis of spatial structure in Upper Paleolithic habitation sites. *British Archaeological Reports, International Series* 205.
Simek, J. and R. Larick. 1983. The recognition of multiple spatial patterns: a case study from the French Upper Paleolithic. *Journal of Archaeological Science* 10: 165-80.
South, S. 1977. *Method and Theory in Historical Archaeology.* New York: Academic Press.
Speth, J. D. and G. A. Johnson. 1976. Problems in the use of correlation for the investigation of tool kits and activity areas. In *Culture Change and Continuity*, ed. C. E. Cleland, pp. 35-57. New York: Academic Press.
Thomas, D. H. 1971. On the use of cumulative curves and numerical taxonomy. *American Antiquity* 36: 206-9.
Thomas, D. H. 1973. An empirical test of Steward's model of Great Basin settlement patterns. *American Antiquity* 38: 155-76.
Thomas, D. H. 1979. *Archaeology.* New York: Holt, Rinehart and Winston.
Vierra, R. K. 1975. *Structure versus Function in the Archaeological Record.* Ph.D. dissertation. Department of Anthropology. University of New Mexico.
Winship, C. and R. D. Mare. 1983. Structural equations and path analysis for discrete data. *American Journal of Sociology* 89(1): 54-110.
Whallon, R. 1973. Spatial analysis of occupation floors I: application of dimensional analysis of variance. *American Antiquity* 38: 266-78.
Whallon, R. 1974. Spatial analysis of occupation floors II: application of nearest neighbor analysis. *American Antiquity* 39: 16-34.
Whallon, R. 1984. Unconstrained clustering for the analysis of spatial distributions in archaeology. In *Intrasite Spatial Analysis in Archaeology*, ed. H. J. Hietala, pp. 242-77. Cambridge: Cambridge University Press.

7

Quantitative Methods Designed for Archaeological Problems

Keith W. Kintigh

Introduction

For purposes of this paper, I would like to draw a distinction between those quantitative techniques that have been developed specifically for archaeological applications and techniques that have been adopted from other fields (such as statistics, ecology, or geology) and are applied in a rather straightforward way to archaeological problems. While this distinction is not always clearcut—a point that I will return to later—I would like to examine the place of these specially designed methods in archaeological research.

Examples of Specially Designed Methods

Before I go any farther, I should provide some examples of the methods I have in mind. In a far from exhaustive list I would include:

First, methods of seriation such as the one originally published by Leslie Spier in 1917 and Ford's (1962) graphical technique (see also Craytor and Johnson 1968). Using complete samples of sherds from stratigraphic excavations and surface collections, Spier was able to seriate sites by ordering them according to the percentage of the major ware present. This simple but elegant method made use of his perceptive understanding of the nature of ceramic change in the Zuni area. Ford's well-known graphical technique relies on the more sophisticated battleship curve model of ceramic change.

Stanley South (1977) has proposed a number of techniques to solve dating problems in historical archaeology. South suggests that if we have counts of dated ceramic types, we can calculate the "mean ceramic date" for the site, a date at which we can assume that the site was occupied. Given the earliest and latest production dates for each type, the "median manufacture date" for that type is the midpoint of the production period. The mean ceramic date is calculated by averaging the median dates of all types present at the site, weighted by the counts for that type. South's methods for dating historic site occupation periods have subsequently been elaborated through use of more complex and more realistic depositional models by Salwen and Bridges (1977), Carlson (1983), and Steponaitis and Kintigh (1985). All of these methods attempt to deal with a strictly archaeological problem through the application of simple mathematics and basic notions of probability.

Based on what was felt to be an inadequacy of existing numerical methods of classification, Robert Whallon (1972) set out to define a quantitative method that would more closely parallel intuitive typologies whose archaeological utility had been adequately demonstrated. He developed a computer program designed around his observation that archaeologically useful ceramic typologies seem to have a hierarchical structure with different definite criteria used at different places in the hierarchy. This program identified types based on the statistical associations among ceramic attributes.

Simulations of human behavior developed by archaeologists might also be considered specialized archaeological methods. Two examples among the many simulations that have been done may be mentioned: First, David Thomas (1973) used Steward's ethnographic description of Great Basin Shoshoneans as the foundation for a simulation that generated testable predictions concerning prehistoric land use. Second, through his simulation of hunter-gatherer demographics, Martin Wobst (1974) was able to examine the relationships among group size, group longevity, marriage rules, and the number of campsites occupied in a thousand-year interval.

Methods of spatial analysis of living floors recently developed by Albert Ammerman and myself (Kintigh and Ammerman 1982) were constructed to facilitate the recognition of behaviorally interesting patterns through the use of heuristic methods developed intuitively by archaeologists (see also Simek and Larick 1983).

My recent work on diversity (1984a, 1984b) is another example of a method that was developed explicitly to solve a troublesome archaeological problem, the problem of disentangling the effects of sample size on diversity. Here, an expected diversity for a given sample size was generated through Monte Carlo methods based on archaeological frequency distributions of artifact classes.

Finally, I might mention James Doran's attempts to use an artificial intelligence approach to interpret archaeological data. His efforts started in the early 1970s (1972), and I am pleased to see that he is continuing his work as evidenced by his paper in this volume.

Techniques from Other Fields

While this list encompasses a broad range of methods, I wish to contrast them with general-purpose quantitative techniques that were developed in other disciplines. These include: standard inferential statistics (such as chi square tests, regression, and analysis of variance); exploratory data analysis; multivariate statistics (such as factor analysis, discriminant analysis, cluster analysis, log-linear models, and multidimensional scaling); and the various quantitative methods developed in ecology and geography that have been applied to archaeological data.

Lest anyone misunderstand my purpose, I am not suggesting that those methods specifically developed for archaeological problems are necessarily better than those adopted from other disciplines; rather, I simply mean to single out the former class of techniques for special consideration. Indeed, I would strongly argue that simple descriptive and exploratory techniques have a critical role in archaeological research, a point that is amplified in Robert Whallon's paper in this volume. Further, I would hasten to agree that many of the techniques developed in other fields are quite well-suited to archaeological problems. In this regard, it may be noted that the original seriation methods mentioned above have largely been supplanted by the more general methods of multidimensional scaling and principal components analysis.

Indeed, it is sometimes difficult to sort out unique archaeological methods from those developed elsewhere. This is sometimes the case when novel applications are worked out that combine standard techniques in nonobvious ways to yield elegant solutions to significant archaeological problems. A good example of this is Whallon's (1984) unconstrained clustering, an innovative, cluster-analysis-based approach to the problem of identifying activity areas on living floors.

Approaches to Archaeological Data Analysis

Let us consider how archaeologists typically approach their data. In most cases we have in mind some rather ill-defined problems or questions, such as the identification and understanding of settlement pattern changes, the determination of activity areas on living floors, or the understanding of intrasite deposits in a village or urban site. Of course, in order to approach these problems analytically, whether quantitatively or not, we must formulate a representation of the data as a set of measures on relevant variables, and we must figure out what methods may be applied using this representation of the data to address the questions of interest.

The problem of representation, the selection of variables as measures of the phenomena of interest, is an extremely important one, although it is not one that I will consider here. It is the next issue that is of concern in this paper, the problem of developing a sequence of analytical steps that will be effective in illuminating the archaeological questions at hand.

In order to make a point, allow me to caricature several approaches to data analysis. Perhaps the most dangerous approach is employed by those who have a small stable of pet methods that they know and love. These methods get applied to every problem and data set, regardless of their appropriateness for the data or their relevance to the archaeological questions.

A related, but slightly less disastrous approach is used by those who, knowing a limited repertory of statistical techniques, modify the research questions until one of the known techniques is more or less applicable. The unhappy result of this approach is that the anthropologically relevant questions may be abandoned in favor of questions that can be statistically managed, and the research ends up answering questions that no one was interested in asking in the first place.

Next, I suggest that I am not the only one who has had occasion to cringe when a graduate student who has just completed several months of painstaking coding of some data says: "Now I'm nearly done with my analysis, all I have to do is give it to the computer to get my results." An almost equally naive view is shown by those who, after having coded their data, see the next step as being simply a search for *the best* method to use in order to examine their problem with reference to their data.

Of course, what we hope is for the archaeologist to realize that there is usually no *single* best method, and that a variety of approaches must be used to gradually gain an understanding of the structure of the data and its relevance to the anthropological questions.

It may turn out that an archaeologist decides that relevant, or sufficiently sophisticated, quantitative methods do not exist, and that there is no alternative to a subjective analysis, informed as much as possible by simple data-display techniques. Sometimes this response is the product of inadequate knowledge of available methods or a lack of creativity in reformulating aspects of the problem in ways that can be handled quantitatively. However, I fear that more often than the quantitative cognoscenti might like to admit, this judgment is an accurate one: that there do not, in fact, exist adequate quantitative methods to deal with many archaeological problems and contexts that have relatively well-developed subjective modes of analysis.

Here I would like to suggest that it is altogether too rare that the dissatisfaction with available quantitative methods has led to the development of new methods tailored to fit our archaeological problems. As I will discuss below, the basis for such methods often exists in our inventory of intuitive techniques.

Troublesome Problems, Innovative Solutions

This brings me to a consideration of the strengths and weaknesses of the quantitative and intuitive modes of analysis that we use, and how these may indicate the important characteristics of archaeological problems for which specially tailored methods may be useful.

Weaknesses of Standard Quantitative Methods

First, some of the more troublesome problems in archaeology have to do with the recognition of spatial patterns in data. It is not coincidental that pattern recognition is an extremely difficult problem to deal with quantitatively. (The fact that robotics has progressed much more slowly than was expected twenty years ago, in spite of a healthy research investment, is testimony to the difficulty of this problem.) Archaeological data are particularly difficult in this regard because we are often not certain just what kinds of patterns we are looking for. Further, spatial patterning may occur at many levels; there may be patterns within patterns.

It is also the case that the human eye is *extraordinarily* good at recognizing visual patterns. The major drawback is that it is difficult to draw objective conclusions on the basis of visually identified patterns, because observers differ in their perceptions, and because the eye is often so anxious to see patterns that random data will appear to be ordered. Here, it appears that a combination of quantitative and visual approaches may be most productive.

Second, although it is perfectly obvious, it seems to me an underappreciated fact that standard quantitative techniques are incapable of using any knowledge that we as anthropologists have learned about human behavior or the formation of the archaeological record in general. Nor are these methods able to make use of any specific knowledge that we may have about the classes of material being analyzed or the specific archaeological context. All any statistical analysis can do is deal with numbers. It matters not whether we are counting deer tibia, waste flakes, ceramic designs, or pollen grains; a statistical analysis treats then all the same.

Of course, this contextual knowledge is generally used in deciding what statistical analyses to perform and in interpreting the results. However, when we intuitively analyze data, this contextual information is available for use during all stages of analysis, not just at the beginning and at the end. Thus we must accept the possibility that the use of contextual knowledge throughout an analysis may, on occasion, lead to better results. Methods specially tailored to archaeological problems (such as seriation) often use as their premise knowledge about the patterning of material culture that we have gained through experience.

Finally, statistical methods often make assumptions about data that simply cannot be satisfied in archaeological situations. In particular, we have trouble with assumptions of randomness and with assumptions about the distributions of variables. Unfortunately, our samples are often not statistically representative, and not all that many of the variables we like to look at have joint normal distributions. Certainly some methods are rather forgiving of violations of their basic assumptions. On the other hand, I fear that a sort of "damn the torpedoes, full speed ahead" attitude sometimes prevails when we should really be worrying about different ways to get at a question.

Weaknesses of Intuitive Methods

Intuitive analyses face problems of objectivity or replicability, and as a result, it is often difficult to assess the significance or reliability of these analyses. These more obvious weaknesses of intuitive analyses have received adequate press. In addition, there are other problems that I would like to briefly discuss.

First, in the previous section, I indicated that we seem to lack adequate cognitive filters to distinguish randomness from pattern. Next, even when the cultural processes involved are fairly well understood, there are lots of probabilistic questions that are difficult to handle intuitively. This is particularly the case when a number of processes that may be considered to be probabilistic are operating in concert. Everyday human intuition about probability is really not very good. In fact, human probabilistic reasoning consistently operates incorrectly in certain ways. (Some interesting work has been done to discover how human probabilistic reasoning operates.) One need only recall that, contrary to most peoples' intuitions, it doesn't take a very large group of people before the odds are pretty good that two of them have a birthday on the same day.

This kind of problem in probabilistic reasoning is illustrated by a simple example. In dating a site on the basis of present and absent types in a surface collection, we use the absence of a type to indicate that a site was not occupied during the time in which that type was produced. However, it is obvious that how important we consider the absence of a type to be is related both to the regional relative abundance of the type and to the size of our collection. While we all recognize these factors, I think that it is safe to say that our intuitive abilities are not up to deciding the point (sample size and degree of relative abundance) at which an absence becomes significant. However, given a reasonable model of the behavioral processes operating, a computer program can be developed that may yield expectations that are quite useful interpretively.

Similarly, we have a difficult time understanding the implications of complex substantive arguments that posit the complex interaction of a number of factors. The experience that archaeologists have had with simulation indicates that lots of arguments that sound perfectly plausible on the surface can't possibly be correct once you operationalize them. Similarly, arguments that may sound most improbable may turn out to work fairly well. These results derive from the limited computational power that we have in our heads—we often need the aid of computer-based simulations to understand complex cultural situations.

Conclusion

We must realize that because the archaeological record is formed by people interacting in complex ways with each other, their environment, and their cultural heritage (to say nothing of postdepositional processes), many archaeological problems are just inherently difficult. Further, we must keep in mind that over the years archaeologists have developed sophisticated intuitive problem-solving strategies whose utility has by no means been eclipsed by the use of statistics and computers.

There is a tremendous potential for us to develop new and better methods for analyzing archaeological data that combine the strong points of intuitive analysis and the strengths of a quantitative approach. In many cases, this will result from an attempt to translate a tried-and-true intuitive method into a quantitative framework with the intent of putting the analysis on a more objective basis, while preserving the degrees of fit among the methods used, the questions asked, and the archaeological context.

While we don't need to reinvent any analytical wheels, we should keep our eyes open for problems that may yield to a new, more contextual, quantitative approach.

References

Carlson, D. L. 1983. Computer analysis of dated ceramics: estimating dates and occupational ranges. *Southeastern Archaeology* 2(1): 8-20.

Craytor, W. B. and L. Johnson. 1968. Refinements in computerized item seriation. *Museum of Natural History, University of Oregon, Bulletin* 10.

Doran, J. E. 1972. Automatic generation and evaluation of explanatory hypotheses. In *Les Méthodes Mathématiques de l'Archéologie*, ed. M. Borillo, pp. 200-211. Marseilles: CADA (CNRS).

Ford, J. A. 1962. *A Quantitative Method for Deriving Cultural Chronology*. Pan American Union, Technical Manual 1.

Kintigh, K. W. 1984a. Measuring archaeological diversity by comparison with simulated assemblages. *American Antiquity* 49: 44-54.

Kintigh, K. W. 1984b. Sample size, significance, and measures of diversity. Paper presented at the 49th Annual Meeting of the Society for American Archaeology, Portland.

Kintigh, K. W. and A. J. Ammerman. 1982. Heuristic approaches to spatial analysis in archaeology. *American Antiquity* 47: 41-63.

Salwen, B., and S. T. Bridges. 1977. Cultural differences and the interpretation of archaeological evidence: problems with dates. In *Current Perspectives in Northeastern Archaeology: Essays in Honor of William A. Ritchie*. Researches and Transactions of the New York State Archaeological Association 17(1): 165-173.

Simek, J. F. and R. R. Larick. 1983. The recognition of multiple spatial patterns: a case study from the French Upper Paleolithic. *Journal of Archaeological Science* 10: 165-180.

South, S. 1977. *Method and Theory in Historical Archaeology*. New York: Academic Press.

Spier, L. 1917. *An Outline for a Chronology of Zuni Ruins*. Anthropological Papers of the American Museum of Natural History 18: 205-331.

Steponaitis, V. P. and K. W. Kintigh. 1985. Estimating site occupation spans from datable artifacts: some new approaches. Paper presented at the 1985 Meeting of the Commission on Data Management and Mathematical Methods in Archaeology of the International Union of Pre- and Proto-historic Sciences, Denver.

Thomas, D. H. 1972. An empirical test of Steward's model for Great Basin settlement patterns. *American Antiquity* 38: 115-176.

Whallon, R., Jr. 1972. A new approach to pottery typology. *American Antiquity* 37: 13-33.

Whallon, R., Jr. 1984. Unconstrained clustering for the analysis of spatial distributions in archaeology. In *Intrasite Spatial Analysis in Archaeology*, ed. H. J. Hietala, pp. 242-277. Cambridge: Cambridge University Press.

Wobst, H. M. 1974. Boundary conditions for Paleolithic social systems: a simulation approach. *American Antiquity* 39: 147-178.

8

Simple Statistics

Robert Whallon

The purpose of this paper is to argue that simple, descriptive statistics and display techniques are indispensable preliminaries to the application of even the most basic inferential statistics or tests. To my knowledge, the vast majority of statistical analyses of archaeological data, published or unpublished, have been done without adequate preliminary scrutiny of the data with such elementary display techniques and descriptive statistics. From my experience, I will be so bold as to put forward the view that this lack of adequate scrutiny of the data renders every one of these analyses, and consequently the studies and interpretations based on them, suspect a priori. In this respect, contrary to our good and familiar moral and legal traditions, such analyses should, in my opinion, be considered guilty until proven innocent.

However, there is another, more positive, pragmatic reason for so strongly advancing the cause of such humble displays and descriptions of one's data, which is that, in almost every instance, one can learn more, more quickly, more clearly, and in more detail about one's data with these techniques than through the use of inferential statistics or tests. It is my opinion that these latter should remain latter in our statistical methodology and should be applied only when an adequate inspection of the data demonstrates and assures that they are appropriate and that they create an accurate representation of the structure or patterns of variability actually inherent in one's data.

In previous publications, I have shown how even "simple" correlation, and certainly the complex data manipulations of principal components analysis, can obscure and hide intricate, multiple patterns of relations among variables in data, including simultaneous positive and negative correlations, nonlinear relations, and relations of discrete disassociation, or presence/absence, as opposed to covariation (Whallon 1984: 249-258). In other work, I have shown how multiple, positive, linear relations between two variables may be indicative of a pattern of multimode distribution of the ratios of the original variables, in which case it is fairly clear that the simplest and most interpretable and interesting patterns in the data must be expressed in terms of new variables, created as ratios of the original measurements (Whallon 1982: 151-154).

In this paper I would like to expand slightly on these topics and show not only what variety and intricacy of data structure may be hidden behind statistical summaries and manipulations of data but also something of the manipulations and effort that often need to go into the display and description of data before one can say that one has adequately discovered and revealed its inherent structure. I hope in this process to show that description and display of data are not just an obligatory tradition in statistical analysis, to be done in a pro forma and perfunctory manner and then forgotten as one plunges ahead into the chic and sophisticated world of "big number crunching." Rather, data description and display can and must be, in a methodologically correct approach, an active, vital, and exceedingly informative component of any satisfactory analysis.

Let us begin with a simple, bivariate analysis. The data are the counts per square meter of all backed elements, Gravette points, Micro-Gravettes, and Lamelles-à-dos, classed as complete, point segments, medial segments, and butt segments, from a single stratigraphic level within the Perigordian VI deposits at the Abri Pataud in southwest France.[1]

If we take a typical first step in "crunching" these numbers, we can calculate a matrix of correlation coefficients in which we find, for example, a moderate, positive correlation of +.54 between medial segments and butt segments (Figure 8.1). A properly prepared cross-plot seems to illustrate this positive, linear relationship satisfactorily (Figure 8.2). Perhaps our next step could be to factor analyze this matrix or to do a principal components analysis of it and proceed directly to the archaeological task of interpreting the results. After all, statistics is only a tool, and we are archaeologists, not statisticians, right?

However, let us take just a minute more and look at these data again, from a slightly different angle. First of all, a look at the total sample sizes for all backed elements from these squares (Figure 8.3) shows a very marked bimodality. Such a strong bimodality ought to make one think immediately of the likelihood that one is dealing with two different populations here; and if this is so, it behooves us to investigate the similarities and differences between these populations before we continue treating them together in our analysis. In fact, in this case, if we calculate the correlation between medial segments and butt segments separately for the mode of small sample size squares and the mode of larger sample size squares, the original moderate, positive correlation of +.54 switches dramatically to −.64 and −.27, respectively.

In dealing with samples of small size, of course, we expect some possible attenuation of correlations that, with large samples, might be strongly positive,[2] simply through the occurrence of random observations of zero in one or the other of the two variables in question. In fact, the strength of the correlation between two variables decreases linearly with the proportion of random zeros found in either one of the variables. In the extreme case where any random zero is matched by a positive observation in the other variable, it takes zeros in only about a third of the observations of each variable to reduce an originally perfect correlation of +1.00 to a negative value (Figure 8.4). However, we do not expect such random zeros to appear in larger samples. Here, therefore, although we might suspect this to be at least partially behind the strong switch in correlation for the small sample size squares, we would not expect such a shift, or even much attenuation, of the correlation observed in the larger sample size squares. However, looking at the cross-plots for these two artifact classes within small sample size and larger sample size squares separately, the negative relationship is fairly clear in both cases (Figures 8.5 and 8.6).

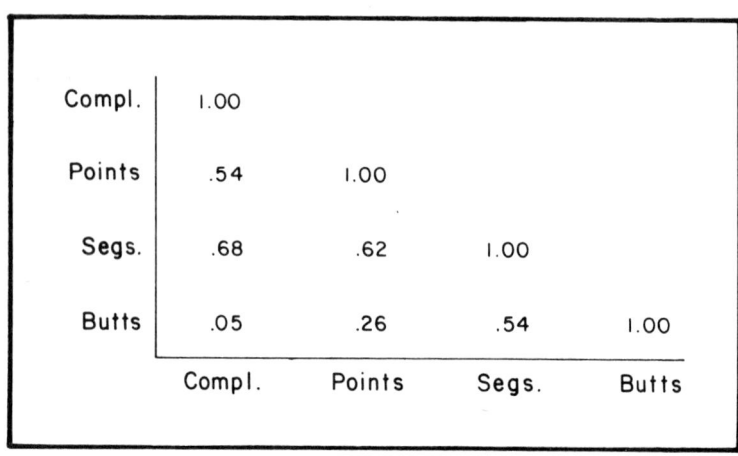

Figure 8.1 Correlations among backed elements, based on counts per square meter within a single Perigordian VI layer at the Abri Pataud.

Putting all this together now, on a single, properly scaled cross-plot (Figure 8.7), we see, indeed, that there is an overall positive relationship between medial segments and butt segments. In larger sample size squares there quite clearly tend to be more of both classes. However, within both of the modal categories of squares, we see, equally clearly, that there is a tendency for a negative relationship between the two artifact classes. In just a few, simple steps we have moved from a single, global, but "blind" statement of "moderate positive correlation" to a more complex, but surely more accurate and informative, understanding of these data, opening more detailed and interesting possibilities for interpretation and further analysis.

These possibilities for further analysis of course include further simple displays and descriptions, as we continue to ask questions, perhaps, about proportionate representation of these artifact classes within each square, and so on. The approach and spirit of inquiry should start by now to be clear.

Before we move on to another example, however, let us examine the first cross-plot I actually obtained for these data (Figure 8.8). If one is used to "reading" such plots, everything we have discussed so far is evident on this plot. At each step, though, I presented other plots that seemed to illustrate better or more dramatically the structure in the data that I was stressing at that moment. In one case I

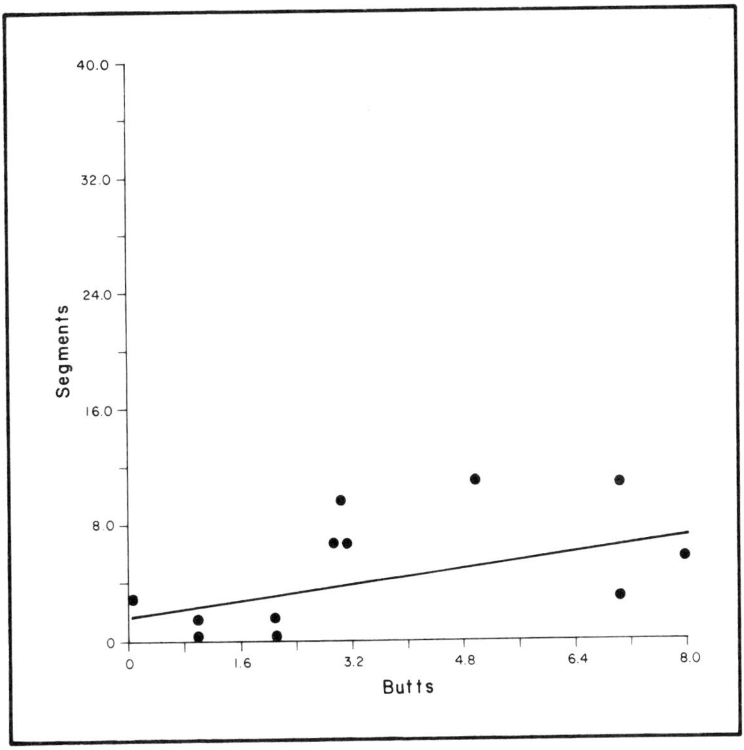

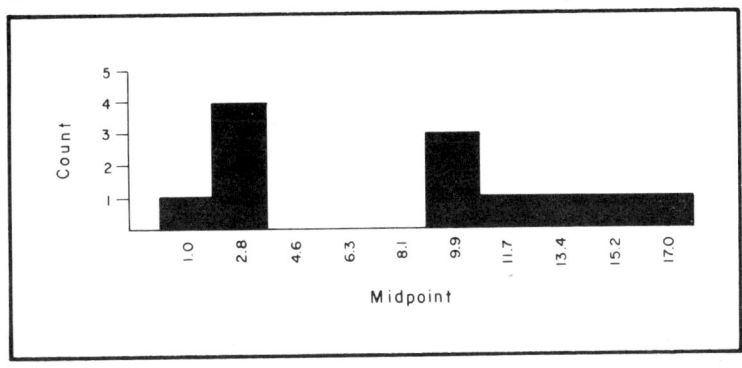

Figure 8.2 Scatter plot of medial segments vs. butts of backed elements—same sample as in Figure 8.1.

Figure 8.3 Sample size by square of backed elements—same sample as in Figure 8.1.

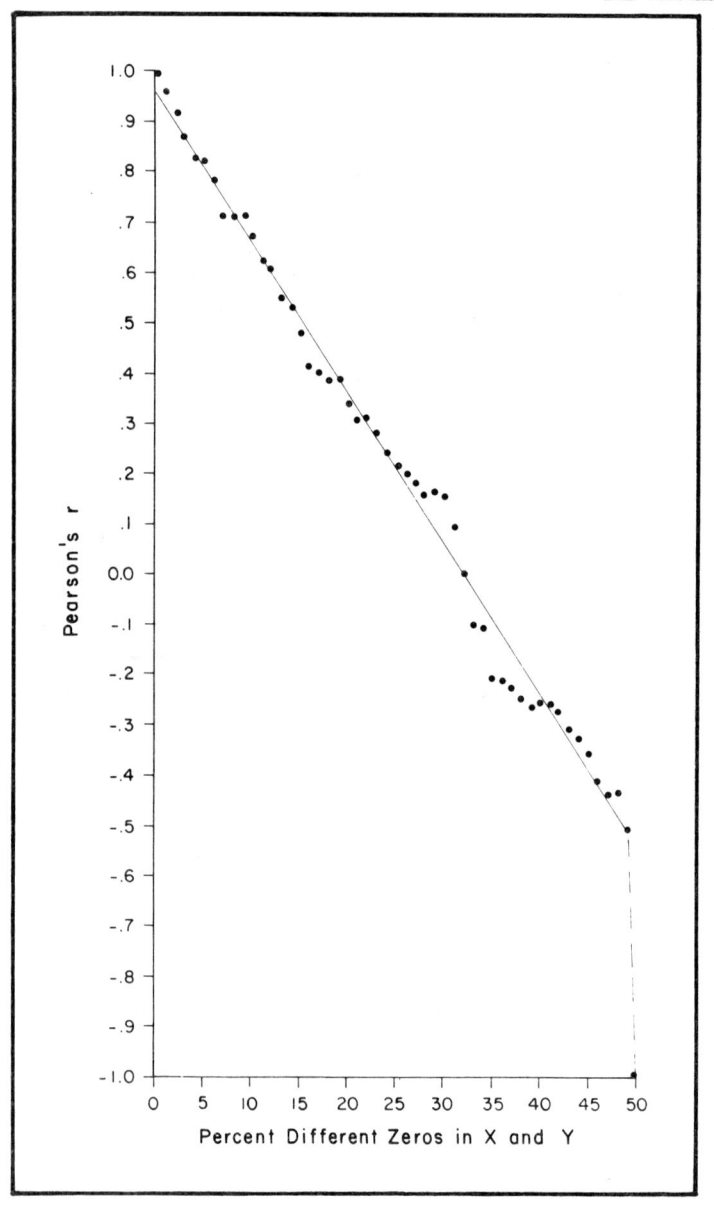

Figure 8.4 Effect of random zeros on a perfectly positive correlation.

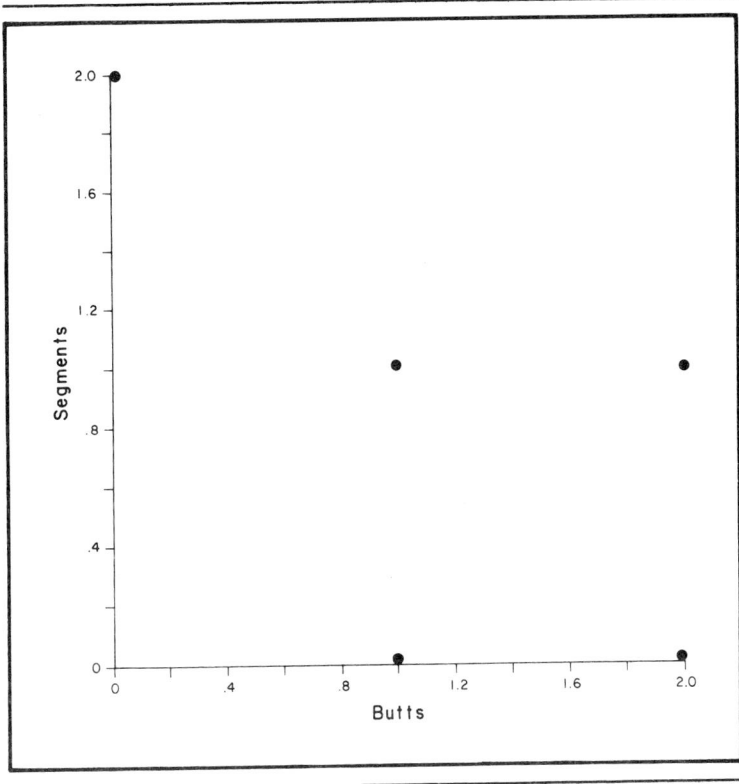

Figure 8.5 Scatter plot of medial segments vs. butts of backed elements—small sample squares as seen on Figure 8.3.

compressed the vertical scale on this plot (Figure 8.2), accentuating the overall positive, linear structure of the data; and in another case, I switched the area of the plot and slightly compressed the new vertical scale (Figure 8.7). The separate plotting of data from the small sample size and the larger sample size squares was, of course, an obvious thing to do.

Was this manipulation of scales and axes legitimate? Or did I "fiddle" the data in an unacceptable manner? To me the answer is clear, and I will defend it strongly: There is nothing sacred about axes or scales in the graphic display of data. To the absolute contrary, these should be, in fact often must be, varied and altered in order to bring out patterns and structure in data. With experience perhaps less

142 Simple Statistics

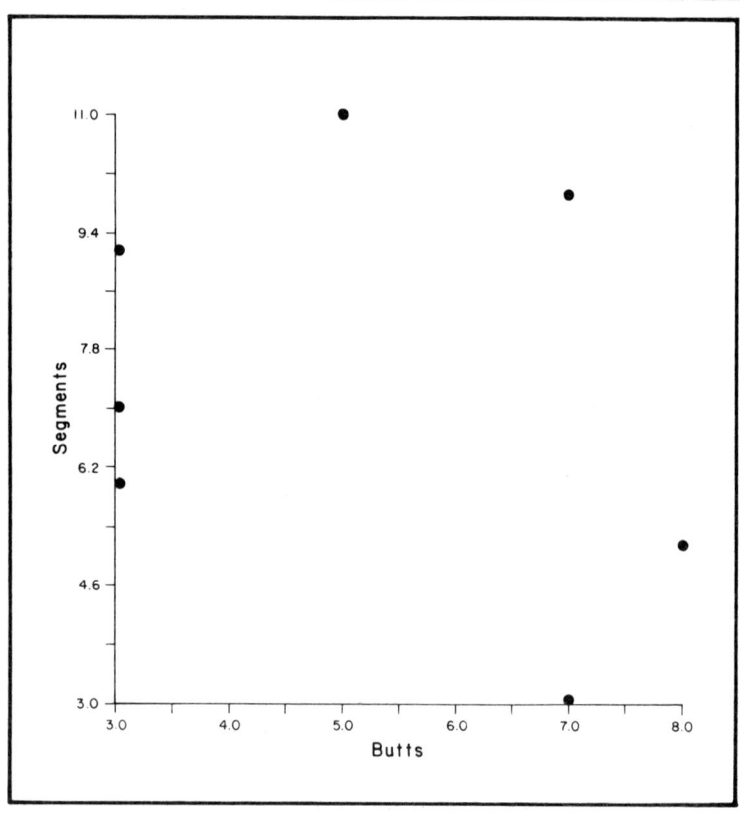

Figure 8.6 Scatter plot of medial segments vs. butts of backed elements–large sample squares as seen on Figure 8.3.

"playing" with these is necessary; but as long as it helps one to see such patterns and structure, it is a useful and legitimate part of the process of exploring one's data. The entire area of "Exploratory Data Analysis" pioneered and championed by Tukey (1977) is nothing but a wide range of techniques for such "playing" with scales, axes, and other "tools" for data display and description with the express purpose of bringing out, and making clear, pattern and structure. In fact, recent studies have demonstrated that there are certain principles of human perception that have important and significant implications for the analysis and interpretation of data organized and displayed graphically (Cleveland and McGill 1985).

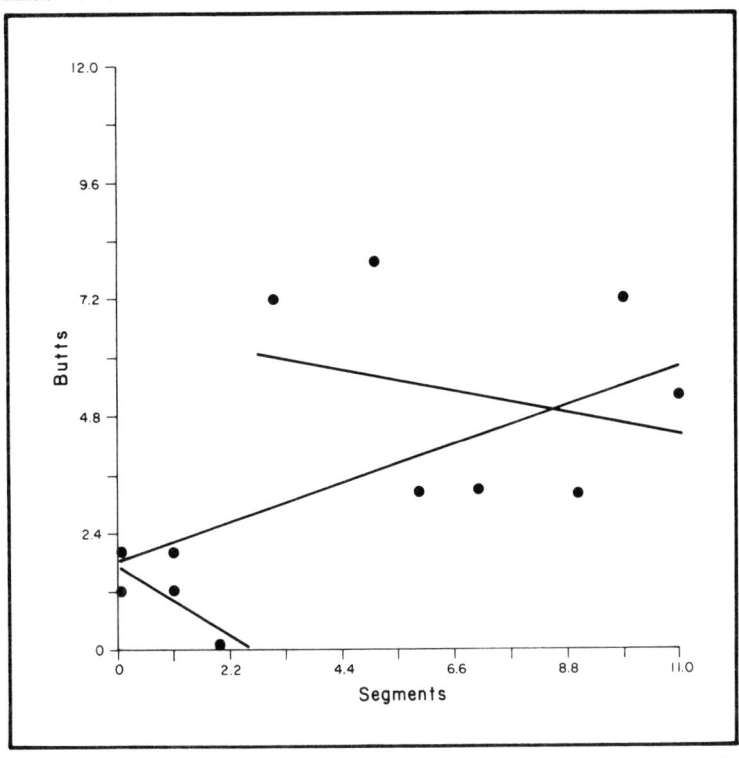

Figure 8.7 Scatter plot of medial segments vs. butts of backed elements—whole sample with regression lines calculated from Figures 8.2, 8.5, and 8.6.

The value of varying the scales at which one looks at data is not confined to bivariate plots, however. To illustrate the interesting things one may do along other lines, we turn now to a simple, univariate example. Some time ago I looked at rim diameters and vessel volumes of Owasco pots (Whallon 1969). A close relationship between these two variables was demonstrated, so that rim diameters, measured from sherds, could be used to study the distribution of vessel volumes in the ceramic assemblages from a number of Owasco sites. Several modal classes of vessel volume were defined, which varied from site to site in relative frequency and through time in mean volume for each mode, leading to various functional and social organizational interpretations. The example I would like to present

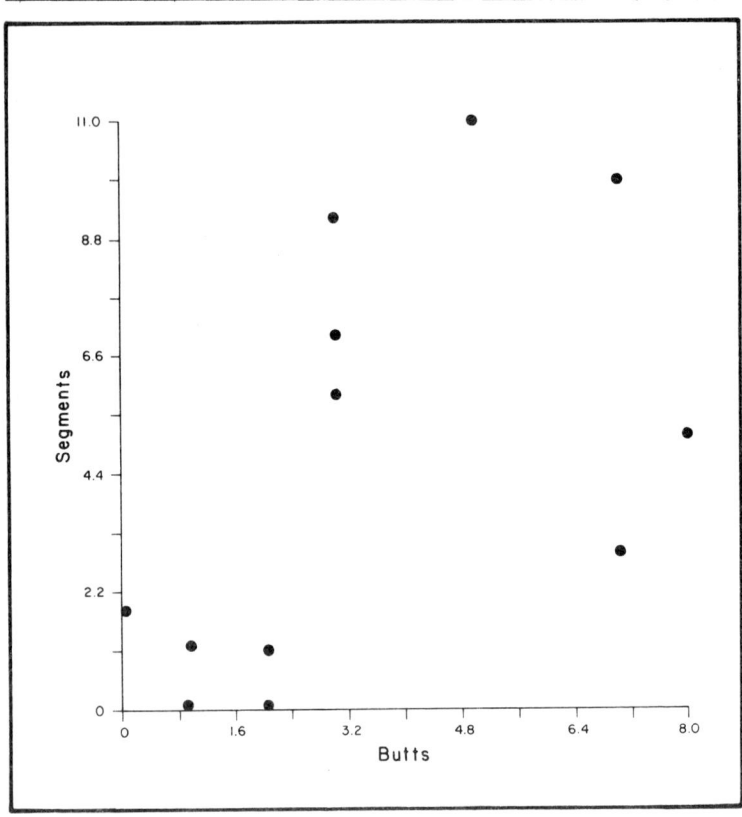

Figure 8.8 Scatter plot of medial segments vs. butts of backed elements—same sample as in Figures 8.2 and 8.7, but scaled as originally produced by a statistical computing program.

here is the vessel orifice data measured on sherds from the Canandaigua Lake site.[3]

The original data are presented in Figure 8.9. This histogram of frequencies of rim diameters seems simple and straightforward enough. There is only one tiny vessel, a great central model into which most sherds fall, and a small group of larger vessels, apparently defining a separate modal class. This is with a class interval of 2.5 cm.

However, if we take a slightly larger class interval, say 4.0 cm, we might get a histogram of this data that shows a pronounced unimodal distribution of rim diameters (Figure 8.10a). At first glance, this

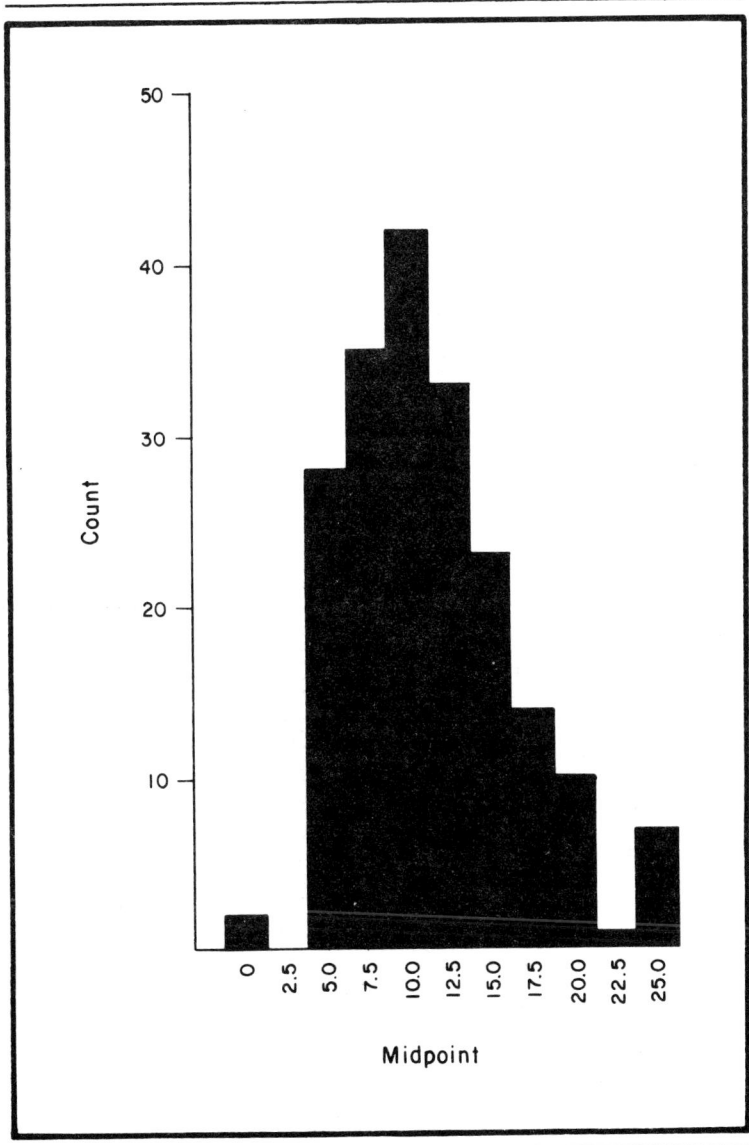

Figure 8.9 Rim diameters of Owasco pots from the Canandaigua Lake site—original data.

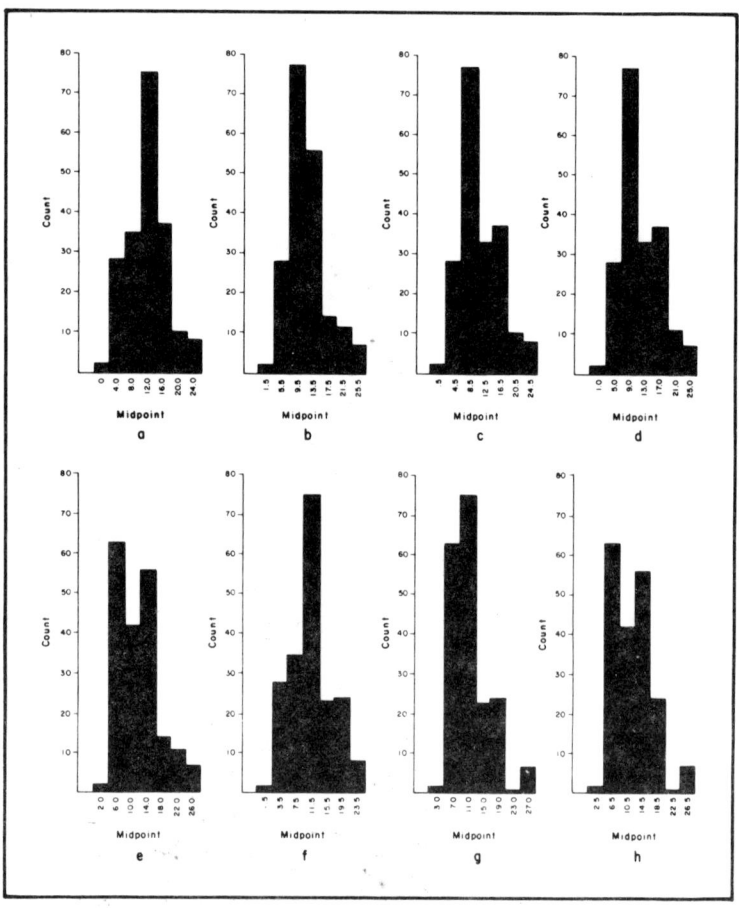

Figure 8.10 Rim diameters as in Figure 8.9, using a class interval of 4.0 cm and varying class midpoints.

might not seem unusual. I think everyone is aware that one can create a unimodal distribution for any data if one expands the class interval of the histogram far enough. But suppose we look just a little more closely at these data? Keeping exactly the same class interval as in Figure 10a, let us shift the class midpoints up and down slightly.

If we shift the class midpoints up by 1.5 (Figure 8.10b), the unimodal character of the distribution is preserved, although the small skew of the distribution shifts slightly. Perhaps we have a stable pattern in the data? Not at all, in fact, since shifting the class midpoints up 0.5 (Figure 8.10c), up 1.0 (Figure 8.10d), or up 2.0 (Figure 8.10e) produces three histograms in which a marked bimodality in the data is evident. Moving the class midpoints down 0.5 (Figure 8.10f)) also presents us with a bimodal distribution, but one with rather different modal values. However, in all these cases, the two modes fall roughly in the middle range of values for rim diameter. Where is the small class of large vessels we thought we saw in the original data? Is it just an artifact of the original scale of observation and a small class interval in the original histogram? Again, in fact, no, because, even with our new and larger class interval of 4.0, we can make it reappear by beginning our class midpoints at 3.0 (Figure 8.10g) or at 2.5 (Figure 8.10h), revealing now three modes in the data. The mode of large vessels is essentially the same in both of these histograms. However, the two other modes are quite different, and we must refer back to the first histogram, at a class interval of 2.5 (Figure 8.9), to see that it is Figure 8.10h that best represents the midrange modes that combine at the original scale of measurement to create the appearance of a single, large, central model with a short but very heavy skew to the right.

I have gone through all this "sleight of hand" with the data not to confuse or to "play games" with histograms, but to show how critical the choices of both class interval and class midpoints are to our perception of the data. Our interpretation of the pattern or structure of these data could be strikingly different, with substantive archaeological consequences, depending upon which of these, or other, histograms we rely on, whether by happenstance or by choice. Thus, here again, as in the example of bivariate cross-plots, scale of display and organization of the display can be of critical importance.

I hope that I have illustrated several things with the above examples, simple as they are. First, we can learn a lot about our data just by displaying it properly. In fact, I would argue that even some of the most commonly and routinely used statistics in archaeology cannot be relied on as good representations of data structure unless adequate examination of well-displayed data assures us that they are appropriate to that. As a case in point, consider the degree to which the single correlation coefficient of +.54 between medial segments and butt segments discussed above does justice to the structure of the data at hand.

Second, I hope that I have shown that varying the scales and axes along which one's data are displayed is not only legitimate but a valuable and essential element in a proper approach to data description, analysis, and interpretation. This is not idle "playing." It should be done consciously, purposefully, and thoughtfully. In fact, one should seldom, if ever, simply accept histograms and cross-plots as they are first produced by the computer (or by hand). Such first displays may be both accurate and adequate, but they always should be evaluated before being accepted, and further exploration of one's data is seldom wasted effort.

Third, I would argue that the approach I have adopted here should be a fundamental part of statistical methodology in archaeology and prior, in this methodology, to all more complex inferential statistics or statistical testing. In this respect, I believe that what I advocate here is essentially identical in its spirit, intent, and place within an overall approach to quantitative data analysis to Tukey's concept and practice of Exploratory Data Analysis (EDA) and is congruent with recent findings concerning human graphical perceptual abilities.

What, then, is the relationship between such simple yet basic statistical methods and the greater subjects of archaeological models or theory? I believe that the relationship is not mutual at all, but rather that these methods, and statistical methodology in general, occupy and should occupy a dependent, subservient position with respect to archaeological models and theory. Perhaps the most that one can say is that the introduction of the computer and quantitative methods in this field has had occasionally a positive effect in the sense of forcing or encouraging some people to think more systematically and rigorously. However, what one thinks about and how one thinks about it at the general level of theory or models ought not to be guided by statistical methods or techniques. The reason is simple: The basic principles in terms of which these methods and techniques have been developed and in terms of which they operate have little or nothing to do with the principles in terms of which we have reason to believe human cultural systems, prehistoric as well as historical or contemporary, are organized and operate. It makes no sense to introduce into archaeological theory or models elements drawn from a methodology whose fundamental principles are essentially unrelated to the subject matter.

In my view, therefore, it must be our archaeological ideas, models, or theory that generates expectations, potentially observable consequences for the archaeological record, which we then can examine against available statistical methods to see if adequate and effective approaches exist that will allow us to test for the presence or absence of such expectations or to observe the degree of congruence to, or deviation from, these predicted consequences. Since most statistical methods have been developed for other applications, many common techniques are seldom useful in archaeology, and archaeological statisticians often have had to develop approaches specifically designed to deal with the characteristics and peculiarities of archaeological models and data. In this respect particularly, simple techniques such as those discussed above often prove to be the most useful and effective.

Thus the relationship of statistical methodology to archaeological/anthropological theory lies not in the techniques and methods of data analysis but, rather, entirely in the areas of (1) what characteristics of the data we choose or are led to look at (i.e., the choice of variables), and 2) what sort of patterns or data structures we look for among those characteristics. The basic, even primitive, but ultimately surprisingly revealing manipulations of a simple display and descriptive statistics then can show us whether there is anything there, whether what we expect or hope to find does or does not exist, whether any more complex analytical manipulations of the data are useful or necessary, and whether they are likely to represent the critical structure of the data adequately and accurately.

Notes

1. The collection of these data was made possible by an NSF postdoctoral fellowship. I would like to thank H. L. Movius, Jr., for permission to record and use these data from his excavations at the Abri Pataud.

2. Actually, in the example presented here, none of these correlations, not even the original, positive correlation calculated over the entire set of data, attains statistical significance at the .05 level. This example is, thus, simply an illustration of how patterns in data can vary, not a demonstration of their statistical significance.

3. I would like to thank C. F. Hayes III and D. M. Barber for permission to use these data and for their help during my study of this collection at the Rochester Museum and Science Center.

References

Cleveland, W. S. and R. McGill. 1985. Graphical perception and graphical methods for analyzing scientific data. *Science* 229: 828-833.

Tukey, J. W. 1977. *Exploratory Data Analysis*. Reading, MA: Addison-Wesley.

Whallon, R. 1969. Rim diameter, vessel volume, and economic prehistory. *Michigan Academician* 11(2): 89-98.

Whallon, R. 1982. Variables and dimensions: the critical step in quantitative typology. In *Essays on Archaeological Typology*, ed. R. Whallon and J. A. Brown, pp. 127-161. Evanston: Center for American Archaeology.

Whallon, R. 1984. Unconstrained clustering for the analysis of spatial distributions in archaeology. In *Intrasite Spatial Analysis in Archaeology*, ed. H. J. Hietala, pp. 242-277. Cambridge: Cambridge University Press.

9

Archaeological Theory and Statistical Methods: Discordance, Resolution, and New Directions

Dwight W. Read

Introduction

As archaeologists began to frame research questions using a quantitative vocabulary, it was natural to turn to statistical methodology for the analysis of quantitatively expressed information (e.g., Spaulding 1960). The introduction of statistical methods into the methodological repertoire of the archaeologist has been a fruitful one (Thomas 1976: 4; Clark and Stafford 1982), despite occasional misgivings and criticisms about improper application of statistical techniques (e.g., Thomas 1978; Hole 1980; Scheps 1982).

Applications of quantitative methods, initially based on univariate statistics, have been shifting toward more complex multivariate procedures in parallel with explanatory arguments becoming structurally more complex. Multivariate procedures are, however, based on complex mathematical manipulations whose implications may not be clearly understood (Benfer and Benfer 1981: 394), thereby giving rise to data that have been manipulated in a manner which the archaeologist cannot justify easily in a more familiar vocabulary. Justification may then revert to analogical reasoning so as to relate the research question to the statistical procedure (see Read 1985). As a result, the reader must often accept, more on faith than anything else, the claim that something worthwhile has been accomplished.

We are assured, it is implied, that if we carefully ensure that our data are a random sample of a population, check each variable for homoscedasticity, joint normality, and so on, then the information spewed forth from the computer will have the meaning we hope to find in it. And so we have developed great concern for ensuring that the purported assumptions underlying the statistical tests are properly met (Hole 1980; Scheps 1982) and have publicly displayed our horror stories of one form of statistical abomination or another (Thomas 1978), all in quest of a kind of holy grail: an error-free, all-assumptions-satisfied statistical analysis that will reveal the truths otherwise hidden and unobservable in our data.

This sometimes myopic attention to the details of statistical methods—details which must, of course, be satisfied—has blinded us to both a far more serious failure and a potentially far more rewarding type of insight into our data. In uncritically taking over a ready-made, theory-free framework for the *application* of statistical methods, we have become seduced unwittingly into a false separation between problem formation and statistical method that unnecessarily limits the latter's usefulness for developing what Read and Leblanc (1977) have called satisfactory explanatory arguments.

Problem formation, since it is an archaeological and not a statistical matter, is taken as an a priori condition (e.g., Thomas 1976: 35), with statistical analysis of data seen as derivative and to be entered into only after the original problem, data base, and data set have been recast into the statistical language of model, population, and random sample so as to linguistically legitimize the application of statistical methods. Statistical methods are viewed as tools to be picked up and applied to the task at hand without seeing that statistical methodology, with its probabilistic conceptual framework, is fundamentally a means to *think logically about data* (Parzen 1960: 8). Yet it is by providing a language through which one can reason logically with quantitative data that the statistical framework is given its analytical power. But realization of this potential requires a different kind of legitimization than is achieved through verification of specific assumptions alone.

When Spaulding stated his oft-repeated definition of a type as a nonrandom association of attributes, he was *reasoning* with quantitative data. When this became translated into chi-square tests based on contingency tables (e.g., Sackett 1966), the quantitative reasoning became subsumed to method. The translation of the concept into method based on contingency tables needed (and needs) criticism, but criticism came primarily at a technical level and thus became virtually vacuous argument over whether one method (contingency table analysis) was better than another method (cluster analysis; e.g., Hodson 1982) for uncovering types without focusing on the implied data structures presumed by each method (c.f. Read 1982). Missing in the arguments has been *demonstration* of what the definition of a type translates into in the language of statistical methodology (e.g., Whallon 1972; Read 1974, 1982; Spaulding 1982) so that assessment can be made of the extent to which statistical methods provide satisfactorily a language for quantitative reasoning about the concept of a type.

But that translation is difficult when separation is made between problem formation and application of statistical methods. This separation of goal and method leads to a disjunction between concept and data, hence to obfuscation of the meaning that can be derived from the statistical analysis of data brought forward for study. The disjunction is not of the archaeologist's making but a consequence of the framework used for the application of statistical theory (Read 1985).

In this paper I will discuss briefly the basis for this disjunction (see Carr 1985 and Read 1985 for a more detailed discussion). Then I outline a resolution and demonstrate, using data on projectile points from a California site (4-VEN39), the manner in which statistical concepts can become part of our means for reasoning about archaeological data. That reasoning leads to a more comprehensive model of an artifact type which relates the type concept to the underlying native cognitive system through which the phenomena in question were given the structure that is being uncovered by the quantitative methods and expressed through the artifact classification.

Disjunction between Statistical Method and Archaeological Theory

A generally accepted schema (e.g., Clarke 1968; Thomas 1976) for using statistical methods in archaeological data analysis is based on a linear progression going from problem definition to hypothesis, then to data analysis, and finally to interpretation of the results of the data analysis. The first steps, wherein a general problem is isolated, are taken as only involving archaeological reasoning (Thomas 1976: 35) since it is the archaeologist, not the statistician, who defines a relevant problem area and data base. The progression from general problem to specific, hypothesized model, and then to test of the model, seems nonproblematic. And at this level, without statistical methods, there is little fault that can be found. But the introduction of statistical methods forces a transformation of the sequence, and one is no longer talking about a *data base for a research problem*, but instead about a *population* and a *random sample* from that population in order that statistical assumptions necessary for statistical inference will be met. This yields the schema shown in Figure 9.1.

The notions of population and random sample are usually defined as equivalent to the data base selected for the research problem (lower part of Figure 9.1). Thus "population" is given an implicit definitional criterion outside of the statistical framework. But the term is also part of the statistical vocabulary; hence a disjunction may arise between the statistical meaning of a population and the *research problem* meaning of a population. And such a disjunction does arise. To see the source of the disjunction, it is necessary to make a short digression and introduce two basic concepts from probability theory.

Probability Space and Random Variables

In their application, statistical techniques are taken from their theoretical context and used as algorithms that define operations to be carried out on a body of data such as a random sample from a population. Here we want to consider the theoretically based conceptual framework of which they are a part. That framework is based on two basic concepts: (1) a probability space and (2) a random variable.

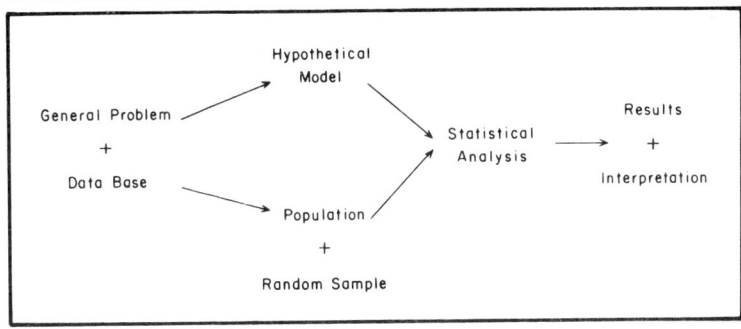

Figure 9.1 Schema depicting data analysis going from a general problem and data base to, on the one hand, formation of a hypothetical model relevant to that general problem and, on the other hand, to a restatement of the data base into the statistical language of population and random sample. These two paths then converge on statistical analysis as a method and interpretation of the results of the analysis.

Consider first the notion of a probability space. Roughly speaking, a probability space is a set of outcomes (or elementary events) along with numbers (or weights) called probabilities that are assigned to each outcome. We can give concreteness to the abstract notion of a probability space by using the conventional model of an *experiment* and its *outcomes* (e.g., Feller 1968).

An "experiment" need not be a laboratory experiment but can be any well-defined process or procedure which leads to a fixed set of outcomes, so that on each performance of the experiment exactly one outcome from that set of outcomes must occur, and each outcome in that set is potentially realizable when the experiment is performed. The experiment need not be under control of the investigator. It may also be a *natural* experiment, in the sense that a real world process that leads to the production of phenomena can be viewed as an experiment (the process) with outcomes (the phenomena or classes produced by the process). Each instance of the production of phenomena via that process can be interpreted as one repetition of the experiment. It is an experiment in this latter sense that is of concern here.

Probabilities are associated with, or assigned to, the outcomes either theoretically (which depends on an appropriate theory relative to the experiment) or experimentally through repeated performance of the experiment. An example of assigning probabilities via an appropriate theory is the following. Let the experiment be: Two individuals, each heterozygous at a locus with two alleles, mate and produce a zygote. Then the outcomes might be taken as the genotype of the zygote. The three possible genotypes, AA, Aa, and aa, would constitute the set of outcomes and probabilities would be assigned to these outcomes on the basis of genetic theory. This theory asserts that each allele, A or a, is equally likely to be passed from parent to offspring, hence the genotypes AA and aa are equally likely to occur and the genotype Aa is twice as likely to occur as either of these, so the probabilities must be ¼, ½, and ¼, respectively. The set of outcomes, {AA, Aa, aa} and the associated probabilities {¼, ½, ¼} form a probability space, Ω.

An example of determining the probabilities experimentally is the following. Let the experiment be: The !Kung San construct a camp in a traditional manner. The outcomes might be taken to be: A camp with one hut, a camp with two huts, a camp with three huts, ... Note that under this definition of an outcome, the outcome is a class of camps, not the camp itself. As we will see below, this shift from the actual *object* (the camp) as the outcome (which is the implicit definition used in most statistical applications) to the outcome being the *class* in which the object is a member has far reaching and important consequences for the statistical representation of a process.

An example of this shift to the class rather than the object as the outcome may be seen in the genetics example given above. There the object is the individual zygote, but the outcome is the genotypic class to which the zygote belongs, not the zygote itself.

To continue with the sample of !Kung camps, each of the probabilities p_1, p_2, ... for having a camp with 1, 2, ... huts, respectively, can be experimentally approximated by observing N instances of !Kung San camp construction and determining the proportion of camps (each constructed in a traditional manner) that have 1 hut, 2 huts, ..., respectively. The limit for each of these proportions as N goes to infinity constitutes the experimentally determined set of probabilities. The complete set of outcomes, {camps with 1 hut, camps with 2 huts, ... }, for the experiment and the associated set of probabilities, {p_1, p_2, ... }, associated with the outcomes from another probability space, Ω'.

The second concept, that of a random variable, is the basic means through which dimensions relevant for characterizing properties of the experiment are expressed. A *random variable* (despite its name!) is a rule (or mapping) that associates with each outcome of the experiment a real number. Thus, for the heterozygous mating experiment, a random variable of interest in genetic theory is the number of alleles of a given type, say the A allele, in the genotype. This random variable assigns the value 2 to the genotype AA, 1 to the genotype Aa, and 0 to the genotype aa.

Another property that must be satisfied by the random variable is that it must associate the same real number to repeated instances of the same outcome. In the second experiment, the definition of an outcome as a class of camps means that a measurement made on an individual camp (such as the area of the camp) will *not* be a random variable since different members of the same class (e.g., 2 camps with 5 huts each) will have unequal values for the measurement but represent the same outcome (i.e., both of the camps are members of the class of camps with 5 huts, but each has a different area). A random variable in this context does not assign a value to the individual object (the camp) but to the class to which the object belongs (e.g., camps with n huts). And if, in addition, the class represents a category relevant to the conceptual system guiding !Kung San camp construction, then such a random variable and its associated properties are informative about that conceptual system.

Random variables are put together in the form of a statistical model, such as the familiar linear regression model for the random variables Y, $X_1, X_2, \ldots, X_n$ whose general form is given by:

$$y = f(x_1, x_2, \ldots, x_n) + \epsilon$$

where:

- y is the value for the random variable Y (taken as the dependent variable);
- x_i is the value for the random variable X_i (taken as an independent variable), 1 i n;
- f is the function expressing the model structure; and
- ϵ is the error term expressing the deviation between the model value, $f(x_1, x_2, \ldots, x_n)$, and the observed value, y.

A model that is valid for the experiment and its associated probability space characterizes the experiment. It is in this sense that the notions of random variables and probability space are basic to the language through which one discusses quantitative properties.

Explanatory Arguments and Statistical Reasoning

The schema for statistical analysis is given in Figure 9.2. None of this scheme appears in Figure 9.1, raising the question of how the two schemas fit together. The procedure for combining them depends on the nature of the experiment.

Consider first the situation as displayed in Figure 9.1. Here the population is defined *prior* to the statistical analysis, hence the population definition is arbitrary from the viewpoint of the analytical techniques. This situation is embedded into the schema given in Figure 9.2 as follows (see Figure 9.3). Define an experiment to be: *Pick an entity or object from the population at random.* Each distinct entity is defined as an outcome (and prior to imposing any theory, each entity is distinct, hence each entity is a distinct outcome). (Observe how this definition differs from the one given above for the !Kung camps, where an outcome was defined as the class to which an entity belongs, not the entity itself.)

Probabilities are assigned in this experiment by taking the probability of an entity's occurrence when the experiment is performed to be the proportion of times it is represented in the population, namely $1/N$, where N is the population size. Any measure on the entity assigns a real number to it, hence assigns a real number to the outcome represented by the entity. Thus any numerical measure can be a random variable in this framework.

Under this definition of an experiment, which is implicitly used in most statistical applications, all of the properties outlined in Figure 9.2 are satisfied. Hence there will be a congruence between the schemas given in Figures 9.1 and 9.2, respectively. For a set of measures taken as random variables, a model may be hypothesized and statistically tested for goodness of fit. But note that according to Figure 9.2, the model characterizes the experiment giving rise to the outcomes. Since the experiment is "pick an entity from the population at random," then the model characterizes exactly that process!

While this experiment has the virtue of allowing statistical methods to be used properly on an arbitrary population, the cost of

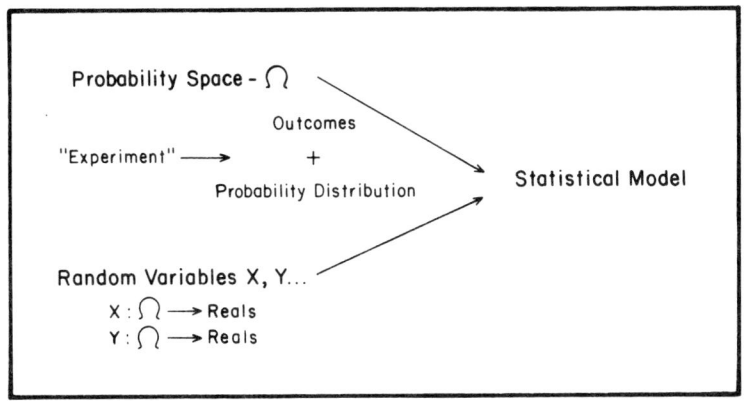

Figure 9.2 A probability space, Ω, may be viewed as an experiment with outcomes and associated probabilities. A random variable is a mapping from Ω to the real numbers. Random variables are organized in the form of a model that includes the probability space as defining the probability distribution for the random variables that appear in the model.

generality is to lose the power of the statistical framework for ascertaining the properties of an underlying process. The generality has been obtained by creating a pseudo-process that, by definition, has the entities in a population as its outcomes regardless of the characteristics of the population. This has the effect of legitimizing the application of statistical concepts to an arbitrary population; but in so doing the desired link between the properties of the statistical model and the properties of an explanatory, underlying process which serves to define an experiment that produces outcomes cannot be maintained. In other words, *the statistical analysis is forced into a descriptive mode for the pseudo-process instead of an explanatory one for the process underlying the production of phenomena, even if the goal is to formulate models with explanatory power.*

The alternative is to recognize explicitly in the analysis the link that can be made between, on the one hand, the explanatory process underlying the occurence of the outcomes that are part of a probability space and, on the other hand, a population in the statistical framework. This may be done by first defining the experiment to be a *single* real world process that gives rise to a delimited set of phenomena. Then the probability space is defined by a set of possible outcomes through the identity, Experiment =

ARBITRARY POPULATION

EXPERIMENT: Select an entity from the population

Ω: {Distinct entities in the population}

PROBABILITY: Proportion of population represented by an entity

RANDOM VARIABLE: Measurement made on an entity

STATISTICAL MODEL: Characterizes experiment of entity selection

---

Figure 9.3 The schemas given in Figures 9.1 and 9.2 are made consistent with each other via an experiment defined as: "pick an entity at random from the population." The probability of an "entity = outcome" is given by $1/N$, where N is the population size. Any numerical measure made over an entity is a random variable. A statistical model in this framework descriptively characterizes this "entity = outcome" experiment.

Process, and the probabilities of the outcomes are now a measure (either determined by theory appropriate to the process or through repetition of the experiment) of the characteristics of the process (see Figure 9.4). Each entity produced by the process may be taken as one repetition of the experiment, so the proportion of times a particular outcome occurs is an estimate of that outcome's probability of occurrence when the experiment is performed.

We may visually express the contrast between this situation and the previous one by means of a Venn diagram. In Figure 9.5 is displayed the universal set U which is the collection of all phenomena produced by the processes of interest—label these processes $P_1, P_2, \ldots, P_n$. (In Figure 9.5 only typical examples of the processes and the phenomena they produce are displayed for clarity in the illustration.) The sets P_i, P_j, and P_k in Figure 9.5 have as elements the entities produced by the processes P_i, P_j, and P_k. These entities can be grouped according to outcomes defined as classes $C_1, C_2, \ldots$, as was done in the example of !Kung camps. (The classes are shown only for

---

EXPERIMENT = PROCESS

Ω: Outcomes from the process

PROBABILITY: Determined by the properties of the process

RANDOM VARIABLE: Should measure a dimension relevant to the process

STATISTICAL MODEL: Characterizes the process

Figure 9.4 An experiment may be taken as a process that produces phenomena. Probabilities are determined through repetition of the experiment (see text for details). A random variable should measure a dimension relevant to the process. A statistical model characterizes the process leading to the observed phenomena.

the set P_k for clarity in the illustration.) The set D in Figure 9.5 is what Cowgill (1969) has called the available data set, namely the collection of entities that is available to the researcher and from which a sample will be drawn.

In the first situation where an outcome is defined to be an entity and which typifies the common application of statistical methods, analysis typically proceeds at the level of a subset of the *entities* in D (the sample data), separate from the pattern of distribution of these entities in the sets . . . P_i, P_j, P_k, . . . and the classes C_1, C_2, ... Here, concern lies primarily with ensuring that the data set brought forward for analysis is a random sample of the entities in D (Read 1985). As discussed above, statistical inference in this situation is directly from the sample data to parameters defined at the level of D and only indirectly, via these parameters, to the population of interest, namely U, and via that population to the processes of interest, . . . P_i, P_j, P_k, ...

The last two steps in this sequence are difficult to realize since the parameters for D bear an unclear relation to the properties of U, hence an even less clear relation to the properties of the processes of interest. The parameters associated with D, though descriptively accurate, are not, in and of themselves, the measure of any process other than the one giving rise to the set D. And that process is only tangentially relevant to the processes of interest.

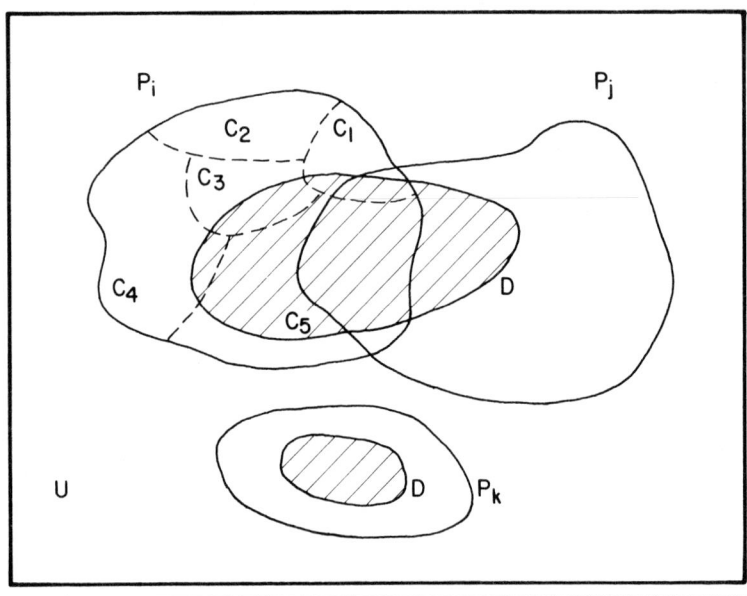

Figure 9.5 Venn diagram showing the relations among phenomena, process, classes, and data base available for analysis. The set U consists of all phenomena that are produced by processes $\ldots, P_i, P_j, P_k, \ldots$ and U has been subdivided into subsets $(\ldots, P_i, P_j, P_k, \ldots)$ that each correspond to the outcomes of a process (these subsets may be overlapping or disjoint). The phenomena produced by process P_k have been further organized into, for example, 5 classes $C_1, C_2, \ldots, C_5$ as indicated by the dashed lines. Of all the phenomena produced by these processes, only a portion, as indicated by the set D (hatched set consisting of two parts), is available for sampling and analysis.

Naroll's (1962) oft-quoted mean value of $x = 10$ m_2 of living space per person is a classic example of the difficulties that arise using this framework. The parameter being estimated by x, namely, the population mean, μ, for all so-called primitive societies, is not directly informative about any single process (i.e., any single society) since the population mean is averaged over all processes (i.e., over all societies).

For the second situation, which I am advocating as the more informative form for quantitative analysis of data aimed at determining the properties of processes, analysis proceeds at the level of the set of *outcomes* in D (e.g., the classes to which the entities in D belong) that are simultaneously contained within a *single* set P_k. Here one uses the property that a process is characterized by its outcomes (i.e., are the outcomes of a single process P_k), and the data set used to make inferences about its properties should thus be a subset of the outcomes for that process alone. Statistical inference is now directly inferential from sample data for that single process to the parameters describing the outcomes of the process, and then from those parameters to the characteristics of that process. The analysis is repeated for *each* process separately. In this manner the descriptive information drawn from the available data set for each process will be directly informative of that process, and these processes together form part of the framework for the formation of the entities in the set U; hence the properties of these processes isolated for analysis are relevant to an explanatory argument about the set U, the phenomena of interest.

Implications for Data Organization and Variable Definition

Two constraints that are part of the just described procedure need to be noted explicitly. First, an experiment properly refers to a situation definable as a *single process and its outcomes*. It is not meant by this that the phenomena are only univariate in nature. Rather, the statistical analysis must focus on a single process at a time (which might be a process at a higher level that organizes several processes at a lower analytical level, as we will see exemplified below). Hence data brought forward at each stage of the analysis must be a consequence of that single process (homogeneity assumption).

The second constraint involves selection of a random variable. Definition of a random variable should be guided by the variable's ability to bring out and identify informative characteristics of the process. Let us examine this second constraint in more detail before considering methods for organizing data consistent with the framework based on an experiment taken as a single process.

As observed above, a random variable, with its definition as a mapping from the set of outcomes of an experiment to the real numbers, is not equivalent to a measure made on an entity. In the experiment defined as the construction of a camp in a traditional manner by the !Kung San, an outcome was a *class* defined via the number of huts in a camp. Consider the *measure* defined as the distance from one hut to an adjacent hut. (Assume for simplicity the idealization that the camps are spatially perfectly uniform so that variation in distance between adjacent huts within a single camp can be ignored.) That measure is not a random variable for the set of outcomes defined as *classes* of !Kung camps since camps with the *same number of huts,* hence instances of the same class and thereby instances of the same outcome of the process, need not have identical distances between adjacent huts.

In place of the numerical measure defined as the actual distance between adjacent huts, we can formulate a model relating the numerical measure to a quantity that is constant across all identical outcomes, hence to a quantity which can be the value for a random variable. In the case of the !Kung camps this may be done by taking advantage of the fact that the !Kung apparently perceive that adjacent huts should be at a *constant distance* from one another, even regardless of the number of huts in the camp (Read 1978). Define a random variable called Adjacent Hut Distance (D) by assigning this constant distance, or *normative value*—call it μ_D—to an outcome, or class of camps. (In this instance, it happens that the same value would be assigned to all outcomes since, empirically, it appears to be the case that the normative or proper distance between adjacent huts is unrelated to the number of huts in the camp. Had this not been the case, and had that distance depended on the number of huts but was constant across all camps with the same number of huts, then the distance between adjacent huts characteristic of a particular class would be the value assigned by the random variable to that class. All members of a class would have the same value assigned, though members of different classes would receive different values.)

The interpretation of the random variable D at the level of the camp is: In each instance of the construction of a camp, a fixed distance, μ_D, is perceived as the proper distance between adjacent huts. When this perceived proper distance between adjacent huts becomes translated into an actual distance through construction of the camp, the measure of the actual distance, call it x, can be modeled as the proper distance (or norm) plus an error term (see also Read 1982, 1985):

$$x = \mu_O + \epsilon \, ;$$

where:
- x is the measured distance between adjacent huts;
- μ_0 is the proper (or normative) distance between adjacent huts; and
- ϵ is the error term.

We may give the following interpretation to the value, μ_0: It is the mean of all measured values, x, of the distances between adjacent huts, where the mean value, μ_D, is computed by taking as a population *all possible outcomes of the process of construction of !Kung camps in a traditional manner* (Read 1985). In order for the parameter μ_D to be a characteristic of the process, and not of some particular set of entities produced by the process, it must be computed not just over all entities that did occur, but over all entities that *could possibly* have occurred using that process: "Even in the simplest of cases the values ... before us are interpreted as a random sample of a *hypothetical infinite population of such values as might have arisen in the same circumstances*" (Fisher 1954: 6-7; emphasis added).

The validity of the model (goodness of fit) may be tested by the form of the distribution for the error terms (residuals) that should occur if the model is valid. If it is correct that a single value is perceived as the proper distance between adjacent huts, so that deviation from this value represents nonsystematic effects, then the error terms ϵ should have a unimodal, approximately normal distribution. And Read (1978) demonstrates that this is the situation for !Kung camps.

The contrast between the consequences of taking a population as arbitrary with respect to the statistical methods and taking the set of outcomes to be the outcomes of a process structuring the data set is striking. When an arbitrary population is used and the experiment is the "selection experiment," one may only properly talk about "population parameters" as properties of the *population in hand*. The probability of an Outcome = Entity is simply the ratio n/N, where n is the number of times the type of entity in question occurs in the population and N is the size of the population. In this framework a random sample from the population is used as a means for estimating parameters that refer only to the collection of entities.

In contrast, for the framework built around Experiment = Process, the real world population of entities which are outcomes of the experiment is not the point of reference for population parameters. Here a probability p is defined as

$$p = \lim_{N \to \infty} n/N,$$

where n is the number of times the outcome in question occurs out of N repetitions of the experiment. Since the real world population is but N repetitions of the experiment, the ratio n/N, even when based on all N members of the real world population, is still an *estimate* of the corresponding probability p. Thus the point of reference for probabilities, and hence for "population parameters," becomes the *process*, not the population in hand. Parameters in a statistical model in this framework are *properties of the process*, not of entities, and a statistical model is a means to characterize the *process directly* and the real world population *indirectly* as signifying the result of N repetitions of the Experiment = Process.

Observe that for the !Kung camp example the probabilities associated with each outcome represent the consequence of yet another process, namely, the dynamics of camp membership. Each family in a !Kung camp has a separate hut, hence the number of huts equals the number of families living together for some period of time. The set of families living together is constrained by cultural rules that reflect both permanent and temporary rights of camp membership (see Marshall 1976: 182; Wiessner 1977; Lee 1979 for a discussion of these rules). The alternative ways in which these rights can be translated into action—which families join together to form a camp—is further affected by demographic parameters, the manner in which marriage acts affect the formation of family units, and the association of family units with camps through membership rights defined in the language of kin relations.

In this example it happens that the random variable D not only assigns the same value, μ_O, to all instances of traditional !Kung camps with a given number of huts, but assigns the same value regardless of the number of huts, hence can be taken as a fundamental observation about !Kung conceptualization of the spatial relations of huts in a camp (Read 1985).

As these comments have illustrated, the framework of Outcome = Entity leads to a narrow result that is divorced from the goal of explanatory arguments, while the framework of Experiment =

Process leads naturally from the specific information obtained through the statistical methods to its interrelation with other processes bearing on the same domain. It is in this sense that I suggest use of statistical methodology as providing an effective language for reasoning quantitatively about phenomena, particularly at an explanatory level.

Realization of this potential has a cost, though, namely the cost of determining that a given data set *does* represent the outcomes of a single process, and that a given random variable is informative of the characteristics of that process. But in the same manner that the population determined *prior* to consideration of a process may fail to be precisely the set of outcomes of that process, the data base (which is identical to the population in the first schema) may also fail to be definable as the set of outcomes formed from repetitions of the Experiment = Process. Similarly, variables selected initially for analysis need not be directly informative of the properties of the process that is being examined. Thus it is necessary to redefine the initial set of information into homogeneous subsets (Read 1974) that are each consistent with the outcomes of some single process and to define and redefine random variables with the goal of forming rules for associating numbers with outcomes in a manner that reflects fundamental properties of the process or processes under investigation (cf. Voorips 1982; Whallon 1982).

Preanalysis of Data

The steps needed for obtaining congruence between a population as a data base and a population as the set of outcomes of a process can be made clearer by making a distinction between a *well-defined* (WD) population and a *not well-defined* (NWD) population. (An analogous distinction is made for variables.) A WD population is a population all of whose entities are the outcomes of a single process, so the entities in the population are viewed as N repetitions of an experiment, where N is the number of entities in the population. All other populations will be referred to as NWD populations. For variables, a WD variable will be one which measures a dimension that directly and satisfactorily characterizes an aspect of the process, and an NWD variable will be any other variable.

The different combinations of WD and NWD variables and populations may be set out as four different modes for preanalysis of data (see Figure 9.6). Mode 1 corresponds to the ideal situation where each entity is the consequence of one and the same process, and each random variable does measure a dimension characterizing the process. No preanalysis is needed for this mode. The other three modes require preanalysis of data with the goal of restructuring the data and redefining measures so that the new subpopulations of entities and measures are all in Mode 1.

The methods used for Mode 2 (NWD populations, WD variable) preanalysis are based on finding "breaks" in the distribution of the WD variables, using the assumption that breaks and "corners" in distributions do not characterize most processes. (Of concern here are the analytical steps that can be taken in the absence of adequate theory for an a priori definition of a WD population.) For variables considered singly, the breaks would be antimodes in a multimodal distribution (with the caveat that multimodality must be sufficiently extreme to warrant subdivision into subpopulations). With variables taken two at a time, scattergram plots can be used and divisions will be made when clear-cut clusters are found (e.g., Figure 3.3 in Read 1985), or when "corners" are found in a distribution (such as would occur if the *ratio* of one variable to the other is bimodal; Whallon, this volume; see also Whallon 1982, Read 1985 for examples). When several variables are considered simultaneously, principal component analysis may be used to reduce the dimensionality of the data structure so that scattergram plots (based on the principal components) will more effectively display natural groups of clusters in the data (see Figs. 3.1 - 3.3, 3.6 in Read 1985 for examples).

Under Mode 3, with a WD population and NWD variables, techniques would include examining ratios of variables (e.g., Whallon 1982), principal component analysis for construction of principal components as new variables fewer in number than the original set and with variable redundancy minimized (e.g., Christenson and Read 1977), and rescaling of variables.

The last situation, Mode 4 with an NWD population and NWD variables, has no single method since the efficacy of each of the methods for Modes 2 and 3 requires the other defining characteristics to be WD. Read (1985) discusses an iterative approach that alternates between the methods for Mode 2 and Mode 3 and demonstrates its efficacy on projectile points from the California Paleo-Indian site,

PRE-ANALYSIS OF DATA

MODE	TECHNIQUE
Mode 1: WD Variables WD Population	None needed
Mode 2: WD Variables Not-WD Population	Cluster analysis, anti-modes
Mode 3: Not-WD Variables WD Population	Dimensionality reduction: factor analysis
Mode 4: Not-WD Variables Not-WD Population	Iterative techniques using above methods

Figure 9.6   The four logically possible modes for well- and not well-defined populations and variables. Possible techniques that may be used to eliminate either not well-defined variables or populations are given for each mode. The fourth mode is the most common, and no single technique applies to this mode.

4-VEN39. (Site excavated by Dr. James Hill using a random sample of excavation units. Data used courtesy of Dr. Hill and the Cultural History Museum at UCLA.) The results of that analysis will be reviewed briefly.

Preanalysis of Data: The 4-VEN39 Projectile Points

The data set from 4-VEN39 consists of 64 projectile points. The variables measured (measurements made by R. Ciolek-Torello) are listed in Table 9.1. That these data are in Mode 4 has been shown in Christenson and Read (1977).

Preanalysis of these data using Read's iterative technique shows that the projectile points can be divided into five types (Read 1985). As discussed in Read (1982), the types are based first on a qualitative shape and then on a quantitative characteristic, except for the fifth type, which is based on qualitative measures alone (see Figure 9.7).

TABLE 9.1
Dimensions Measured on Projectile Points

Variable	Definition
Length	length of point in cm
Maximum width	maximum width in cm
Thickness	maximum thickness in cm
Base height	vertical length (in cm) of base section of point; negative if concave and positive if convex
Base width	maximum width of point base in cm
Edge convexity	radius of circle (in cm) that best fits curvature of the point edge
Tip angle	angle of the tip of the point measured to the nearest 5 degrees
Proximal limits	distance in cm from the base "corners" to the edge location for the maximum width of the point
Flake Removals	number of "small" flake scars per cm along the point edge

Two of the types are based on a triangular shape, and the quantitative characteristic is the base width. As a metric value, base width has a bimodal distribution for the triangular points and so can be reduced to a nominal distinction: Narrow (base) and Wide (base).

The third and fourth types have a leaf shape and are distinguished by overall size. Size takes on a bimodal distribution within this group of points and so may be reduced to a nominal distinction: Small or Large.

The fifth type has an inverse relation between length and width, but without a bimodal distribution for any of its dimensions. The shape varies from more leaflike for the smaller points to more needlelike for the larger ones. This type is distinguished solely on the basis of shape.

The five-class typology has a natural hierarchy going from projectile points as a class, then to shape differences, and finally to nominal distinctions within a shape class. The hierarchy is given in Figure 9.8.

RESULTS OF PRE-ANALYSIS

TYPE	STATISTICAL MODEL
Triangular shape, narrow base	$\omega = \mu_N + \varepsilon$
Triangular shape, wide base	$\omega = \mu_W + \varepsilon$
Leaf shape, small size	$S = \mu_S + \varepsilon$
Leaf shape, large size	$S = \mu_L + \varepsilon$
Leaf/Needle	continuous distribution

Figure 9.7 The preanalysis of the 4-VEN39 data led to the definition of five types using both qualitative and quantitative distinctions. The types represent three shape classes, and two of the shape classes are subdivided by a quantitative variable with a bimodal distribution within a shape class. The statistical model represents this bimodal form of the distribution within a shape class.

Conceptual Basis for the 4-VEN39 Typology

While the hierarchy does define more inclusive sets of points as one moves from the bottom to the top, it also reflects differentiation at a conceptual level. It is useful to divide the hierarchy into two parts, as has been done in Figure 9.8, with one part referring to the ideational domain and the other part, the actual points, referring to the phenomenological domain (following Dunnell 1971). In the ideational domain we are going from the concept, projectile point, to the assertion that this concept is part of the cultural repertoire of the inhabitants of 4-VEN39, then to a qualitative model of the concept, and finally to an imposition of normative values as parameter values for the qualitative models (see Figure 9.9). The ideational domain is linked to the phenomenological domain through the manufacture of projectile points at 4-VEN39 and the Experiment = Process becomes a model for that manufacturing process in the context of this

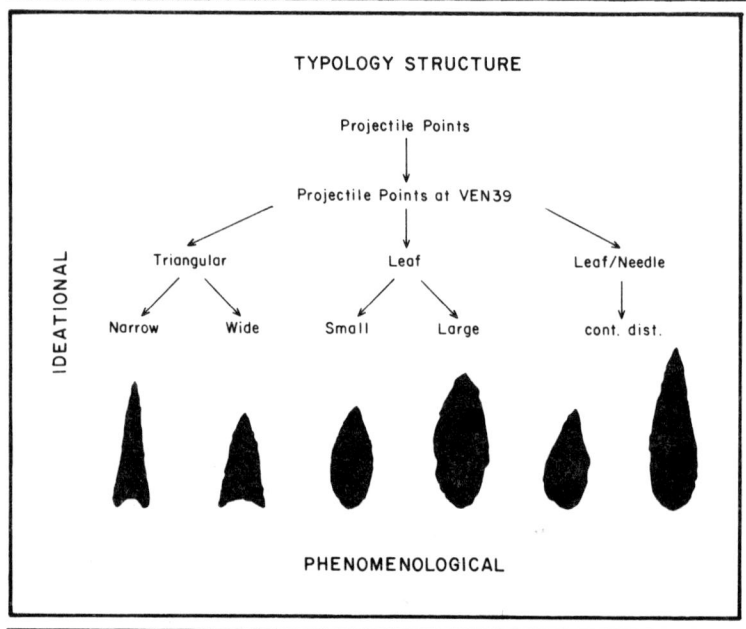

Figure 9.8 The five types may be organized in the form of a typology structure. The typology structure begins with the concept "projectile point" and uses different criteria for subdivision at each level until the five types are represented. The points below the five types are "typical" examples from each class, with the exception of the fifth type. For that type the extremes of the range of variation are shown. The typology structure is part of the ideational domain; the actual points are part of the phenomenological domain.

conceptual domain. To see this more clearly, consider first the implied ideational structure in more detail.

A projectile point is both an object and a concept. For the ideational domain we want to consider the concept. What I mean by a projectile point as a concept is not necessarily some kind of "mental template" but rather certain attributes and relations expressed over the entity that must hold for it to be considered what we label as a projectile point. As Leone (1982) has noted, "while the details and particulars of a past culture may be lost, *the principles of that organization, or structure, may be suggested through what remains*" (p. 743, emphasis added).

IDEATIONAL STRUCTURE

CONCEPT ⟶ CULTURAL CONTEXT ⟶ MODEL - QUALITATIVE ⟶ NORMS AS MODEL PARAMETERS

CONCEPT	CULTURAL CONTEXT	MODEL - QUALITATIVE	NORMS AS MODEL PARAMETERS
Pointed - penetration	4-VEN39	Triangular Shape	Narrow Base - μ_N
Base - hafting		Leaf Shape	Wide Base - μ_W
Shape - aerodynamics Weight		Leaf/Needle Shape	Small Size - μ_S
Rigidity - structural stability Hardness			Large Size - μ_L
Edge Sharpness - penetration, killing			

Figure 9.9 The ideational structure is based on a transformation going from concepts that are part of what makes for an effective projectile point (extracultural concepts) to their embedding into the cultural repertoire represented by 4-VEN39, then to a qualitative model which expresses these concepts, and finally to parameter values for the models (norms).

The attributes and structural relations are: (1) Point—a projectile point must be able to penetrate, hence must be pointed. Further, there will be constraints on the range of pointedness for the object to be able to perform its task effectively (cf. Read 1982). (2) Base—a projectile point will be hafted to a shaft when it is used. The base will be opposite the point in order to maximize the conversion of thrust into force of penetration. Constraints on the shape of the base will be in terms of the method of hafting. (3) Shape and Weight—a hafted projectile point must be aerodynamically stable (at least in the minimal sense of allowing it to be targeted), hence must have certain shape and weight characteristics. (4) Rigidity and Hardness—a projectile point must remain structurally stable during use, hence must have certain mechanical properties. Minimally, it must be rigid so that it maintains its shape, and it must be hard so that that shape is maintained during use and penetration. (5) Edge Sharpness—the edge sharpness of the projectile point will affect its ability to penetrate and to remain in the animal, hence affect its killing power.

These five attributes conceptually define a projectile point in the sense that an entity must be pointed, have a base for hafting, have a weight and shape consistent with aerodynamic properties, have a rigidity and hardness consistent with structural stability during use, and have edges that enhance penetration and/or the killing power for the entity to be effective and efficient in the tasks associated with a projectile point.

The range of variation in actual design that is acceptable under these five attributes and relations will, of course, depend on the specifics of the situation. Is the point + shaft part of an arrow or an atlatl? If an atlatl, is it to be thrown or jabbed into the animal? If it is to be jabbed, will it have a detachable point? And so on. Each of these and other alternatives will differentially affect the specific configuration that will yield an effective projectile point under the stipulated usage. Further, manufacturing error will make each point distinct as a physical object. But constant across the specific points are these five attributes and structural relations which then give the point unity at the conceptual level of attributes and relations.

Thus, in order that there be projectile points at 4-VEN39, the *concept* of a projectile point must be part of the cultural repertoire at 4-VEN39. That is, the artisans of 4-VEN39 and the users of the products produced by the artisans must, in some sense, be conceptualizing entities that are pointed, aerodynamically stable, can be hafted, have sharp edges, and so on. What "they" might call this category, or even if it has a linguistic label, is irrelevant. To assert that there are projectile points at 4-VEN39 only entails the claim that at some level a "cognitive category" which can be etically described (as has been done via statistical analysis [Read 1985]) is relevant to "their" emic conceptualizations. Thus the second step in the hierarchical structure embeds the concept "projectile point" into the cultural context of 4-VEN39 and thereby provides a bridge between the emic and the etic in the analysis of artifactual material, as Renfrew (1983: 14) has suggested is a necessary step.

As a set of attributes and relations, the concept projectile point does not lead to any specific form. The third step in the hierarchical structure translates the concept into a *qualitative* model in which these relations hold true. The specific qualitative model will, in part, reflect the interrelation of the projectile point as a physical object with the cultural domain. The design of the point may include characteristics symbolic of, or reflecting, relations expressed in different aspects of the cultural domain.

Such an information load is possible since the range of shapes and materials that satisfy the definitional criteria (where the main constraint is effectiveness and efficiency of use) is sufficiently broad so as to allow for subdivision of a continuum into discrete states (see Read 1982 for a discussion and example of how these states may be statistically identified using the concept of efficiency of use of an artifact), whether deliberate ("iconistic") or merely through craft traditions ("isochrestic") (Sackett 1982, 1985).

The qualitative shape is culture specific, or perhaps more accurately, reflects the extent to which there is common sharing of a similar perception of the form of a projectile point. Within the selected shape certain dimensions may be transformed from a continuous to a discrete range of values at the ideational level. We see this in the 4-VEN39 projectile points with the triangular points. Here base width has been dichotomized. There is a clear separation of the triangular shape points into two groups using the base width dimension (Figure 3.4 in Read 1985). It seems reasonable to posit, then, that base width, as a metric measure, became transformed into a discrete measure with two values through normative ascription on the part of the artisans of 4-VEN39.

The triangular points thus are divided into two classes, Triangular Shape + Wide Base and Triangular Shape + Narrow Base. The metric measurement, base width, now represents two processes: first, the ideational one which defines the normative value, and second, the manufacturing process through which the point is produced. Under this interpretation the mean base width within each class of triangular points is an estimate of the respective normative values, and when the outcome is taken to be Narrow or Wide, the corresponding random variable is the rule that assigns the normative value, Narrow, to the narrow triangular points and the normative value, Wide, to the wide triangular points.

The Experiment = Process is not just the translation of the ideational structure into the phenomenological domain (which suffices for both the definition of the outcomes and the normative values) but is also, through the probabilities associated with the outcomes, the translation of the material conditions of 4-VEN39 into the ideational domain wherein these material conditions affect and constrain the frequency with which certain outcomes are selected by the artisans (see Figure 9.10). For example, if the Small and Large leaf-shaped points reflect differences in the physical applications of these two types of points, i.e., reflect the respective tasks which they may effectively perform, then the probabilities associated with these outcomes refer to the frequency of these tasks. The probabilities define the relative frequency with which the categories of the ideational structure became instantiated as concrete objects. The tasks determine the frequency of use, hence the frequency of manufacture (attenuated by differential rates of wear, breakage and so on), and thus the probabilities associated with the set of outcomes for the process of projectile point manufacture at 4-VEN39.

Outcomes as Analytical Constructs

The set of outcomes is not fixed analytically but can be taken at different levels. The base level is that of the projectile points as physical entities. At this level the characterization of the points as outcomes becomes identical to that which accrues when the projectile points are taken as an arbitrary population and the experiment is the "select an entity" experiment.

The next level higher in abstraction has as outcomes the elements of the set [Narrow, Wide, Small, and Large], with corresponding statistical parameters μ_N, μ_S, μ_W, and μ_L, all interpreted as signifying

```
                    EXPERIMENT

IDEATIONAL STRUCTURE
                        MANUFACTURE OF
        +           →                    → OUTCOMES
                        PROJECTILE POINTS
MATERIAL CONDITIONS


PHENOMENA       Level 0: Actual Points

NORMS           Level 1: Outcomes = N, W, S, L

EMIC MODELS     Level 2: Outcomes = Triangular, Leaf,
                                   Leaf/Needle

CONCEPTS        Level 3: Outcomes = Projectile Point
```

Figure 9.10 The process = experiment may be defined through the ideational structure and the material conditions of 4-VEN39 at time of occupation. The ideational structure determines the outcomes that will be realized when points are manufactured, and the material conditions determine the probabilities of the outcomes. Outcomes can be viewed at four different levels: phenomena, norms, emic models (etically specified), and concepts.

normative values that have been (emically) imposed on the corresponding continuous dimensions to give them nominalization in the form of a dichotomy. At this level the probabilities reflect the frequency with which these normative values come into play according to the processes underlying them. For example, consider the fact that the outcomes Narrow and Wide occur with almost identical frequency (Read 1985). The most straightforward explanation for this difference, namely that the dichotomy is a functional difference, can be rejected for the following two reasons. First, the Narrow/Wide dichotomy is not reflected in any other aspect of the morphology of these points. The other dimensions for the two types of points do not distinguish the two groups (Read 1985). Second, though it might be argued that the width difference could relate to differences in the width of the arrow shaft to which a point was hafted, it is unclear why two different shaft diameters would be used when all other aspects of the morphology of the points in the two classes are identical. And, as Thomas (1978b) has demonstrated, there is only a weak correlation ($r = 0.48$) between point base width (his neck width) and shaft diameter.

If the dichotomy does not reflect a simple functional difference, then it may reasonably be concluded that there is a relatively wide range of width values that lead to essentially equally effective usage of the points. In other words, a plot of the dimension Base Width versus efficiency or effectiveness of tool use would have a broad, flat peak (see Figure 4.6 in Read 1982).

Such a dimension is open to arbitrary (i.e., nonfunctional) subdivision into subranges by the artisans, with each subrange characterizing a particular group of artisans (be it a subgroup within a society, or at the society level, as Wiessner finds with the San points [1983]). The mean value for a subrange may be taken as a normative value that characterizes that subrange.

To illustrate, Read (1982) finds, using Scottsbluff points as a data base, that some dimensions whose values a priori would be expected to have substantial impact on the effectiveness of usage of the point (such as the angle of the tip of the point) have the same mean value across several different sites, along with a highly constrained range of values (low coefficient of variability). On the other hand, dimension with little relationship to the functioning of the point divide into two groups: (1) those dimensions with the same mean for each site and a high coefficient of variability, and (2) those dimensions with a different mean for each site but a low coefficient of variability. The former can be interpreted as dimensions which have unrealized potential for stylistic "input" and the latter as dimensions which have had stylistic input (whether it be iconic or isochrestic in form).

These observations suggest that it is useful to interpret the Wide/Narrow dichotomy for the 4-VEN39 points as an example of stylistic differentiation within a single social group, the inhabitants of 4-VEN39. In addition, the dichotomy is time independent in that it is found at all levels of the site (data not shown). Since the dichotomy occurs within a single site and at all levels of the site, it seems reasonable to interpret this as an instance of iconic, and not isochrestic, stylistic input. If iconic, then what is its "meaning"? The fact that the two groups of points, Narrow Base Points and Wide Base Points, are virtually identical in numbers (17 versus 18 [Read

1985]) suggests that the Narrow/Wide dichotomy may reflect a moiety division in the Chumash society in which the inhabitants of 4-VEN39 were a part (Christenson, personal communication).

While there is no definitive information on the social organization of the Chumash, Kroeber (1971 [1918]) considered it likely that they would have had a moiety structure as did the groups north and south of them. And Harrington (1942: 32) in his cultural trait list for the Chumash indicates that they had moieties, but the names of the moieties are unknown.

A moiety structure divides the living group into approximately equal halves, with each half doing the same subsistence activities. Hence the frequency of implements "owned" by the members of one moiety should be about equal to the frequency of implements "owned" by members of the other moiety. If an implement is imbued with an iconic attribute which "marks" the moiety to which one belongs, there will then be two states for that attribute, and the implements, when sorted according to those two states, will divide into two groups of approximately the same size. And that is precisely the situation with the triangular points and the attribute Base Width with its two states: Narrow and Wide.

One might object to the argument on the analytical grounds that the division into two groups of the same size could be due to factors separated from the manner in which the two classes of points were conceptually embedded into the cultural system of which 4-VEN39 was a part. But if this were the case, then other classes of points should have a similar frequency distribution. However, the Leaf Shape points have also been dichotomized, in their case into two size categories, Small and Large; but here the categories are not about the same in size. Instead, the former is about twice as plentiful as the latter. Hence the division of the triangular points into two equal-sized groups on the basis of base width is specific to the properties of this class of implements.

Admittedly, the suggestion that the two varieties of triangular points may reflect a moiety structure is speculative and needs further confirmation, even if circumstantial. To pursue the topic further, though, leads away from the main thrust of the argument being developed here, and so no further corroboration will be developed.

In contrast to the Triangular points, the size difference, Small and Large, for the Leaf Shape may reflect a functional difference in usage within a general task (e.g., if these points were used as atlatl darts, the size difference might reflect two size classes of animals being hunted), and so here the probabilities would relate to the relative frequencies of the activities in which the points were used; hence it is unlikely that these frequencies would be the same, and in fact they are not.

At the next higher level of abstraction, the outcomes are qualitative shapes—Triangular, Leaf, and Leaf/Needle. It seems plausible to posit that these shape differences reflect different types of general tasks (e.g., the Triangular points might be arrow points, and the Leaf Shape points might be atlatl darts [or possibly knives]), so the probabilities associated with these outcomes measure the relative frequency of these general tasks at 4-VEN39 (e.g., if the difference posited above is valid, the relative frequency of bow hunting versus, say, atlatl hunting, corrected for any differential rate in breakage, wearing out, and preservation of the two shape classes).

The last level of abstraction has a single outcome, Projectile Point, and is at the level of the concept. It identifies the category of relevance to the main process and distinguishes this set of data from other sets of data at 4-VEN39. It also provides a level of abstraction at which meaningful comparison may be made from one context to another. Different cultures share the concept Projectile Point, yet differ radically at the level of qualitative models and values of norms as parameters for these models.

Conclusion

The examination of projectile points at 4-VEN39 presented here is not exhaustive but suggestive of the way in which the statistical analysis of these points can be presented in a language that permits a more explicit discussion of the interface between the artifact and the culture for which the artifact is a material representation. Traditional statistical analysis which permits the use of arbitrary populations is limiting, rather than expanding, in its application. Statistics-as-method only utilizes a small part of the repertoire that is available through statistical modeling.

The methods discussed here for the preanalysis of data are part of the philosophy of exploratory data analysis, but with a significant difference. The difference is in the goals. I suggest that the goal is to develop models that characterize processes said to structure the problem domain and its attendant data base. The methods needed to achieve this task include exploratory data analysis techniques, but they put them into an organized framework and delve into the conceptual framework used in archaeology to provide that organization. Carr (1985) has called this type of exploratory data analysis "constrained exploratory data analysis."

The preanalysis of data does not provide meaning by itself. Meaning is at many levels, and the challenge is to develop an adequate language and interpretative framework that can make these different levels of meaning explicit and delineate their interconnections. The statistical framework of experiment and outcomes can aid through providing a language and conceptual framework for exploring the logic of the interconnection between the ideational and the phenomenological levels, but only when there is congruence between population and process, and the latter appears to inevitably lead into the arena of native cognition and native categorization of phenomena.

The statistical analysis has led to a hierarchy of classes, with classes defined, in the final analysis, by nominal distinctions. The dichotomization of a continuum (base width in one case, point size in the other) must relate to a native constructed dichotomy, such as Spaulding (1977) has discussed and Gould (1980: 119-121) has noted for Australian aboriginal tool classification. In the latter situation, Gould notes that the working edge angle is dichotomized into two size ranges, or states, with corresponding linguistic classes, *tjimari* (x = 40 degrees) and *purpunpa* (x = 67 degrees).

The model developed by Read (1985) and discussed above (Equation [2]) exactly characterizes the ethnographic data that Gould reports. Curiously, Gould concludes that "these categories, *whether conscious or not*, cannot be reliably inferred in the absence of living informants" (p. 121, emphasis added). The pessimism is obviously not warranted since the statistical analysis done here on the 4-VEN39 points has established classes whose locus must reside in the maker's and user's conceptualizations and behavior, since the distinctions are not imposed but uncovered through the analysis.

If Gould had simply been concerned with whether or not the archaeologist can uncover categories which were also given linguistic labels by the artisans and users of the tools, his cautionary remarks would be warranted, since we have no way of knowing, for example, if the classes uncovered in the 4-VEN39 material were linguistically marked or not. But as Gould's data demonstrate, there need not be an isomorphism between linguistically labeled categories and emically "recognized" categories, as evidenced by differential behavior patterns with respect to the members of the respective classes.

Gould notes that the tjimari are never hafted, while the *smaller* purpunpa are hafted, though the *larger purpunpa are not* hafted, i.e., a small versus large dichotomization in the latter class is "recognized" but not linguistically marked. This does not imply, as Gould concludes, that the latter distinction is emically irrelevant—"Hafting was correlated more closely with size and use than with any particular emic category" (p. 119)—unless one narrowly construes an emic category only as a category that is linguistically marked, which does violence to the concept. One could add other ethnographic examples of emically recognized, but not linguistically marked, categories, such as the data on the San points reported by Wiessner (1982), but the point does not need belaboring.

Instead, it is more useful to recognize the interplay between statistical analysis as a method, on the one hand, and the framework of interpretation that appears to be necessary for significant statistical analysis, on the other. The position taken here is similar to that expressed by van der Leeuw (1982) in his discussion of the meaning of objectivity in archaeological reasoning. Namely, statistical methods—if they are to transcend the particulars of simple description—require a context that can be given interpretation in the form of "experiment" and "outcomes," where the former may be interpreted as the process through which material phenomena arise, ranging from the specific objects to the (emic) classes represented by the objects. The process(es) in question is not just the technological one but must include the conceptual framework within which that technological process is embedded.

The technological process is informative about the variance, the conceptual framework about the mean. Together, these inform us about the manner in which a continuum is (arbitrarily) subdivided into contrasting aspects. While we cannot recover the linguistic labeling, we can recover the consequences of the conceptual categorizations as these become translated into specific artifacts. The discontinuities that appear in our measurements—sometimes qualitative, sometimes in the form of the distribution such as a nonoverlapping bimodal distribution—are a manifestation of choices made by the artisan, hence of conceptual categories that guide the artisan's production. And that implies, as Renfrew (1983) and van der Leeuw

(1982) have discussed, that we must come to grips with how the cultural context wherein those categories lie is structured, and how the cultural context relates to the phenomena that we observe and study. Statistical reasoning is one means to express these relations so that their consequences can be drawn out and expressed.

Acknowledgments

I would like to thank Marty Biskowski, Ruth Leiserson, and Sami Omar for comments on an earlier draft of this manuscript.

References

Benfer, R., and A. Benfer. 1981. Automatic classification of inspectional categories: multivariate theories of archaeological data. *American Antiquity* 46: 381-396.

Carr, C. 1985. Getting into data: philosophy and tactics for the analysis of complex data structures. In *For Concordance in Archaeological Analysis: Bridging Data Structure, Quantitative Technique, and Theory*, ed. C. Carr, pp. 18-44. Kansas City: Westport Press.

Christenson, A., and D. W. Read. 1977. Numerical taxonomy, r-mode factor analysis and archaeological classification. *American Antiquity* 43: 163-179.

Clark, A., and C. Stafford. 1982. Quantification in American archaeology. *World Archaeology* 34: 61-72.

Clarke, D. 1968. *Analytical Archaeology*. London: Metheuen.

Dunnell, R. 1971. *Systematics in Prehistory*. Glencoe: Free Press.

Feller, W. 1968. *Introduction to Probability Theory and Its Applications*. Volume 1. New York: Wiley.

Fisher, R. 1954. *Statistical Methods for Research Workers*. London: Oliver & Boyd .

Gould, R. A. 1980. *Living Archaeology*. Cambridge: Cambridge University Press.

Harrington, J. 1942. Culture element distributions XIX: central California coast. *Anthropological Records* 7(1): 1-46.

Hodson, F. R. 1982. Some aspects of archaeological classification. In *Essays on Archaeological Typology*, eds. R. Whallon and J. A. Brown, pp.21-29. Evanston: Center for Amer. Arch. Press.

Hole, B. 1980. Sampling in archaeology: a critique. *Annual Review of Anthropology* 9: 217-234.

Kroeber, A. L. 1971 [1918]. Elements of culture in native California. In *The California Indians: A Source Book*, ed. R. F. Heizer and M. A. Whipple, pp.3-65. Berkeley: University of California Press.

Lee, R. 1979. *The !Kung San*. Cambridge: Cambridge University Press.

Leone, M. P. 1982. Some opinions about recovering mind. *American Antiquity* 47: 742-760.

Marshall, L. 1976. *The !Kung San of Nyae Nyae*. Cambridge: Harvard University Press.

Naroll, P. 1962. Floor area and settlement pattern. *American Antiquity* 37: 587-589.

Parzen, E. 1960. *Modern Probability Theory and Its Application*. New York: Wiley.

Read, D. W. 1974. Some comments on typologies in archaeology and an outline of a methodology. *American Antiquity* 39: 216-242.

Read, D. W. 1978. Towards a formal theory of population size and area of habitation. *Current Anthropology* 19: 312-317.

Read, D. W. 1982. Toward a theory of archaeological classification. In *Essays on Archaeological Typology*, eds. R. Whallon, and J. A. Brown, pp. 56-92. Evanston: Center for Amer. Arch. Press.

Read, D. W. 1985. The substance of archaeological analysis and the mold of statistical method: enlightenment out of discordance? In *For Concordance in Archaeological Analysis: Bridging*

Data Structure, Quantitative Technique, and Theory, ed. C. Carr, pp.45-86. Kansas City: Westport Press.

Renfrew, A. C. 1983. Divided we stand: aspects of archaeology and information. *American Antiquity* 48: 3-17.

Sackett, J. R. 1966. Quantitative analysis of Upper Paleolithic stone tools. *American Anthropologist* 68: 356-394.

Sackett, J. R. 1982. Approaches to style in lithic archaeology. *Journal of Anthropological Archaeology* 1: 59-112.

Sackett, J. R. 1985. Style and ethnicity in the Kalahari: a reply to Wiessner. *American Antiquity* 50: 154-159.

Scheps, S. 1982. Statistical blight. *American Antiquity* 47: 836-851.

Spaulding, A. C. 1953. Statistical techniques for the discovery of artifact types. *American Antiquity* 18: 305-313.

Spaulding, A. C. 1960. Statistical description and comparison of artifact assemblages. In *The Application of Quantitative Methods in Archaeology*, ed. R. Heizer and S. Cook, pp. 60-92. New York: Wenner-Gren Foundation.

Spaulding, A. C. 1977. On growth and form in anthropology: multivariate analysis. *Journal of Anthropological Research* 33: 1-15.

Spaulding, A. C. 1982. Structure in archaeological data: nominal variables. In *Essays on Archaeological Typology*, ed. R. Whallon, and J. A. Brown, pp.1-20. Evanston: Center for Amer. Arch. Press.

Thomas, D. 1976. *Figuring Anthropology*. New York: Holt, Rinehart and Winston.

Thomas, D. 1978a. The awful truth about statistics in archaeology. *American Antiquity* 43: 231-244.

Thomas, D. 1978b. Arrowheads and atlatl darts: how the stones got the shaft. *American Antiquity* 43: 461-471.

van der Leeuw, S. E. 1982. How objective can we become: some reflections on the nature of the relationship between the archaeologist, his data and his interpretations. In *Theory and Explanation in Archaeology*, ed. C. Renfrew, M. J. Rowlands, and B. A. Segraves, pp.431-458. New York: Academic Press.

Whallon, R. 1972. A new approach to pottery typology. *American Antiquity* 37: 13-33.

Wiessner, P. 1977. *Hxaro: A Regional System of Reciprocity for Reducing Risk Among the !Kung San*. Ann Arbor: University of Michigan.

Wiessner, P. 1983. Style and social information in Kalahari San projectile points. *American Antiquity* 48: 253-276.

10

Removing Discordance from Quantitative Analysis

Christopher Carr

Since the mid-1960s, American archaeology has witnessed an exponential increase in the use of quantification, basic statistics, and multivariate methods in research (Clark 1982:225). These advances have crosscut many topics, including subsistence analysis (Reidhead 1981; Keene 1981; Winterhalder and Smith 1981), settlement analysis (Winters 1969; Limp 1981; Parker 1985; Kvamme 1985), intrasite spatial analysis (Peebles 1971; Whallon 1973, 1974, 1984; Carr 1984, 1985b), mortuary analysis (Brown 1971; Braun 1979), demographic analysis (Zubrow 1975), exchange (Greber 1976), artifact typology (Spaulding 1953; Whallon 1972; Christensen and Read 1977; Hoffman 1985), seriation (Hole and Shaw 1967; Johnson 1968; Marquardt 1978; Braun 1985), and sampling (Muller 1974; Lafferty et al. 1981). The developments have helped archaeologists both to express complex ideas succinctly in the language of mathematical structures and to model and simulate complex archaeological and behavioral variation.

Simple experimentation with and mastery of *technique* has been a predominant concern in these efforts (Thomas 1971, 1978; Cowgill

1977; Speth and Johnson 1976; Hole 1980; Vierra and Carlson 1981; Scheps 1982). More recently, however, a systematic interest in the logic of analysis has developed. In particular, attention is being given to formally developing and maintaining, during analysis, logically consistent relationships between the nature of archaeological and behavioral phenomena, the structure of data expressing them, technical assumptions, and theory (e.g., Carr 1984, 1985a, 1986; Martin 1983; Moore and Keene 1983; Whallon 1984; Whallon and Brown 1982; this volume). Such efforts facilitate an analysis becoming relevant, accurate, meaningful, and efficient, whereas mastery of technique, alone, does not.

This chapter summarizes the problems involved in developing and maintaining logical consistency during analysis. First, it clarifies the ways in which theory, quantitative technique, and data can be discordant with each other and a phenomenon of interest during analysis. Second, it enumerates various sources of discordance from statistical, philosophical, and psychological perspectives. Next, several methodological strategies for removing discordance from analysis are described. Finally, I mention how explicit statement of the procedures used in bringing concordance to analysis is critical to theory development. Abstract concepts and frameworks are illustrated with examples pertinent primarily to intrasite spatial analysis. This is the subject for which I have thought about these issues most thoroughly (e.g., Carr 1984, 1985b, 1986).

Philosophical Assumptions and Context

Only certain aspects of the logical, philosophical basis of meaningful scientific investigation are considered in this paper. It is desirable, therefore, to place its content in a larger, philosophical perspective.

First, it is necessary to comment on the nature of meaningful scientific investigation that is assumed. Informally and intuitively, a scientific study and its results can be taken to be meaningful if they allow or lead to the assignment of appropriate meaning to phenomena or to explanation of them. More formally, a meaningful scientific investigation will: (1) give accurate insight into a problem and lead to the development of theory, (2) allow the accurate and logical testing of models or hypotheses that represent extant theory, or (3) allow a particular case to be accurately and logically subsumed under extant theory, constituting a valid explanation. The accuracy of insight, test, or logical subsumption and the appropriateness of an assignment of meaning, of course, are not absolute qualities. They can be assessed only within the limits of the researcher's guiding paradigm.

By implication, the theories, models, or hypotheses that are developed or evoked in a meaningful scientific investigation and that allow or lead to the assignment of appropriate meaning must, themselves, be meaningful. A meaningful proposition or construct is taken here to be not only *testable and confirmable* in the minimal, least demanding usage of the term in philosophy of science (Carnap 1936: 420-427) but also *nontrivial*. It is taken to have "worthwhile" content from the perspective of the goals of the researcher's paradigm (Read and LeBlanc 1978: 307-308, 332; Salmon and Salmon 1979: 72) and to organize information efficiently and parsimoniously (Hemple 1966: 40-45; van der Leeuw 1978: 328).

For a scientific investigation to produce results that are meaningful within the limits of a researcher's paradigm, three conditions are minimally required:

> *Condition 1.* At least some aspects of the data brought forward for study must be relevant to the researcher's problem domain and accurately represent the phenomenon of interest (i.e., a population or process) and its nature.
> *Condition 2.* Those aspects of the data's structure that reflect the phenomenon of interest and its nature must be identified, and then accurately represented when summarized as patterning.
> *Condition 3.* These patterns must be interpreted in a manner consistent with the nature of the phenomenon of interest.

These minimal requirements, in turn, necessitate that the theories, models, hypotheses, test implications, mathematical techniques, data collection methods, and/or the data that are involved in an investigation be relevant to and logically consistent with each other, and ultimately to the empirical phenomenon of interest.

How to develop and maintain relevance and logical consistency between these entities at different levels of abstraction is a subject matter of philosophy of science that involves a great diversity of topics. Some examples include the correct forms of a logical deduction and induction; the role of auxiliary hypotheses and assumptions in operationalizing higher-level abstractions in terms of observables; the use of bridging arguments in making logical deductions and inductions; and the setting of boundary conditions to generalizations, hypotheses, models, and theories.

This chapter focuses on only a small subset of these issues but also some that philosophers of science typically have not explored in depth. In particular, I will discuss the *choice and logic of application of quantitative methods* of analysis to archaeological data and *choice of data*, each within the context of theory and the empirical world.

Terminology

To be precise about concordant relations in the discussions to ensue, it is necessary to define several terms. These refer to different categories of information or portions of reality: (1) a portion of the real world, (2) a phenomenon of interest, (3) data brought forward for study of a problem domain that includes the phenomenon of interest, (4) aspects of the data that are truly relevant to only the phenomenon of interest, and (5) aspects of the data that are expected to be relevant to the phenomenon of interest. These categories hold a nested, hierarchical relationship to each other. Higher numbered (lower level) categories embody decreasing amounts of information on the real world as a result of the partially controllable processes of selective observation and analysis.

A portion of the real world. Of the several categories of information, this is the broadest. It is the subset of entities or objects in the real world that the researcher selects for study in relation to his paradigmatic orientation and his more particular problem domain. Similar concepts are the research universe or study area.

A portion of the real world may be selected for study with a purpose in mind and in regard to certain of its characteristics. However, it is taken to have, simultaneously, a very large number of characteristics (properties, structures, organizations, natures) that are determined by a very large number of processes. This gives any portion of the world many *facets* or *phenomena*, such that it can be explored from many different perspectives and paradigms.

An example of a portion of the real world is an earthen archaeological site. This land parcel would have a large number of characteristics—e.g., artifactual, topographic, pedological, hydrological, archaeomagnetic, and others. Only some of these might serve as a basis for selecting it for study. The site could be studied from many different perspectives and paradigms.

Phenomenon of interest. This is the one facet within a portion of the real world—among its many facets—that is the object of study. Like the portion of the real world that is selected for study, the phenomenon of interest is chosen in relation to the researcher's paradigmatic orientation and problem domain.

A phenomenon of interest can be either a homogeneous population or a single process. If the phenomenon is a population, its organizational nature is determined by the process(es) that structure it—one or several of the many processes that structure the portion of the world of which it is a part. If the phenomenon is a process, its form is determined by the constraints that define it—a subset of the many constraints within the portion of the world of which it is a part.

An example of the phenomenon of interest is a population of several toolkits of some one kind within the behavioral domain, e.g., a collection of hide-working sets of knives, scrapers, and borers. This population is the set of outcomes of a single process—an activity, hide-working. The organizational nature of the population of tool kits—for example, whether their constituent tool types covary or only co-occur among the multiple toolkits and whether the tool types are symmetrically or asymmetrically distributed among the toolkits (Carr 1985)—is determined partially by the nature of the hide-working process.

A phenomenon of interest can also be a set of *multiple, parallel,* and *coterminous* processes or the population they generate. By these concepts is meant several processes that operate over and affect the same range of observations, so as to still define only one organizationally homogeneous population rather than multiple, organizationally differentiated populations (Carr 1986). In other words, the multiple processes are concatenated, with the output of one serving as the input of the next so as to effectively define a single process and a homogeneous population of final outcomes that can be treated as such analytically. This occurs despite whatever conceptual distinctions among the processes may be made.

Continuing the toolkit example, above, two parallel processes can be envisioned. One would be the activity of hide-working, involving the repeated use of knives, scrapers, and borers and defining a population of several toolkits of these in the behavioral domain. The second process would be one or more depositional formation processes and postdepositional disturbance processes that operate over the same toolkits and result in their being transferred into the archaeological domain as a population of deposits. The first process might involve the use and organization of knives, scrapers, and borers in constant proportions among the toolkits. The second group of processes might systematically alter the tool types' organization to simple co-occurrence relationships. However, because the two processes are parallel, coterminous, and concatenated, they effectively define a single process and a homogeneous population of outcomes (deposits of "toolkits" in the archaeological domain), which can be treated as such analytically.

Data brought forward for study. This category usually involves more and less information than that pertinent to the single phenomenon of interest. Data brought forward for study often include variables and cases that pertain to multiple phenomena (populations or processes), rather than a single phenomenon. They also may exclude critical variables or certain observations that reflect the phenomenon of interest. These circumstances have analytic, physical, and practical causes, all to be discussed later.

An example of data brought forward for study, to elaborate our toolkit illustration, would be the spatial locations of knives, scrapers, and borers that were used for multiple purposes—hide-working, woodworking, and bone-working. These data would reflect multiple phenomena of potential interest—multiple populations of toolkits that organizationally reflect multiple kinds of activities (processes). The data also might lack locational information on some items as a result of their not being recovered during excavation or other postdepositional processes.

Relevant data structure. In contrast to a data set brought forward for study are those aspects of it that are relevant to some one phenomenon of interest. These may be simply a subset of pertinent variables, observations, and relationships within the data. The relevant aspects may also be more complex dimensions or components of the data matrix that can be extracted only analytically (e.g., with factor or Fourier analysis). Note that those aspects of the data that are relevant to the phenomenon of interest often express only a portion of the information that is potentially available and pertinent to it. This is a product of the constrained manner in which data that are brought forward for study are collected and selected.

Examples of relevant data structures within a data set brought forward for study can be found in the case of the artifact palimpsest of multipurpose knives, scrapers, and borers just described. One relevant data structure would be spatial locations of only those artifacts that were used and deposited together as hide-working toolkits (the population of interest) during hide-working (the defining process). A second relevant data structure would be the locations of only those artifacts that were used and deposited together during woodworking, and a third would pertain to the locations of only bone-working artifacts that were deposited together. Use-wear or Fourier procedures (Carr 1986) might be used to analytically segregate these several relevant subset structures within the data brought forward for study.

It is important to realize that a single population of observations (a phenomenon of interest) can have any of several organizations and can be represented by any of several relevant data structures. This is possible when the observations are the outcomes of parallel, coterminous processes and when some of those processes are optional. An example would be a population of toolkits (deposits) in the archaeological domain. These might exhibit and be definable by ratio, ordinal, nominal, or polythetic scale relationships among the artifact types comprising them. The scale of the defining relationships would depend on the kinds and number of formation and disturbance processes responsible for them. The nature of generation of the archaeological toolkits would determine their organization and the kind of relevant data structure that would represent them accurately. The potential for phenomena of interest to have multiple organizations and representations stands as the basis of the "entry model" strategy of analysis, which is discussed later.

Expected relevant data structure. It is necessary to distinguish those aspects of a data set's structure that are expected to be relevant to a phenomenon of interest and its nature from those that are actually relevant. Aspects that are expected to be relevant are derived from some theoretical-interpretive framework and are expressed in the form of a model of relevant structure (Read 1985, schema D; Carr 1985b). They may bear little similarity to aspects of the data that actually reflect the phenomenon of interest, depending on the adequacy of both the primary premises and the auxiliary assumptions within the theoretical framework. For example, in our toolkit illustration, the population of hide-working toolkits (phenomenon of interest) might be manifested empirically as nominal scale spatial relationships between knives, scrapers, and borers as a result of the particular nature of the hide-working activity and other depositional processes. In contrast, the researcher might expect, on the basis of theoretical postulates (Carr 1984), that the population of toolkits would be defined by ratio scale spatial relationships.

The Need for Concordance in Analysis and Causes of Discordance from a Statistical Perspective

Meaningful scientific investigation requires the researcher to choose data and an analytic technique such that logical consistency is developed and maintained during analysis in three kinds of relationships. There must be concordance between: (1) the structure of the *data* to be investigated vs. the empirical phenomenon of interest; (2) the assumptions about the phenomenon of interest that underlie a chosen *technique* vs. the aspects of the data that are relevant to the phenomenon and the nature of the phenomenon itself; and (3) assumptions about the phenomenon of interest that are made by the *theoretical framework* that guides or emerges from analysis vs. technical assumption, relevant data structure, and the nature of the phenomenon. The need for logical consistency in each of these relationships is equivalent to the three conditions for successful scientific investigation that were discussed more informally, above.

Concordance in the first relationship ensures simply the *relevance* of analysis. Concordance in the first and second ensures the relevance and *accuracy* of analysis. Concordance in all three allows analysis to be *meaningful* as well as relevant and accurate—the most difficult state to achieve. I will elaborate on these three points after discussing each relationship in greater detail.

The Relation of Data Structure to the Phenomenon of Interest

If a quantitative analysis is to be relevant, which is a minimal requirement for its success, at least some aspects of the data brought forward for study must accurately reflect the empirical nature of the phenomenon of interest. Relevant variables must be designed, and relevant observations must be selected for use.

Data that are brought forward for analysis in early stages of a scientific project, however, usually have a great potential for reflecting both more and less information than that pertinent to some single phenomenon. This results from several conditions.

First, the variables and observations that are initially chosen for analysis are usually selected for their potential pertinence to a *broad problem domain* that involves *multiple, potential phenomena of interest*, rather than a single phenomenon. As Cowgill (1982: 39) notes:

> In theory we may base our selection of variables and their possible values entirely on considerations of their relevance for specific purposes, but in practice ... the tendency seems to be begin with a sizable number of *possibly relevant* variables and to decide that the truly relevant ones are those variables that in fact do, in terms of their patterning within the assemblage, show some sort of structure. (stress by Cowgill)

Second, data that are initially chosen for analysis often are selected deductively on the basis of the *expected* nature of the potential phenomena of interest rather than their *actual* nature, which remains to be investigated and understood. If the theoretical framework employed to make such deductions is weak, any single phenomenon of interest may manifest itself in unsuspected sets of variables and observations that may be left out of analysis, and extraneous data may be thought relevant and analyzed. Similarly, if a strong theoretical framework is improperly used beyond its boundary conditions, the variables and observations that are predicted to be relevant to a phenomenon may differ from those that are actually relevant.

Third, variability that is irrelevant to a phenomenon of interest may reside in the data initially presented for study because of the researcher's inability to physically isolate the phenomenon from others in the real world. Sometimes, the isolation of a phenomenon is possible only analytically. For example, consider three spatial distributions of simple backed blade knives within a site: one comprised of knives used for woodworking, another of knives for butchering, and a third of knives for cutting hides. Although a researcher might be interested in only the population of woodworking knives (the phenomenon of interest) and their spatial distribution, these might be impossible to isolate physically without information on use-wear. The researcher would have to begin analysis with distributional data on backed blade knives of all kinds (multiple phenomena). The single knife population of interest might be definable only analytically, perhaps with factor analysis (Schiffer 1975) or Fourier and filtering methods (Carr 1986).

Fourth, data brought forward for study may include information on undesirable processes such as observation and data-recording biases and errors. These may or may not cause a phenomenon of interest to not be physically isolatable.

Finally, practical limitations—economic, legal, or otherwise—may prevent a researcher from developing a data set that is fully pertinent to the phenomenon of interest. "Stand-in" or "proximate" populations or variables may have to be used for those actually pertinent (e.g., Winterhalder 1981: 20; Smith 1981: 38). Also, "summary variables," which describe aggregate behavior and one hopes are "sufficient" (Levins 1966: 427-430), may have to be used in place of detailed measures that are directly relevant to the phenomenon of interest (e.g., Winterhalder 1981: 19; Smith 1981: 52).

When data presented for analysis do not fully pertain to the empirical phenomenon of interest, two undesirable circumstances may arise. Both involve a loss of relevance. First, and obviously, the analysis may measure or characterize some phenomenon other than the one of interest or may reflect the one of interest only obliquely. If the latter is the case, the researcher may be able to compensate for quantitative irrelevance at the level of qualitative interpretation of results, providing that he is aware of the problem, can estimate the amount of irrelevant variability in the analytic results, and the problem is not too great.

The second problem that can arise when data do not fully pertain to the empirical phenomenon of interest is less direct and harder to compensate for. It is the logical discordance that is caused between the data's actual structure and the structure of the data that is assumed by the analytic technique. Being chosen in relation to a broad problem domain, the variables and observations that are brought forward for analysis typically reflect *multiple processes* that define *multiple populations*, i.e., multiple phenomena. In contrast, many statistical techniques assume a statistical model that specifies some *single process* as responsible for the variability within the data and a *homogeneous population* defined with respect to that process, i.e., a single phenomenon (Read 1985). For example, tests of model sufficiency in linear regression assume that the analyzed observations and variables refer to a single, multivariate normal population. Equivalently, many statistical techniques can be viewed as assuming a statistical model that allows multiple processes to be responsible for the variability within the data; however, these processes must be *parallel* and *coterminous* in the range of observations that they affect, so as to still define only one homogeneous population rather than multiple populations (Carr 1986).

To the extent that the model that underlies a statistical technique assumes a single process and population, or parallel processes and a single population, whereas the deducted set of possibly relevant variables and observations pertain to multiple processes and populations, technique and data will be logically discordant with each other. This discordance will be additional to that which occurs between the data's structure and the empirical phenomenon of interest. It will lessen not only the relevance of analytic results, but also their accuracy in representing any one phenomenon. Results will reflect an uncontrolled mix of several kinds of relationships among observations: relationships among observations within populations, which may differ from one population to another, and the relationship of populations to each other (Christensen and Read 1977: 170).

A good illustration of the effects of discordance between data structure and technique that can arise when data are not fully relevant to a single empirical phenomena of interest is purposefully provided by Whallon (1984). Using correlation analysis, he measured the similarity of the spatial distributions of several artifact classes within the Mask site, a Nunamiut Eskimo hunting stand. A global analysis and several local analyses were performed, each using local proportional artifact type densities (similar to proportions of artifact types within grid cells) as the observations. In the global analysis, a set of intertype correlations were calculated for density observations distributed over the whole site, as if the densities constituted a single population; however, they actually came from several different kinds of "activity zones." In contrast, the local analyses each involved the calculation of a separate set of intertype correlations using density observations from only one of the several kinds of activity zones. The global correlation coefficients differed from the local ones and were presumably less relevant to and a less accurate representation of past activities than the local coefficients. The global analysis involved a discordance between (1) the technique of correlation, which assumed a homogeneous population of observations (here, density observations) generated by a single process or parallel processes (an activity and/or other depositional processes) and (2) the data's actual structure, which encompassed multiple populations (density observations from multiple kinds of activity zones with different type-proportions), each generated by different processes (activities and/or other depositional processes). The local analyses minimized this discordance, and hence, gave different results.

Thus *relevant quantitative analysis requires a logical concordance between data structure and the empirical phenomenon of interest.* The data must reflect, as much as possible, no more nor less than the process or population of interest. This concordance is seldom found in the initial stages of analysis. Its development is the subject of later sections of this chapter.

The Relation of Technique to Data Structure and the Phenomenon of Interest

For a quantitative analysis to be both relevant and accurate—a more demanding requirement for analytic success than simple relevance—there must be concordance between more than data structure and the phenomenon of interest. These must be consistent with analytic technique. More exactly, the technique that is chosen for analysis must make assumptions about the organization of the phenomenon of interest that are concordant with those aspects of the data's structure that reflect the phenomenon's actual organization. This can be seen in the following way.

(1) A data matrix can explicitly and implicitly contain many different kinds of relationships between variables and observations. These include nominal, ordinal, and ratio scale relationships among variables, monothetic and polythetic relationships among observations, and overlapping and nonoverlapping relationships among observations. These various kinds of relationships can represent different phenomena or some single phenomena with varying degrees of accuracy. Any one phenomenon of interest will be accurately represented by only certain aspects of the data matrix's structure. Which aspects of the data's structure are relevant to the phenomenon will depend on the phenomenon's nature of organization.

For example, consider two artifact types that covaried in their frequencies when used in the behavioral domain. This covariation would reflect the nature of their functions and organization for use and the nature of organizations of the toolkit (phenomenon of interest) in that domain. However, as a result of parallel, coterminous depositional formation processes and postdepositional disturbance processes, the two types might only co-occur in the archaeological domain, and the toolkit (the same phenomenon of interest) would have a different organization: a *nominal* scale of organization rather than a *ratio* scale organization. Now consider a data matrix composed of the densities of each of the two artifact types within grid cells over the site. The membership of the two types in the same toolkit and the existence of the toolkit would not be expressed accurately by the ratio scale relationship among the densities of the two types over the grid cells. Instead, they would be indicated by the nominal scale relationship among the presence-absence states of the types over grid cells that is *implicit* in the density data. The phenomenon of interest would be expressed in only certain aspects of the total information that is contained within the data matrix.

(2) A quantitative method, by the nature of its procedures and design, can be sensitive to and accurately represent only certain aspects of the total structure of the data to which it is applied. In this regard, the application of a technique to data implies assumptions that only certain, specific aspects of the data are important for representation and interpretation whereas others are not. It implies that certain aspects of the data accurately reflect the phenomenon of interest and its nature whereas others do not. For example, an R-mode technique, operating on relationships among variables, might be sensitive to ratio scale patterns of covariation among variables, but not to nominal scale patterns of association among them. Application of such a technique to a data set would imply an assumption that only ratio scale patterning in the data is of interest, is concordant with the nature of the phenomenon of interest, and accurately reflects it. Likewise, a Q-mode method, operating on relationships among observations, might be sensitive to monothetic relationships of similarity among items as opposed to polythetic ones. Application of such a method to a data set would imply an assumption that only the monothetic relationships in the data are of interest, are concordant with the nature of the phenomenon of interest, and accurately reflect it. In either case, if those data patterns that actually reflect the phenomenon of interest are not those to which the applied technique is sensitive, the results of analysis will not

be accurate. Results will not reflect the relevant patterns in the data accurately, nor will they allow accurate insight into the phenomenon of interest. Consequently, choice of technique is critical.

For example, continuing the toolkit case, above, suppose that a researcher expects that artifact types in the same toolkit will covary in their frequencies over a site as a result of their use and discard in constant proportions while achieving a task. Suppose that he also expects the randomizing effects of postdepositional disturbance processes on artifact organization to be minimal. He then might logically use the above-described matrix of artifact type densities within grid cells as given, along with correlation analysis, to search for covarying artifact types and toolkits over the site. The use of correlation analysis, however, would be discordant with the actual nominal scale organization of the archaeological toolkits containing the types and with those aspects of the total information implicit in the density matrix which reflect that organization. Not being consistently sensitive to nominal scale patterning among variables, correlation methods would not necessarily lead to the discovery of the toolkit.

During early stages of analysis, there is a high potential for discordance between relevant aspects of a data set that reflect the phenomenon of interest and technique. Often at this stage, the researcher knows little about the nature of organization of the phenomenon and how it is expressed in the data. He must choose an analytic technique deductively, on the basis of the *postulated* organization and expression of the phenomenon rather than its *actual* organization and expression. Any discordance between the postulated and actual nature and expression of the phenomenon will, in turn, result in the choice of a technique that is discordant with the relevant aspects of the data's structure and that cannot accurately represent them. Such was the case in our toolkit example just cited.

In sum, when applied to data, a technique makes assumptions about which aspects of the data reflect the phenomenon of interest and its organizational nature. These assumptions should concord with those aspects of the data's structure that actually do reflect the phenomenon and its nature empirically. Only under this condition will analytic results characterize the phenomenon of interst accurately. *Accurate quantitative analysis requires logical concordance between technical assumption, relevant data structure, and the phenomenon of interest.*

The Relation of Theory to Technique, Data Structure, and Phenomenon of Interest

For a quantitative analysis to be meaningful as well as relevant and accurate, the theoretical framework that guides or emerges from it must be logically concordant with the empirical phenomenon of interest, aspects of the data that reflect it, and the assumptions that the technique makes about it. Only if the theoretical framework concords with these entities can the data pattern that emerges from analysis be assigned an appropriate meaning. If the patterns within a data set that are relevant to the phenomenon of interest are accurately revealed using an appropriate technique with one set of assumptions, but the patterns are interpreted within a theoretical framework that makes a different set of assumptions, then the meaning assigned to the patterns will probably be incorrect. For example, two tool types within the same toolkit might only associate rather than correlate in their spatial distributions over a site as a result of certain postdepositional disturbance processes having operated over that same area. Appropriately, they might also be found to associate using spatial techniques that are sensitive to nominal scale relations among types and not to correlate using techniques that are sensitive to ratio scale relations. It is unlikely, however, that these results would be assigned appropriate meanings—the existence of the toolkit and the operation of the postdepositional processes—if it were expected theoretically that tool types within toolkits always covary over space and that the effects of disturbance processes on this relationship are minimal (Carr 1977, 1984). Thus it is possible to identify, with appropriate techniques, data patterns that accurately reflect the phenomenon of interest but to then impart inappropriate meaning to the patterns if one's guiding theoretical framework is not consistent with the phenomenon of interest, aspects of the data's structure that are relevant to it, and assumptions that the applied technique makes about the phenomenon. *Meaningful quantitative analysis requires logical concordance among theory, technique, relevant data structure, and the phenomenon of interest.*

The logically consistent relationship between technical assumption and theoretical framework that is necessary to meaningful scientific investigation can be envisioned in a manner that is different from the above and more in line with discussions of philosophy of science. The assumptions that are implied by the application of a technique to data and that pertain to which aspects of the data reflect the phenomenon of interest and its nature can be treated as *auxiliary assumptions* within the employed theoretical framework (Hempel 1966: 22-23; Salmon 1982: 36). This is true whether one is building hypotheses and theory, testing them, or using them to explain a particular case. Thus meaningful investigation can be said to require logical consistency between these auxiliary assumptions and other aspects of the theoretical framework, i.e., *internal* theoretical consistency.

This viewpoint is strictly correct. However, it focuses undue attention on the need for concordance between technical assumption and theoretical constructs; it does not imply the equally important need for concordance among technique, data, and the phenomenon of interest. It also makes it difficult to visualize and discuss the need for and the nature of concordance among technique, data, and phenomenon separate from consideration of other aspects of the theoretical framework. Consequently, in this chapter technique and technical assumptions about the nature of the phenomenon of interest that a technique is expected to monitor during its application are considered to constitute an ideological construct in their own right—separate from theory, model, hypothesis, and test implication and serving to interface test implication with data.

Summary

Quantitative analysis within the context of scientific investigation is a complex thought process involving many entities at different levels of abstraction. These include the empirical phenomenon of interest, aspects of a data set's structure that are relevant or irrelevant to it, technical assumptions about it, and theoretical assumptions about the phenomenon of interest as expressed in test implications, hypotheses, models, or theory. An analysis will vary in the degree to which it is successful, depending on how many and which of these entities are related to each other in a logically consistent manner during the thought process. An analysis may be simply relevant; relevant and accurate; or relevant, accurate, and meaningful in the most successful circumstances (Figure 10.1).

Many discordances among the phenomenon of interest, data structure, and technique result from the processes of selecting data and technique. These problems can be summarized by defining more

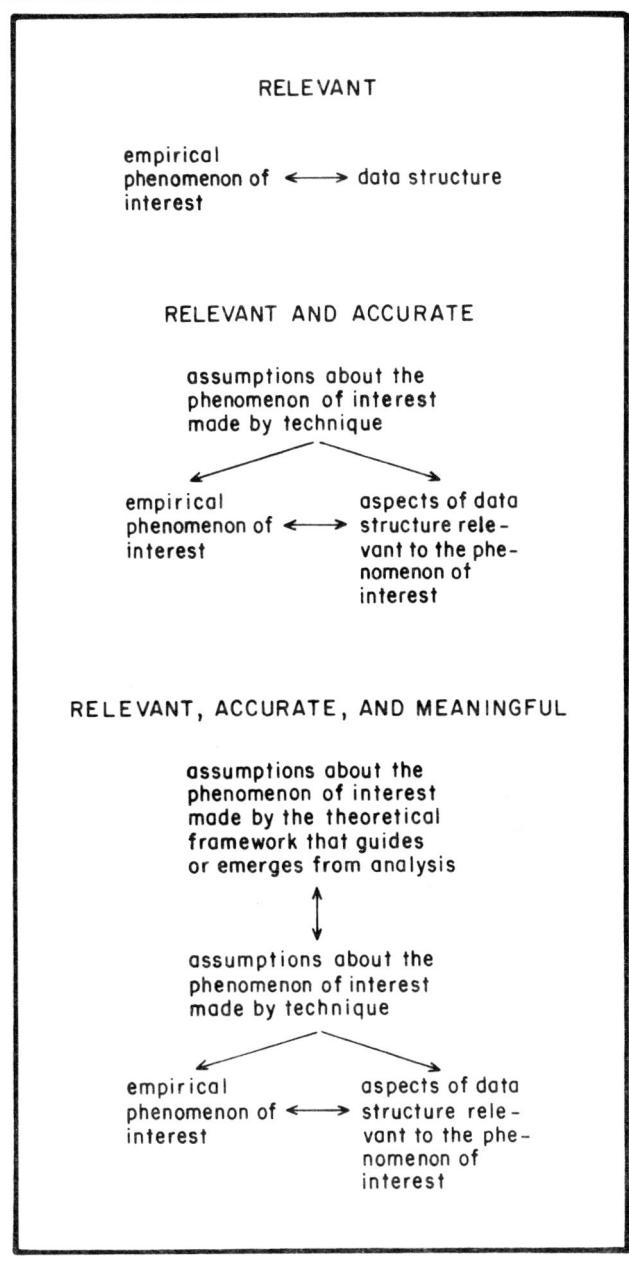

Figure 10.1 Relationships of concordance required for an analysis to be relevant, accurate, and meaningful.

completely and differentiating some of the terms presented at the beginning of this paper, using a matrix perspective. Two pairs of contrasting terms are offered. They are: all data brought forward for analysis, or simply *data structure* vs. *relevant data structure*, and (2) *relevant subset structure* vs. *relevant relational structure*.

Data structure. This term is used to refer to all the variables, observations, and the relationships among them that occur within a data set brought forward for study, regardless of whether or not they reflect the population or process of interest. A data structure may include "extra" variables or observations and relationships among them that are not pertinent to a single process (or parallel processes) and a single population of interest, as well as those that are. It may also include, simultaneously, multiple kinds of relationships among the *same* variables or observations (e.g., nominal scale and ratio scale relationships, monothetic and polythetic relationships)—only some relationships of which reflect the organization of the phenomenon of interest. For example, ratio scale data simultaneously express interval, ordinal, and nominal scale relationships among variables, not all of which need be relevant. Finally, a data structure may lack crucial information on the phenomenon of interest as a result of theoretical or practical limitations on data collection.

Relevant data structure. In contrast to the term "total data structure," this term is reserved, as defined before, for those aspects of a data set that reflect the single phenomenon of interest and its nature of organization. A data set's relevant structure includes only those variables and observations that pertain to a single process or parallel, coterminous processes that define a homogeneous population. It also includes only those kinds of relationships among variables and observations that reflect the form of organization of the phenomenon of interest.

A data set's relevant structure, particularly for archaeological data, usually will not have a physical correlate in a specific set of data items. This results partly from the fact that a single variable may reflect multiple processes (underlying dimensions of variability) and stochastic variation. It also relates to the fact that data at a measurement level higher than the nominal scale simultaneously reflect relationships at that higher level scale and relationships at all lower-level scales. Finally, it can reflect a more fundamental circumstance: the organization of the phenomenon of interest in the physical world, as opposed to data about it. A phenomenon may not exist separate from other phenomena; it may be possible to isolate it only analytically, not physically.

Relevant subset structure vs. relevant relational structure. The relevant structure of a data set has two distinguishable, usually cross-cutting components. These are its relevant subset structure and its relevant relational structure. Consider a matrix of variables and observations that have been selected in regard to a broad problem domain rather than as a reflection of some single phenomenon of interest. The relevant subset structure of that matrix can be defined as the *subset of data items* that pertains to variables and observations reflecting the phenomenon of interest, although not necessarily only that phenomenon (see above). A data matrix that is defined in regard to a problem domain will usually have multiple relevant subset structures, each pertinent to different phenomena.

In contrast, the relevant relational structure of a data matrix is comprised of those particular *relationships* among variables and observations that are of a kind that reflect the organizational nature of the single phenomenon of interest. A data matrix may simultaneously contain several relational structures pertinent to several phenomena, even if the matrix has but one relevant subset structure. The value of each data item may reflect multiple underlying dimensions of variability pertinent to different phenomena; multiple, implicit levels of variability and relationships at different scales of measurement which are pertinent to different parallel, coterminous processes; and stochastic variation. For example, a matrix of cell densities of two artifact types contains a nominal-scale relevant relational structure, which might be pertinent to their organization as a toolkit in the archaeological domain, and a ratio-scale relevant relational structure, which might be pertinent to the disorganization of the types by postdepositional disturbance processes.

Two general kinds of discordance between data and technique can be summarized using the above distinctions. One pertains to the way in which *data* are selected, the *number of phenomena* that a data set reflects, and the number of relevant *subset structures* that comprise it. During early stages of research, variables and observations are usually chosen in regard to some general problem domain, reflect multiple phenomena (processes and populations), and are composed of multiple potentially relevant subset structures. This multiphenomenal nature of the data is logically discordant with the theoretical bases of many statistical techniques, which assume a model of the data positing a single population produced by a single process.

The second kind of discordance pertains to the way that *technique* is chosen, the assumptions that the technique makes about *the nature of organization* of the phenomenon of interest, and the particular relevant *relational structure* of the data to which the technique is sensitive. During early stages of research, technique is often chosen deductively, with its assumptions reflecting the expected nature of organization of the phenomenon of interest and its expected expression as a relevant relational structure within the data. These expectations often will not concord with the actual nature or organization of the phenomenon and its expression as a relational structure in the data.

Both kinds of discordance typify early stages of research, when a single phenomenon of interest has not been envisioned and little is known about the number or nature of the phenomena that are responsible for the data or their manner of expression in the data. However, the discordances can also occur in later stages of analysis, depending on the success that the researcher has had in formulating specific questions, focusing on a single phenomenon, and coming to understand the kinds and causes of variability in the data.

A General Cause of Discordance from a Philosophical and Psychological Perspective

In this section, a cause of discordance among data structure, technical assumption, and theoretical framework is described in philosophical and psychological terms. The cause is made clear by comparing the logical processes that are involved in analyzing *complex* data sets, which requires mathematical pattern recognition procedures, to those involved in analyzing simple data sets, which requires only mental pattern recognition abilities.

The complexity of a data set is defined here to be a function of its size (number of variables and observations), the number and complexity of patterns within it, and the strength of patterning. A complex data set can be either of two kinds. The first is a *multivariate* data set in which the number of variables, observations, and patterns among them are too large for the patterns and meaning of variation among data items to be assessed mentally. A data set having a structure resolvable only by principal components analysis would be an example. The second kind of complex data set is a univariate response to multiple factors, which form a *time or space series* that is too complicated for mental dissection. To investigate a data set having this structure, Fourier analysis, spatial filtering techniques, or time series analaysis would be required (Carr 1982b, 1986; Braun 1985). In contrast to these complex data sets, a *simple* data set is taken to be one having a very limited, mentally manageable number of variables and observations that exhibit uncomplicated patterning.

It is important to emphasize that the dichotomy drawn here between complex and simple data sets pertains to only those of their characteristics that determine whether mathematical procedures are necessary to *recognize patterns* within them. The distinction is not used to refer to other data characteristics, which determine the *ease with which appropriate meaning is assignable* to the patterns found within them. These additional characteristics include, for example, the number and complexity of assumptions involved in collecting, subsampling, and/or screening the data. In regard to these kinds of characteristics, all data sets are more or less complex (Schiffer, personal communication 1983).

With these qualifications in mind, let us now consider a general cause of analytic inconsistencies. Archaeology seeks to reconstruct and understand *nonobservables* (past behavior and ideas) through the discovery and investigation of patterning among *observables* (archaeological phenomena). This places archaeological method within the realm of scientific method, which involves the generating and testing of hypotheses or models (complexes of hypotheses). Hypotheses or models that are concerned with nonobservable activities and ideas are formulated through the discovery of patterns (generalizations) and are tested through the seeking of specific patterns (test implications) in archaeological observables.

The logic that is involved in formulating or testing hypotheses can vary in its consistency and potential for leading the researcher to relevant, accurate, and meaningful conclusions. The degree to which these desirable circumstances are realized depends on the three conditions for successful analysis discussed at the beginning of this chapter.

The arguments to follow pertain to Conditions 2 and 3. They regard the proper identification, accurate summarization, and appropriate interpretation of relevant data structure within a total data set. However, focus will be on the identification and summarization of relevant data structure, and particularly whether pattern-seeking *mathematical techniques* (e.g., factor analysis) are required for this and the logical effect of this requirement. Also, it will be used to assign meaning to recognized data patterns, and the data and empirical phenomenon of interest pertains to the framework's *primary propositions* (hypotheses, laws, or models) rather than its auxiliary assumptions (e.g., sample representativeness). The difficulties posed by erroneous auxiliary assumptions are considered at the end of this discussion.

During hypothesis development and testing, two kinds of situations can arise, varying in the logic that they involve. In the first, a researcher studies relatively simple phenomena of interest. Observables and data on them pattern themselves clearly such that the researcher can observe the patterns without the aid of mathematical pattern-searching algorithms. In this case, the logic involved in the formulation or testing of hypotheses can be carried out with consistency among data structure, generalization/test implication, and hypothesis and can lead to accurate and meaningful conclusions. This can be done in the manner envisioned by philosophers of science (Hempel 1966; Hanson 1972). In the second situation, the phenomena that are studied are relatively complex. Observables and data observations pattern themselves in ways that require the researcher to use pattern-finding mathematical techniques rather than his own senses and mental capabilities, alone, to search for pattern. In this case, logical inconsistencies among the phenomenon of interest, data structure, technique, test implication, and hypothesis can creep into the analysis. Inaccurate quantitative results and distorted understanding may result.

Let us see how the study of complex phenomena and patterning among observables with mathematical techniques presents a problem in logic, whereas the study of simpler phenomena and patterning among observables with one's own mental capabilities does not, by comparing the two.

In the analysis of either simply or complexly structured data, the researcher's task is twofold: to *find* patterns inherent in the data and *interpret* them with regard to the phenomena that produced them. Finding a pattern can involve choosing subsets of variables and observations as well as defining relationships among them. Interpreting an empirical pattern can be achieved in two ways. The first involves comparing the empirical pattern to those patterns implied by extant predictive laws or models and then matching it to one of the expected patterns (Toussaint 1978: 191-192). This allows the logical subsumption of the specific case under the accepted general law or model (i.e., explanation). Alternatively, interpretation of a pattern can be achieved through the formulation of a new hypothesis/model that implies an expectable pattern which matches the one found (theory/hypothesis building), followed by logical subsumption of the specific case under the new general principle. This amounts to explanation only if the new principle can be confirmed with other, independent data. The problem with the logic of analysis of complex data sets is most apparent in those analyses that require the second means of interpretation—hypothesis generation—but also is an aspect of analyses that involves the application of extant laws/models for interpretation. Analysis involving hypothesis generation will be considered first.

For simply structured data sets with simple patterning among observations, the tasks of finding patterns and interpreting them through the generation of adequate explanatory hypotheses can be done with a *single* mental operation called *abduction* (Hanson 1972). Abduction is the simultaneous discovery of a *pattern* and its *significance* in suggesting a hypothetical cause of the pattern, as one searches data. Abductive reasoning is the simultaneous dawning that a pattern exists in one's data, and that "the pattern could be explained if hypothesis X were true."

Abduction is more than induction, the process by which generalizations (patterns) are formulated (Hempel 1966). Abduction involves the realization of the higher-level *meaning* of a generalization (i.e., the development of a hypothesis) as well as the formulation of the generalization, itself. Abduction is also more than retroduction, the process of understanding that a pattern could be explained if a given, new hypothesis were true. Abduction involved the *perception* of a new pattern—previously unperceived—as well as the retroduction of a new explanatory hypothesis. Abduction, then, is the seeming "conceptual gestalt" by which, simultaneously, new hypotheses are born and patterning in data suddenly becomes clear and explicable. (Here I have departed from Hanson's [1972] use of the term retroduction.)

For more complexly organized observables, the processes of discovering patterns among data items and inferring the phenomenon that produced those patterns in a more intricate, *multistep, serialized* task. In the most common approach to analysis, first sophisticated, pattern-finding mathematical techniques are used to search the data for multidimensional patterns and to summarize those patterns in two- or three-dimensional representations that humans can visualize, or with a few statistics. (An exception is the "entry model" approach to data analysis, described below.) This step, which involves the generalization of patterns among observables, is equivalent to logical *induction*. Second, the patterns that are found and summarized are then interpreted in terms of the phenomena that produced them. This step, which involves the logic that a pattern would be explicable if a given, new hypothesis were true, is equivalent to logical *retroduction*.

The difference between the multistep, serialized logic of analysis of complex data structures and the single-step logic of analysis of simple data structures is critical. It involves a separation of the process of *finding patterns* from the process of interpreting patterns by the mathematical technique used to search the data. *This separation and serialization has the fundamental consequence of leaving room for the development of logical inconsistencies among the phenomenon of interest, data structure, pattern-finding technique, and interpretive framework during the course of analysis. These inconsistencies, in turn, may result in the definition of patterns that do not accurately reflect the phenomenon of interest and the drawing of false conclusions.*

To elaborate on this point, in the simple abductive process, data are searched for patterns by the human mind. The mind both *knows* what kinds of data and patterns are possibly meaningful and expectable from an interpretive standpoint, and *selects and searches* the data for precisely those patterns in some appropriate way. At the same time as the data are selected and searched, the interpretive framework, the set of possibly meaningful patterns, the data's subset and relations structures that are considered relevant, and the mode of search all are questioned and reformulated continuously in light of the patterns found in the data. Feedback is instantaneous and continuous among phenomena of interest, data structure, mode of pattern searching, and interpretive framework. This helps to bring and keep all four into logically consistent relationships with each other. Such feedback and logical consistency are possible only because the mental activities of finding patterns and interpreting pattern occur simultaneously, in parallel, as part of the process of abduction.

In the case where mathematical techniques are used to search for patterns in complexly structured data items that pertain to complex phenomena, such feedback does not occur on a continuous basis. Data are not searched for patterns by a human mind with a *variable* search strategy, a variable theoretical framework, and a variable list of potentially relevant data structures—all of which may change as knowledge is gained about the data's structure during the search. Rather, data are examined using a mathematical technique with a *fixed* search strategy that is consistent with a fixed interpretive framework. A fixed list of variables, observations, and relationships in the data is considered potentially relevant. None of these change as the technique is applied to the data. Critically, in a single pass over the data, results that accurately represent the data's relevant structure and the phenomenon of interest may or may not be derived, depending on the degree of logical consistency among the subset of data that is assumed relevant for analysis, the relational aspects of the data that are assumed relevant by the technique and revealed by it, and those aspects of the data that are truly relevant. Interpretation only *follows* the search for patterning *after* logical inconsistencies between the phenomenon of interest, relevant data structure, technique, and implied theoretical framework, as well as misrepresentation of the data, have had a chance to be incorporated in the analysis. Interpretations and conclusions of questionable relevance, accuracy, and meaning may be derived. Thus logical inconsistencies in analysis and erroneous conclusions can result from the *separation and serialization* of the processes of searching for pattern and interpreting pattern. This removes the opportunity in a single search-pass over data for feedback between currently known aspects of its structure and the nature of the search technique and the interpretive framework.

The separation of the processes of searching for pattern and interpreting pattern by technique, and the undesirable effects of this on the logic of analysis, characterize not only analyses that involve the formulation of new hypotheses for interpretation. They also characterize analyses that involve the application of extant laws/models for interpretation. First, test implications are deduced from alternative models/laws that might have interpretive value for the specific case under investigation. Then a data subset that is thought to be relevant according to the theoretical framework is chosen and searched by a mathematical technique that has assumptions also thought to be relevant. This is done in order to find patterns that match one or more of the test implication(s) and that allow the logical subsumption of the specific case under one or more of the explanatory models/laws. The patterns that are found may or may not accurately represent the phenomenon of interest and the data's relevant structure, depending on whether there is consistency among the data's subset structure that is assumed relevant and used, the data's relational structure that is assumed relevant by the applied technique, and those aspects of the data that are actually relevant to the phenomenon of interest. The matches obtained between found patterns and deduced test implications, and the interpretations made, will correspondingly vary in their accuracy and meaning. Once again, in a single search-pass over the data, there is no opportunity for feedback between currently known aspects of the data's structure and the search technique and interpretive framework. Logical inconsistencies are allowed to develop, and erroneous conclusions are allowed to be drawn.

In a real analysis, an interpretive framework involves uncertain auxiliary assumptions in addition to potentially erroneous hypotheses, laws, or models. The problem of how to analyze complex data with logical consistency and how to define relevant data patterns that have potential for being assigned appropriate meaning becomes all the more apparent and troublesome. In a real analysis, choice of data and technique and the patterning of the data that is revealed may be influenced by the auxiliary premises as well as the primary premise assumed true. A delay in the feedback between known aspects of data structure and the interpretive framework (including the auxiliary assumptions) may result in poorer choices of data and search techniques, a greater potential for inconsistency in analysis, and the definition of less relevant and accurate patterning. This circumstance will increase the possibility of assigning inappropriate meaning to analytic results, additional to the effects of any inaccuracies in the auxiliary assumptions themselves.

In sum, maintaining logical consistency during the analysis of a complex data set often cannot be achieved for any single pass over the data. This problem does not result from the use of a pattern finding technique per se. Both mental scanning of simple data sets and mechanical scanning of complex ones require the use of some search technique, yet the effectiveness of the latter may not match that of the former. Rather, the problem with the analysis of complex data, as typically approached, results from separating and serializing the processes of finding pattern and interpreting pattern. This does not allow continuous feedback among the phenomenon of interest, data structure, search technique, and theoretical framework. For circumstances involving hypothesis formulation as opposed to hypothesis testing, the problem posed by complex data sets, compared to simple ones, can be summarized in logical terms. *Analysis of complex data requires inductive and retroductive logic, whereas analysis of simple data can be achieved through abduction.*

The "Methodological Double Bind"

The serial process of finding pattern and interpreting pattern that is commonly involved in the analysis of complex data sets can result in the two potential kinds of discordances that were described earlier in this chapter. In brief, an analytic technique and the interpretive framework with respect to which it is chosen may assume the data of interest to pertain to a single process and population (relevant subset structure) and have a certain organization (relevant relational structure). In contrast, the data may actually reflect multiple processes and populations and have a different relevant relational structure.

These discordances can occur at any stage in the analysis of complex data sets. They are particularly problematic, however, at the beginning of the analytic process. At this point, little may be known about the data's relevant structure. As a consequence, the researcher is put in a double bind. He cannot choose an appropriate technique of analysis and an appropriate subset of the data for analysis without some knowledge about the data set's structure; at the same time, he cannot obtain this knowledge without applying some pattern-searching technique to summarize the data's structure in a simpler form that is comprehendable by the human mind.

A very simple example of this bind during the initial stages of analysis of complex data is given by Christenson and Read (1977: 171). Concerned with the typology of a set of projectile points, they note that they could not do an R-mode factor analysis of the data to determine relevant dimensions of morphological variability without first identifying and eliminating extreme cases and defining a homogeneous population. (To not do so would introduce distortions in the magnitudes of the correlation coefficients serving as a basis for the factor analysis.) At the same time, proper multivariate (as opposed to univariate) identification of the outliers required that the dimensions of variability present in the data be known.

The methodological double bind has the unfortunate effect of encouraging the researcher to proceed directly with fine-grained analysis using unscreened data and standard techniques that have not been chosen in relation to the case-specific nature of the phenomenon of interest and its particular expression in the data. If the data and technique are not concordant with each other and the phenomenon of interest, the patterns that are found may be irrelevant or inaccurate. At worst, the results are accepted at face value and as final, with little attempt to evaluate the degree of discordance in analysis and possible distortions in the representation of the data and phenomenon. At best, fine-grained analysis is undertaken in order to obtain information about the data and phenomenon, which then is used to choose relevant data and techniques for subsequent reanalysis. However, if the initial analysis produces distorted results, these may serve as a poor basis for modifying the choice of data and techniques. Convergence on relevant and accurate results through repeated analysis alone is not guaranteed.

Thus complex data pose the researcher with the problem of how to "open" them and learn about their structure without violating their relevant aspects.

Overcoming the Methodological Double Bind and Developing Analytic Concordance

On "General Knowledge"

In order to begin overcoming the methodological double bind and developing concordance in analysis, it is necessary for the researcher to secure what I term (Carr 1986) "general knowledge" about the data's relevant structure. By general knowledge is meant an understanding of the general *classes* of observations, variables, and relationships among them that most likely do and do not reflect the phenomenon of interest accurately. General knowledge about a data's structure contrasts with the detailed understanding of particular observations, variables, and relationships that result from a concordant, fine-grained analysis. For example, in intrasite spatial analysis, general knowledge about a spatial distribution of artifacts would include insights into the approximate range of scales of artifact clusters, whether clusters typically overlap, and whether or not they tend to contrast greatly in artifact density with the background artifact scatter. It would also include information on whether coarranged artifact classes (depositional sets) are organized on a ratio, ordinal, nominal, or polythetic scale of measurement and whether they tend to overlap. This general knowledge would contrast with documentation of the precise limits, positions, and density contrasts of specific clusters and the precise relationships among artifact types as members of specific depositional sets, which would be revealed in a fine-grained, concordant analysis. General knowledge is not restricted to deductively derived postulates about the phenomenon of interest and the data, although it may include information having this origin (see below).

The methodological double bind seems insurmountable if it is assumed that the particulars of a relevant data structure must be known prior to analysis to choose an appropriate data set and technique (see above). However, this is not so. It is possible to overcome the problem by: (1) somehow developing a general knowledge of the data's relevant structure, (2) choosing data and technique in relation to this knowledge, which guides analysis initially in the right direction, (3) using robust tactics and techniques rather than assuming, fine-grained ones to initially explore the data and gain knowledge about the more detailed aspects of its relevant structure and the phenomenon of interest, and (4) examining the data multiple times, with feedback of new insights about details from early steps to later steps. These means for overcoming the methodological double bind and developing analytic concordance can be achieved with four complementary tactics of analysis:

(1) deductive specification of potentially relevant variables and observations, and an appropriate technique;
(2) "constrained" exploratory data analysis;
(3) the "entry model" approach; and
(4) stepwise, cyclical analytic designs.

Each of these strategies allows the researcher to develop general knowledge about the data brought forward for analysis and the phenomenon of interest. They aid him in selecting a relevant subset of variables and observations and an analytic technique that is sensitive to the data's relevant structure.

Deductive Specification of Potentially Relevant Variables and Observations and an Appropriate Technique

One direct strategy for developing general knowledge about a data set and a phenomenon of interest is the evoke extant theory about the nature of the kind of phenomenon in general. On the basis of such theory, the subset of the data and the technique that are most *likely* to be relevant to the phenomenon of interest can be deduced. To the extent that the expected nature of the phenomenon of interest does not concord with its actual nature, irrelevant variables and items may be included in analysis, and some relevant ones may be deleted. In addition, the technique that is chosen for analysis may assume that certain kinds of relationships among variables or observations are relevant when in fact other kinds reflect the phenomenon of interest more accurately.

This strategy is usually employed at the very beginning of a multistep analysis, when little is known about the structure of the data presented for analysis or the causes of their variability. It can be followed and checked by inductive exploration using data and techniques that are justified on the basis of the insight that is gained initially and deductively.

In archaeological studies, middle-range theory (e.g., Binford 1977a; Schiffer 1976; Raab and Goodyear 1984) is frequently used to deduce the subset of data and/or the technique that is likely to be appropriate for analysis. Middle-range theory is useful for this because it specifies the archaeological observables that are expected to manifest particular phenomena of interest, and/or their expected nature of organization. Let us consider some examples of this application of middle-range theory.

Middle-Range Theory Used to Specify Relevant Subsets of Variables and Observations

One area of currently active research in which middle-range theory has been used to deduce potentially relevant variables and observations for analysis is artifact style analysis for the purpose of testing or formulating propositions about prehistoric social organization. Wobst's (1977) information exchange theory of style specifies the kinds of items that are likely to indicate group affiliation through their design, thereby suggesting the *observations* in any particular case that are probably relevant to the study of prehistoric social organization. Items having this potential are those that: (1) probably were used in contexts ensuring their visibility to all members of the group and members of other nearby groups, as opposed to items used in the domestic sphere; (2) are long-lived, making their expression of group affiliation efficient over time; and (3) probably were not exchanged between groups.

Voss (1980a: 4), following Wobst, goes on to specify for such items the different kinds of stylistic *variables* that are often useful for determining group affiliation vs. group interaction. Discrete characteristics that are highly visible and that thus can function effectively as symbols, such as discrete design elements and configurations (Fredrick 1970; Stanislawski and Stanislawski 1978), are more likely to be accurate measures of group affiliation. In contrast, continuous variables that encompass the "nuances" of style, such as the dimensions of design zones and counts of design element repetitions, are more likely to be accurate measures of group interaction. In addition, Braun and Plog have suggested that the stylistic characteristics of an artifact define a hierarchy. Attributes at different levels of the hierarchy represent different stages of the decision process that is involved in the manufacture of the artifact (Plog 1978: 161) but are also sensitive to different social factors and groups (Braun and Plog 1982: 511), perhaps at different geographic scales (Braun 1980: 12-13).

A framework for more systematically isolating the different style variables within an artifact that can reflect different kinds of processes has been offered by Carr (1984b, 1985c). Carr defines four correlated hierarchies of observable and measurable characteristics of style variables: a hierarchy of manufacturing decisions involving the variables, a hierarchy of manufacturing execution steps involving the variables, a hierarchy of the visibility of variables' states, and a hierarchy of the geographic extent of alternative states taken by variables under the assumption of no artifact exchange. The visibility of a variable's states is measurable in relation to their absolute size, their color, textural, and size contrasts from each other and their background, the number of alternative states the variable can take, the social context of use, and other considerations. The place of an attribute in each of these hierarchies constrains its potential for operating in and reflecting any of a hierarchy of processes. These include processes that are pertinent to solely technological or raw material constraints, active symbolization of boundaries between groups of various expanse, active symbolization or passive reflection of cooperation within social groups of various expanse, expression of individual identity and personality, and individual motor habits. The systematic dependency of the hierarchy of processes upon the hierarchy of characteristics of style variables allows the researcher to predict the one or few processual meanings that a style variable can have on the basis of its observable characteristics. Those attributes of an artifact that are most likely to be relevant to a technological, social or individual-level process of interest can be isolated.

In total, the middle-range principles of these several researchers define a very powerful framework. From them, the kinds of observations and variables in an artifact style data set that are likely to be relevant to prehistoric social organization can be deduced with a great degree of specificity. When applied within the bounds of their limitations (Wiessner 1983), these principles suggest the data's relevant subset structure, which in turn would tend to be concordant with statistical techniques assuming some single process. Thus, here is a case where deductive specifications of variables and observations can improve the likelihood of concordance between data structure and technique.

Some studies of prehistoric social organization that have used these principles in this manner include those of Braun (1977, 1980), Plog (1976, 1978, 1980), Voss (1980a, 1980b), and Hinkle (1984). We may also note that Spaulding's emphasis on using nominal scale measures (or higher-scale measures reduced to a nominal scale) as a basis for artifact typologies derives from conclusions of his that are concordant with the information exchange theory. Spaulding (1982: 5-6, 10) argues that it is nominal scale (discrete) variables that indicate culturally imposed patterns of artifact manufacture and that may be used to define types having cultural significance (i.e., types indicating the group affiliation of the artifact's makers).

Another field of study in which middle-range theoretical arguments have been used to deduce variables and observations that are probably relevant to some phenomenon of interest is mortuary analysis. Braun (1979: 69) has argued that the archaeological variables that are relevant to the identification of ascriptive, hierarchical social distinctions include grave good classes that do not occur in village middens, that occur rarely overall within burials, that involve a relatively substantial labor input to produce, and that do not associate with age or sex. He also argues (p. 67) that it is qualitative rather than quantitative burial ritual attributes that symbolize formal authority and hereditary ranking. These arguments were then used by Braun to select a potentially relevant subset of variables from a burial set for analysis.

**Middle-Range Theory Used to Specify
the Nature of the Phenomenon of Interest,
Relevant Relational Data Structure,
and Appropriate Technique**

Middle-range theory does not deal only with the archaeological indicators of past phenomena, that is, with the variables and observations that comprise relevant subset structures. It also addresses the nature of organizations of such indicators—relevant relational structures—and by implication, appropriate techniques of analysis.

An example of a field in which linkages have been specified among the organization of archaeological observables, relevant relational data structure, and technique is intrasite spatial analysis. I (Carr 1984) have constructed a model of intrasite artifact organization that commonly typifies archaeological sites. The model posits the internal and external set organization of archaeological "toolkits," or "depositional sets," as polythetic and overlapping. It also specifies that archaeological "activity areas" or "depositional areas" may vary in their size, shape, orientation, spacing, artifact density and composition, border crispness, and in whether they overlap and are hierarchically arranged in space. Most spatial quantitative methods that have been used in intrasite studies then were reviewed for their concordance with this model, providing an assessment of their appropriateness for application to most sites. In a later publication (Carr 1985b), I expand the set organizational model to a continuum of 12 models, which specify depositional set structures ranging from monothetic, ratio scale form to highly polythetic forms, and from completely nonoverlapping to overlapping. Then, some behavioral and natural contexts in which depositional set organization can be expected to be similar to those stipulated by the models are enumerated; also, some quantitative techniques (new and old) that are appropriate for use when depositional sets are organized in these ways are specified. In this way, with a limited understanding of the behavioral and natural context of a site, it is possible to deduce the probably relevant organization of artifacts within it and the techniques most likely concordant with that organization. Similarly, Whallon (1984) has enumerated many kinds of variability encompassed by depositional areas. He then evaluated the use of factor analysis and other global methods for their concordance in analyzing artifact distributions. Finally, Whallon's and my efforts have involved the development of new spatial analytic techniques, which are designed specifically to be concordant with archaeological organizations and relevant data structures of a kind likely to be encountered (Whallon 1979, 1984; Carr 1977, 1981, 1982b, 1984, 1985, 1986).

The progress that has been made in these studies is based on nearly a decade of previous research that has focused on evaluating the response of various techniques to different spatial organization of artifacts (see Carr 1984 for references). These earlier studies, however, did not involve the construction of models of artifact organization and relevant relational structures, making their results difficult to apply in other analyses. In contrast, the development of middle-range theory and models about artifact spatial organization, and the enumeration of techniques concordant with them, allows particular sites to be subsumed under the models and appropriate techniques to be identified more easily.

Another example of middle-range theory providing a model of organization and being used to deduce concordant analytic techniques pertains to mortuary analysis. Braun (1977, 1979: 67) has argued or implied that ascribed and achieved status and leadership positions differ in two ways. First, ascribed status positions require greater predictability and temporal continuity (institutionalization) of the behaviors of those who occupy them than do achieved status positions. This constancy in behavior is postulated to be symbolized at death by a more coherent, stable set of mortuary rituals and burial treatments, some of which are manifested archaeologically. Second, ascribed positions of status and leadership involve more social roles, which are symbolized at death by more numerous, redundant, and associated ritual practices and burial treatments. On the basis of these two different multivariate, *dimensional* characteristics of ascribed and achieved status positions and their mortuary remains, Braun deduced that factor analysis is an appropriate technique for investigating mortuary data sets. It can be used to define within them a status dimension of social organization and for assessing whether status was ascribed or achieved.

In sum, during initial stages of analysis, the nature of the phenomenon of interest and the relevant subset and relational structures of the data in hand often are not well known. In this circumstance, middle-range theory can be used to deductively specify the most likely nature of the phenomenon, the subset of data that has the greatest potential for reflecting it, and a technique that concords with it and the data's relevant relational structure. As middle-range theory develops, we can expect this means for overcoming the methodological double bind to become more reliable.

"Constrained" Exploratory Data Analysis

Extant theory and deductive arguments can help the researcher to develop general knowledge about a data set's relevant structure and a phenomenon of interest. However, they are seldom sufficient. Individual data sets need not—usually will not—conform to expectation in every way. If the theory to make deductions does not have strong predictive capabilities, the phenomenon of interest may manifest itself in unsuspected sets of variables and observations and forms of relationship among them. The same problem can arise if the predictive theory is incorrectly applied beyond the limits of its boundary conditions or if the auxiliary assumptions that are made when relating the theory to the data at hand are wrong. For example, consider the auxiliary assumptions that are made about sources of variation that are supposedly controlled during data collection. When unsuspected extraneous factors as well as those of interest affect the measurements brought forward for study, the data set's relevant structure may take an unexpected form. An expected linear relationship between two natural environmental variables, for example, might instead take the form of a cyclical function with a linear trend, as a result of the compounding of diurnal variation with the variation of interest. Thus totally deductive specification of the variables and observations to be analyzed and the techniques to be used need not ensure their complete relevance to the phenomenon of interest nor the concordance of the technique to the data's relevant structure.

To compensate for these problems, it is necessary to supplement the deductive strategy with an inductive one that examines the data on its own terms. "Constrained exploratory data analysis" (CEDA), having at least two variants that differ in the kinds of techniques they employ, is useful for this purpose.

CEDA vs. Exploratory Data Analysis

As defined here, CEDA includes all the analytic methods that comprise exploratory data analysis (Tukey 1977; Hartwig and Dearing 1979; Clark 1982) but only a portion of the philosophy of exploratory data analysis that motivates their use. Like exploratory data analysis, CEDA is an inductive approach to recognizing patterns in a data set. Both have the goal of finding "any unanticipated structures or relationships that occur within a data set, regardless of expectation" (Tukey and Wilk 1970: 371). Both involve searching for any patterning in the data in order to reach a better understanding of the nature and causes of its total structure. Unlike exploratory data analysis, however, CEDA aims at developing this understanding of the data's structure in order to *isolate* the relevant aspects of it—*those that reflect some one explicitly specified phenomenon of interest as defined deductively* within the larger theoretical framework or paradigm of the researcher. In contrast, exploratory data analysis aims at developing an understanding of the data explicitly in order to generate new ideas, problem areas, and hypotheses (Tukey 1979: 122, 1980: 23-24) within a primarily inductive framework. Discovery of *many* relevant data structures pertinent to many phenomena, rather than the *single* structure pertinent to the single phenomenon of interest, is the goal of exploratory data analysis. Because CEDA is undertaken within a larger deductive framework and is more focused in its aim, whereas exploratory data analysis occurs within an inductive, less focused context, the designation *constrained* exploratory data analysis is used.

Whereas exploratory data analysis was developed by Tukey in reaction to the strongly deductive, "confirmatory" mode that has dominated theoretical statistics (Tukey 1979), CEDA is meant to articulate with it. Analysis is begun in a deductive manner with the specification of variables and observations that are probably relevant to the phenomenon of interest. Data items that are thought to be irrelevant are dropped from analysis. The search for relevant and irrelevant data items is continued in an inductive manner with CEDA procedures. The subset of the data that results from *both* the deductive and CEDA steps can then be used in either hypothesis testing or hypothesis formulation. In either case, both "data-screening" steps are motivated by the researcher's larger theoretical framework, which specifies the phenomenon of interest. *CEDA, then, is an inductive middle-step within a stepwise analytic design that has an overall deductive orientation and that is begun with deduction.* In contrast, exploratory data analysis is an inductive approach for initiating analytic process. (See Carr 1985a, for a discussion of the strengths and weaknesses of exploratory data analysis in this capacity.)

To examine the total structure of a data set and determine those aspects of it that are probably relevant to the phenomenon of interest, CEDA uses the same methods as exploratory data analysis, plus some additional ones. First, to view the multiple structures within a data set, CEDA involves the reexpression of the data on various scales of measurement (e.g., nominal, ratio, logarithmic, square root) and the examination of the reexpressed data with different techniques that are concordant with those scales of measurement (Tukey 1979: 24; Hartwig and Dearing 1979: 10). Also, techniques assuming multiple mathematical models are used to investigate the data from multiple perspectives. An effort is made to find any patterns in the data, regardless of whether they reflect the phenomenon of interest, and to consider how potentially relevant structure in the data then might be isolated from irrelevant patterning (e.g., removal of outliers, selection of variables, expression of the data on a particular scale, use of a technique that is sensitive to the scale most likely appropriate to the relevant structure). Second, CEDA, like exploratory data analysis, stresses the importance of graphic representations of the data (e.g., histograms, crossplots, the box and whisker, and maps) as aids in searching for patterns (Tukey 1979: 373; Hartwig and Dearing 1979: 9).

CEDA vs. Data Screening

CEDA and exploratory data analysis involve many of the same techniques and operations traditionally used to screen and restructure data in preparation for applying higher-level statistical techniques. These include: histograms; crossplots; simple univariate descriptive statistics; bivariate techniques of association, rank correlation, and correlation analysis; elimination of outlying observations; segregation of modalities for separate analysis should the data be composed of observations within several suspected populations; and transformation of the form of the frequency distributions of individual variables or the functional relationships between variable pairs. All of these techniques and operations can be used in CEDA to obtain a basic understanding of the data to be analyzed.

However, CEDA departs from traditional data screening in that these methods are not applied primarily to transform the structure of the data into one that concords with some analytic technique that has been chosen a priori. Data are not screened to *fit a technique*. Rather, the data set is examined to find and isolate the potentially relevant aspects of its structure *in regard to which an appropriate technique of analysis is chosen or developed.*

Two Forms of Constrained Exploratory Data Analysis

CEDA encompasses two variants that differ to some extent in the nature of the techniques they encompass. One emphasizes the use of techniques that make *minimal assumptions* about the data's structure when displaying them for patterning-searching. The second variant emphasizes the use of techniques that are capable of handling and dissecting a *heavy load of irrelevant variables or observations, or variation in general within the data.* This is a common characteristic of data sets initially presented for analysis or modified only by deductive selection.

A good example of a technique that makes minimal assumptions and that might be used within a CEDA framework, but which to date has been used in only an exploratory data analysis framework, is Whallon's (1984) *unconstrained clustering* method of intrasite spatial analysis. As Whallon (p. 35) notes, unconstrained clustering "is hardly more than an elaborate approach to a descriptive summary or display of the data or a series of such summaries and displays." (For a more detailed discussion of the method in relation to exploratory data analysis, see Carr 1985.) Other examples include other graphic displays such as the stem-and-leaf display, the box-and-whisker, and scatter plots, and certain "resistant" descriptive statistics such as the trimmed mean, the Winsorized mean, and the median absolute deviation (Tukey 1977; Hartwig and Dearing 1979: 16-26). These techniques can be used to determine the variables, observations, or the relationships among them that are probably relevant to the phenomenon of interest.

One example of a technique that is capable of handling a heavy load of irrelevant variables but that does not make minimal assumptions, is *R-mode factor analysis*. Although it can be used for multiple purposes, R-mode factor analysis is ideally suited for defining clusters of variables, making it "easier to decide upon their relevance to a problem" (Christenson and Read 1977: 174) within a CEDA framework.

Christenson and Read (1977: 167, 170-174) have used factor analysis along with a multivariate identification-of-outliers program explicitly to prepare for developing a projectile point typology with cluster analysis. A factor analysis of projectile point data was used to identify two dimensions of morphological variability (groups of variables) that seemed relevant to the researchers' typological goals and other dimensions that seemed irrelevant. The two relevant dimensions were then selected as the "variables" to be used in creating the point typology. Read (1985) illustrates how factor analysis and scatter plots of factor scores can be used in an alternating, interactive manner to refine the selection of variables (factors) and set of observations that are chosen to represent the one or more phenomena of interest potentially reflected in a data set's structure.

A second example of a technique that is capable of handling a heavy load of irrelevant variation and that does not make minimal assumptions is *spectral analysis*. This technique allows the researcher to identify multiple forms of variability of different scales that are compounded within the track of a *single* response variable over time or space. The results of a spectral analysis can be used by a researcher to design "filters" that allow the extraction and isolation of these individual forms of variation from the compound response variable, which in turn are defined as new variables. Those of the new variables that are considered to reflect the phenomenon of interest can then be subjected to further analysis, free of the confusing effects of the other, irrelevant sources of variation. I (Carr 1982a) have used spectral analysis in this manner to identify and analyze several sources of variability within an intrasite resistivity survey data set. I have also suggested its application to composite artifact distributions (palimpsests) that have been formed by the partial spatial overlap of multiple depositional processes (e.g., different kinds of activities of different scales), in order to identify artifact density variables attributable to the different processes. Density variations that are thought pertinent to each of the processes of interest (relevant data structures) can then be extracted from the palimpsest using filtering techniques so that they can be studied individually (Carr 1982b, 1984, 1986.)

In conclusion, analysis of complex data sets often requires inductive as well as deductive specification of the variables, observations, and relationships among them that are potentially relevant to the phenomenon of interest and a potentially concordant analytic technique. In this regard, for complex data those phases of scientific investigation that are concerned with hypothesis testing and that are supposedly "deductive" are seldom *completely* deductive. Theory may be used to deduce a model or hypothesis. However, the formulation of a test implication—which states an expectable relationship among observables in *terms of the variables, cases, and technique that are selected for analysis*—is a process that often requires both deductive and inductive logic. The expectable relationship follows from the theoretical framework, but its expression depends on the data and technique to be used, which often must be selected in part by induction.

Entry Models

A third strategy for familiarizing oneself with an unknown data set while maximizing consistency between its relevant structure and technical assumption involves what may be termed *entry models* and *parallel data sets*. This strategy uses both inductive and deductive logic and requires the development and use of middle-range theory. It gives the researcher insight into the organizational nature of the phenomenon of interest and the relevant relational structure of the data that represent it. This allows the researcher to choose an analytic technique which is more concordant with that form of organization. It does not necessarily involve the selection of relevant observations and variables (relevant subset structure), though it may. The strategy is summarized in Figure 10.2.

The entry model approach centers around the development of several alternative entry models. Each implies a concordant pairing of a relevant data structure that potentially represents the phenom-

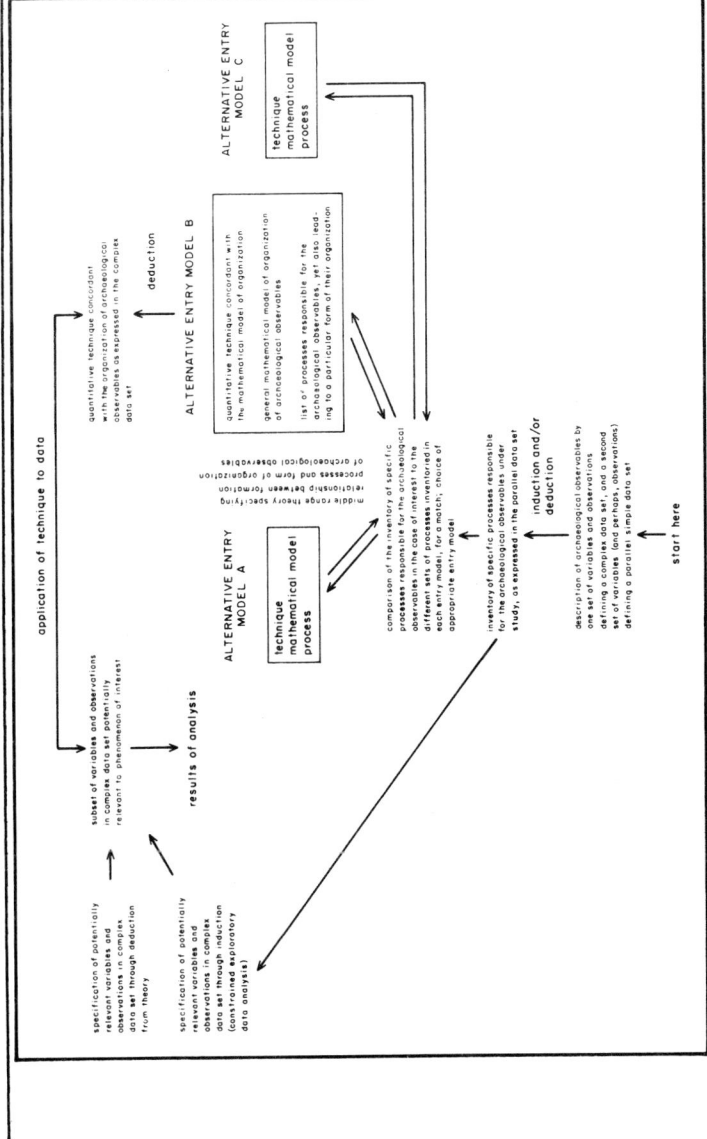

Figure 10.2 The use of entry models and parallel data sets to become familiar with a complex data set.

enon of interest, one or a few techniques, and the formation processes responsible for the data's relevant structure.

Each entry model has three essential components. (1) The most critical is a *general mathematical model* or description of the *form of organization* that might be taken by the archaeological observables representing the phenomenon of interest. If the archaeological observables in a particular study area do empirically have this form of organization, then the model of their organization will imply the relevant relational structure of the data describing them. In intrasite spatial analysis, samples of alternative mathematical models would be ones specifying the various forms of spatial organization that coarranged artifact types (observables) representing "toolkits" or "depositional sets" (the phenomena of interest) within archaeological sites might have. These would include models of ratio scale, ordinal scale, nominal scale, or various polythetic scale forms of organization (Carr 1985b). If, at a particular site, a series of artifact types were actually coarranged in accordance with one of these models, then the data describing the artifacts' locations would have a relevant relational structure of the form implied by the model.

(2) The second component of an entry model, concordant with the first, is an *enumeration of the kinds of processes* that can lead to the archaeological observables being organized in the way that the mathematical model specifies. These would be processes postulated to be responsible for the organizational nature of the phenomenon of interest and its archaeological satisfaction. If the archaeological observables in a particular study area are empirically organized in the way the model specifies, these will also be the processes responsible for the relevant relational structure of the data describing the observables. The processes will always include cultural and natural formation processes of the kind documented by middle-range archaeological theory (e.g., curation, lithic reduction and maintenance processes, means by which rank is symbolized in mortuary remains). However, they may also include "formation processes" to which general anthropological theory pertains (e.g., the pattern and tempo of fission-fusion of hunter-gatherer bands). Continuing our intrasite spatial example, one of several alternative entry models might describe a polythetic form of spatial organization of artifact types within "toolkits" in the archaeological domain and include a list of formation processes that could lead to that organization. These might include differential artifact preservation, artifact curation,

artifact recycling, misclassification of artifacts, or the occurrence of alternative tool types within a toolkit.

Although specification of such linkages among forms of archaeological organization and processes may be difficult, it is currently the subject of active research on middle-range archaeological theory. Use of the entry model approach, by its very nature, encourages the development of middle-range theory.

(3) The last component of an entry model is an inventory of the *quantitative techniques* that are concordant with the mathematical model of organization of the archaeological observables. If, in a particular study area, the archaeological observables are empirically organized in the way the model specifies, these will also be the techniques that are concordant with the relevant relational structure of the data describing the observables. For example, continuing from above, the one entry model describing a polythetic form of spatial organization of depositional sets might list a "polythetic association" method of spatial analysis (Carr 1985b). Polythetic association is concordant with that form of organization.

An entry model usually is one of a series of such models. Each entry model specifies a different mathematical model of the organizational form that the archaeological observables might take and implies a different relevant relational structure that the data describing them might have. The differences among the entry models in the organization of observables and the relevant data structures that they postulate or imply reflect the effects of the different formation processes or higher-level processes that the entry models enumerate as responsible for the observables and data. The differences also can reflect the fact that a single phenomenon of interest can have multiple organizations and representations when it is the product of parallel, coterminous, and optional processes. This was discussed at the beginning of this chapter. Similarly, several alternative entry models will specify different quantitative techniques that are concordant with the different mathematical models of organization.

An example of a set of alternative entry models and their application is given in Carr (1985b). This study involves twelve entry models, six to be discussed here. These postulate six different mathematical models of the internal set organization of spatially coarranged artifact types (observables) that comprise a depositional set or "toolkit" in the archaeological domain. Figure 10.3 and Table 10.1 illustrate and define the characteristics of these different

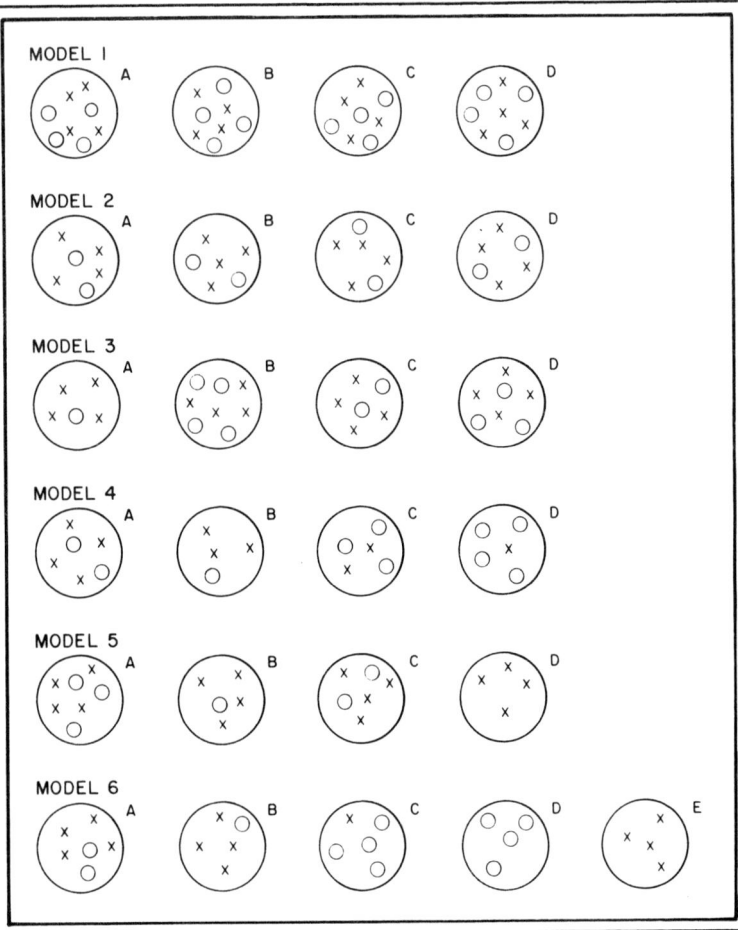

Figure 10.3 Six models of the internal set organization of artifact types among archaeological deposits fall along a monothetic-polythetic continuum. Only one pair of types within the same set of deposits is shown; other types are assumed to have analogous forms of organization. The organizational characteristics of each model are described in Table 10.1

organizational forms. The several structures are alternative possible manifestations of the one phenomenon of interest—depositional sets as representations of artifact types that were manufactured, used, stored, or deposited together in the behavioral past. Their different

TABLE 10.1
Mathematical Characteristics of the Six Models of Organization of Artifact Types in Figure 10.3

Characteristic:	Asymmetry within groups of artifacts allowed for one or more pairs or types	Differences among groups in the magnitudes of their asymmetries allowed for one or more pairs of types	Differences among groups in the directions of their asymmetries allowed for one or more pairs of types	Asymmetry within groups taken to the extreme, where one type, of one or more pairs of types, does not occur in some groups	Global monothetic or polythetic organization using A, B, C, D, E as groups of interest	Local monothetic or polythetic organization using pairs of items as groups of interest
Models:						
1.	−	−	−	−	Monothetic	Monothetic
2.	+	−	−	−	Monothetic	Polythetic
3.	+	+	−	−	Monothetic	Polythetic
4.	+	+	+	−	Monothetic	Polythetic
5.	+	+	−	+	Polythetic	Polythetic
6.	+	+	+	+	Polythetic	Polythetic

organizations reflect their generation by different kinds of formation processes, which also are enumerated by the entry models but not shown here. Finally, the six entry models specify different sets of quantitative techniques that are concordant with the different forms of depositional set organization and that might be used to search archaeological data for patterns that indicate depositional sets (Table 10.2). These techniques vary in the scale of measurement of spatial coarrangement to which they are sensitive—from ratio scale coarrangement to the loosest forms of polythetic coarrangement.

A second example of a set of alternative entry models is given in Carr (1986). Here, six entry models are defined. Each postulates a different mathematical model of the spatial and content characteristics of clusters of artifacts (observables) comprising depositional areas or "activity areas" and their background artifact scatters in the archaeological domain. For example, depositional areas are modeled as to whether they overlap spatially, the degree to which their artifact densities contrast with those of their background, and their degree of boundary crispness. The different structures are alternative forms that the single phenomenon of interest—depositional areas—can take. Each structure is then associated with some archaeological formation processes that might generate it and spatial analytic techniques that are concordant with it, completing the entry models. The techniques include various Fourier and spatial filtering methods for enhancing the "visibility" of depositional areas and segregating different kinds of areas.

Entry models are useful when two circumstances occur. (1) The data set that is slated for analysis, and that describes the archaeological observables representing the phenomenon of interest, is very complex. As a result, the researcher is unable initially to specify—by simple inspection of the data—the aspects of its structure that are likely to be relevant, the probable organization of the archaeological observables that represent the phenomenon of interest, and an analytic technique that probably is appropriate. (2) There exists a simpler, parallel data set that gives the researcher insight into the processes that are responsible for the archaeological observables, their consequent organization, and the relevant and irrelevant structural aspects of the complex data set.

In these two circumstances, it is possible for the researcher to learn something about the complex data set's relevant relational structure

TABLE 10.2
Similarity Coefficients Appropriate for Analyzing Spatial Arrangements of Artifact Types Having Various Forms of Organization Along the Monothetic-Polythetic Continuum

Form of Organization*	Appropriate Coefficient for Item Point Location Data**	Appropriate Coefficient for Grid Cell Data**
Model 1	AVDISTM	–
Model 2	–	Pearson's r
–	–	Kendall's tau and tau-b, Goodman and Kruskal's gamma, Spearman's rho
Model 3	–	–
Model 4	AVDISTLP1	Jaccard similarity coefficient, Cole's C-7, Hurlebert's C-8
Model 5	AVDISTGP	–
Model 6	AVDISTLP2	–

*Models shown in Figure 10.3 and described in Table 10.1.
**References to the coefficients are given in Carr (1985b).

and to specify a potentially concordant analytic technique by examining the *parallel data set* and using the entry model. This is done in lieu of *directly*, but possibly discordantly, examining the *complex* data with a higher-level pattern-searching technique (p. 208). In this way, the researcher is removed from the bind of not being able to choose an appropriate analytic technique without knowledge of the complex data set's structure, yet not being able to obtain this knowledge without applying some pattern-searching techniques to it.

The logical and analytic process involved in using a parallel data set and entry models is shown in Figure 10.1. It can be described as follows.

(1) Two data sets are established. The first is a complex one that is the ultimate target of analysis and that describes the observables representing the phenomenon of interest. The second is a simple, parallel data set that is sensitive to the processes of formation of the archaeological observables described in the complex one.

An example of a complex data set would be a matrix of point locations of artifacts of many classes within a hunter-gatherer site.

An example of a simple data set that parallels this complex one and gives insight into its organizational nature would be one that documents various indicators (Schiffer 1983) of archaeological formation processes that affect artifact deposition and disturbance and, thus, the matrix of point locations. The parallel data set might contain information on intrasite spatial variation in soil acidity, which would reflect the potential for differential preservation of bone artifacts over space; and/or the orientation and dip of artifacts, which would indicate the possibility of disturbance in the artifacts' spatial distribution by fluvial activity; and/or the grain of the surrounding environment, which would suggest the likelihood of tethered mobility patterns, repeated reuse of the site, and the palimpsest nature of the artifact distribution.

(2) The processes that are responsible for the archaeological observables described in the complex data are reconstructed on the basis of information in the parallel data set. This reconstruction can be accomplished by logical deduction, in which case the specific patterns within the parallel data set are subsumed under general, accepted models of the observable consequences of formation processes. For example, in deductive mode, the disturbance of an intrasite artifact distribution by fluvial processes might be determined by noting patterns in the orientation, dip, and size sorting of artifacts and then subsuming such patterns under established models of fluvial displacement of artifacts (Behrensmeyer and Hill 1980; Shackley 1978). Reconstruction can also be achieved by abduction from patterns within the parallel data set, followed by testing of one's conclusions with other, independent data that also comprise the parallel data set. This step conforms to Schiffer's (1983) call for "up front" identification of the processes that are responsible for archaeological observables prior to behavioral interpretation.

(3) The specific processes that are found to be responsible for the organization of the archaeological observables of interest and that determine the relevant structure of the complex data set are then matched with processes that are enumerated in a more general way in one or more of the entry models.

(4) Several conclusions are reached based on: (a) the association of the archaeological observables of interest and the complex data set with a particular entry model via common processes, (b) the entry model's specification of the effects of such processes on the organization of archaeological observables of the kind described by the

complex data set, and (c) the entry model's specification of the analytic techniques that are concordant with that organization. First is the probable general nature of organization of the archaeological observables described in the complex data, which is specified in mathematical terms. By implication, general knowledge of the complex data's relevant relational structure can also be inferred. Finally, the techniques of analysis that are most apt to be appropriate for investigating the archaeological observables in the complex data set can be concluded. Note that information in the *parallel* data set is used to determine the appropriate entry model, whereas information on the relevant structure of the *complex* data set is derived from the entry level. Also note that the process of associating the archaeological observables in the complex data set with a given entry model is equivalent to logically subsuming them under the entry model.

An example of the steps that have been outlined is given in Carr (1985b). Here, the target complex data set is composed of the spatial locations of many artifact types (observables) within a French Magdalenian reindeer hunting camp, Pincevent habitation no. 1. The phenomenon of interest (to be discovered) is sets of artifact types that were manufactured, used, stored, or deposited together in the behavioral past and that are similarly arranged in the archaeological domain according to some relevant scale of organization. Initially, the organization of whatever depositional sets might exist at the site, and the relevant structure of the complex distributional data manifesting them was unknown. Nor were these conditions obvious from the data upon their visual inspection. It consequently was unclear what spatial technique would be appropriate for analyzing the data.

Various kinds of information constituting a parallel data set were used to identify formation processes at Pincevent that would have affected the nature of organization of any depositional sets and the relevant relational structure of the complex data. Some examples of the kinds of parallel data evoked include: tool morphology, which indicated patterns of tool recycling and reuse; spatial patterns of conjoined pieces of broken artifacts, which indicated patterns of refuse disposal and cleaning; anomalously low counts of some reindeer bone elements relative to those expected on the basis of estimated minimum number of individuals, which indicated differential preservation patterns; site seasonality as an indicator of expectable general patterns of refuse generation and disposal; etc.

The formation processes reconstructed from the parallel data then were compared to those enumerated in six alternative entry models, each of which also postulated a mathematical model of relevant depositional set organization (Figure 10.3, Table 10.1). On the basis of matches between the formation processes reconstructed for Pincevent and those specified in the entry models, and the linkage among process, data structure, and technique in the entry models, it was concluded that most depositional sets at the site were probably organized like mathematical models 4 or 6 (Figure 10.3, Table 10.1). It was also concluded that the two techniques most apt to be concordant with depositional set organization at Pincevent and that should be used to analyze the complex data set of artifact spatial distributions were AVDISTLP1 and AVDISTLP2 (Table 10.2). These measure the degree of spatial coarrangement of artifact types using certain polythetic scales of measurement.

(5) The one or few quantitative techniques that are determined to be most probably concordant with the relevant relational structure of the complex data set are applied to that data or some subset of its variables and observations that is thought to be relevant to the phenomenon of interest. The potentially relevant subset can have been specified by deduction from theory or by inductive examination of the parallel data set (Figure 10.3). In the Pincevent case, for example, artifacts (observations) of the type flint pebbles were considered for deletion from the complex data set of artifact locations and from the search for depositional sets. This was done inductively on the basis of a piece of information in the parallel data set: the fact that many of the smaller pebbles were probably of natural, fluvial origin, and thus irrelevant to behavioral reconstruction. Finally, having established the most probably relevant subset structure of the complex locational data and concordant techniques, one of the methods was applied to the data. Twenty-one depositional sets were defined.

In sum, the entry model strategy can be a powerful approach for a researcher to familiarize herself or himself with a complex data set without violating relevant aspects of its structure with some quantitative technique. The strategy allows the researcher to determine the probable general nature of the data set's relevant structure (general knowledge), and thus the technique(s) that are most likely appropriate for its analysis, *without directly analyzing it with some possibly discordant method*. This is accomplished through the examination of a simple, parallel data set for the processes of formation of the archaeological observables described in the complex data set, rather than through a direct, inductive examination of the many facets of the complex data set's structure using multiple techniques. In essence, the strategy allows one to gain insight into complex data obliquely, by reconstructing the history of their development rather than by affronting them with a technique.

Although the entry model strategy can be more powerful and bring greater concordance between data and technique than the deductive or CEDA strategies, it has a limitation. It requires a good foundation of middle-range theory on the processes that are responsible for the archaeological and behavioral variability of interest, and also processes that are not of interest. As this foundation broadens—in part through the development of entry models themselves—the strategy will become more practicable (see Schiffer 1983).

Stepwise, Cyclical Analytic Designs

A final means for improving consistency among data structure, technique, and theoretical framework during analysis is the well-known stepwise, cyclical process of scientific investigation (Figure 10.4). This process requires repeated analysis of a data set. Each analysis involves modifications of the data, the analytic technique(s), and/or the interpretive framework that guides analysis such that all three approach greater concordance with each other. Modifications of these three entities with each cycle are made in light of: (1) discrepancies between expectable results and those obtained (external inconsistencies), (2) discrepancies between the interpretive implications of different subsets of the results that are obtained (internal inconsistencies), (3) whether the discrepancies increase or decrease from trial run to trial run, and (4) the general knowledge, and ultimately, the detailed knowledge that is gained about the phenomenon of interest and the data's relevant structure. The deductive approach, CEDA strategy, and entry model approach all may be involved in various cycles of analysts.

In short, the stepwise approach to data analysis is a logical process that *simulates*, in serial format, the continuous, simultaneous feedback between data, technique, and theoretical framework that characterizes the mental process of abduction.

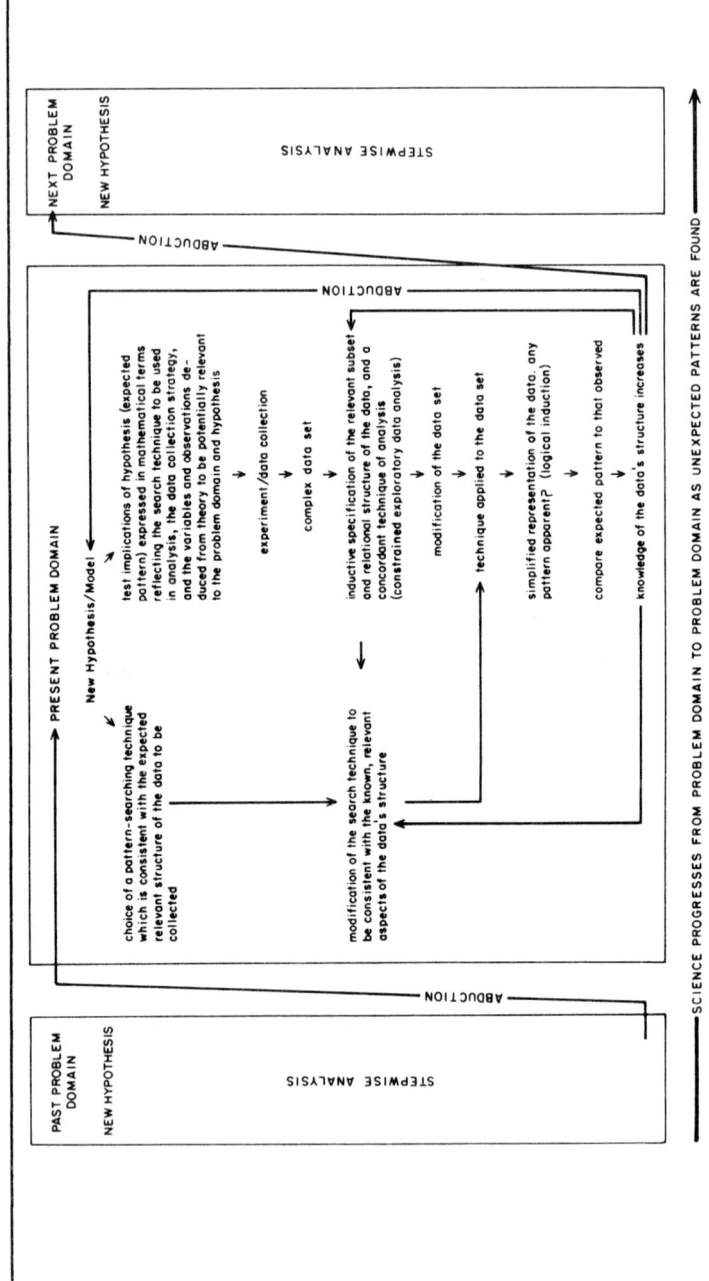

Figure 10.4 The sequential, stepwise, cyclical process of scientific investigation.

Conclusion

Analysis is a complex thought process that requires the researcher to choose appropriate data and techniques if it is to be relevant and accurate. These must be chosen such that the population or process of interest, the data expressing them, technical assumptions about them, and theoretical assumptions about them all concord with each other as much as possible.

In early stages of analysis, this condition is difficult to secure. The researcher may not have narrowed the scope of study to a single phenomenon or may know little about the number or nature of the phenomena that are reflected in the data. Also, any investigation of the data to overcome these deficiencies must be done sequentially, without feedback between the processes of finding pattern and interpreting pattern during any one analytic step. This allows discordance between data structure and technique to occur. The researcher thus has a problem of how to initiate analysis without violating its relevant structure.

Two kinds of relevant discordance can arise between data structure and technique during the analysis of complex data. First, the data may pertain to multiple processes that define multiple populations, whereas the statistical technique of analysis may be based on a model specifying some single process as responsible for the data and some one homogeneous population defined in respect to that process. The data may have multiple relevant subset structures, whereas the technique may assume it to have only one. Second, the employed analytic technique may imply that the phenomenon of interest has an organization that is different from its actual organization and the expression of this in the data. The technique may assume the data to have a relevant relational structure different from the one it has.

Deductive specification of potentially relevant data or techniques using middle-range theory, constrained exploratory data analysis, entry models, and stepwise cyclical analysis can be used to minimize these two kinds of discordance during initial stages of analysis or to reduce them from analytic step to step. These tactics encourage the researcher to explicitly state the single phenomenon that is of interest and its nature or organization, and to justify the data and analytic technique to be used in relation to it, to each other, and/or to theory.

The tactics involve the formalization of *bridging arguments* (Hemple 1966: 72-75) that link phenomenon, data, technique, and theory to each other.

Explicit statement of bridging arguments between these entities and justification of analytic choices is an extremely important scientific activity. Not only does it aid in making specific analyses relevant, accurate, and meaningful, but it goes hand in hand with the refinement of theory and scientific advance generally (e.g., Read 1974). Bridging arguments pertain, in part, to the relevant structure of a data set and the nature of a phenomenon of interest. Their formalization provides a means by which logical inconsistencies and false premises in current theory about a phenomenon are uncovered and new theories can be developed.

In a well-established scientific discipline, bridging arguments that link regularly investigated phenomena, data, techniques, and theories to each other are well known and part of accepted theory and methodology. Though they may be evoked in designing an analysis, it is superfluous to report them in detail. However, in a quickly growing and groping discipline like archaeology, where such bridges are not yet formalized and accepted, it is critical that they be thought about, stated explicitly, and reported openly and systematically for criticism. Only within such a milieu can archaeological knowledge advance in an orderly manner.

Acknowledgments

This chapter was presented at the International Union of Prehistoric and Protohistoric Sciences Meetings, Denver CO, April 1985, and the Society for American Archaeology annual meetings, Denver CO, May 1985.

The ideas in this chapter stem from conversations I have had with W. Fredrick Limp, Michael Schiffer, Robert Whallon, David Braun, Dwight Read, Lewis Binford, and many graduate students. For their stimulation, for the way they have enriched my life, I am most grateful. I also wish to thank David Braun, Dwight Read, and Michael Schiffer for a number of excellent comments on this paper that helped me to revise it. Ishmael Williams, Mary Herrington, and Connie Kloecker helped in the editing and typing of the manuscript.

References

Behrensmeyer, A. K., and A. P. Hill (eds.). 1980. *Fossils in the Making: Vertebrate Taphonomy and Paleoecology*. Chicago: University of Chicago Press.

Binford, L. R. 1968. Archaeological perspectives. In *New Perspectives in Archaeology*, eds. L. R. Binford and S. R. Binford, pp. 5-32. Chicago: Aldine.

Binford, L. R. 1977. *For Theory Building in Archaeology*. New York: Academic Press.

Binford, L. R., and J. A. Sabloff. 1982. Paradigms, systematics, and archaeology. *Journal of Anthropological Research* 38(2): 137-153.

Braun, D. P. 1977. Middle Woodland-early Late Woodland social change in the prehistoric midwestern U.S. Unpublished Ph.D. dissertation. Department of Anthropology. University of Michigan.

Braun, D. P. 1979. Illinois Hopewell burial practices and social organization: a reexamination of the Klunk-Gibson mound group. In *Hopewell Archaeology: the Chillicothe Conference*, eds. D. Brose and N. Greber, pp. 66-79. Kent, OH: Kent State University Press.

Braun, D. P. 1980. Neolithic regional cooperation: a midwestern example. Unpublished paper presented at the annual meeting of the Society for American Archaeology, Philadelphia.

Braun, D. P. 1985. Absolute seriation: a time-series approach. In *For Concordance in Archaeological Analysis: Bridging Data Structure, Quantitative Technique, and Theory*, ed. C. Carr, pp. 509-539. Kansas City: Westport Publishers.

Braun, D. P., and S. Plog. 1982. Evolution of "tribal" social networks: theory and prehistoric North American evidence. *American Antiquity* 47(3): 504-525.

Brown, J. A. 1971. Approaches to the social dimensions of mortuary practices. Society for American Archaeology, *Memoirs* 25.

Carnap, R. 1936 Testability and meaning. *Philosophy of Science* 3(4): 420-471.

Carr, C. 1977. The internal structure of a Middle Woodland site and the nature of the archaeological record. Unpublished preliminary examination paper. Department of Anthropology. University of Michigan.

Carr, C. 1981. The polythetic organization of archaeological tool kits and an algorithm for defining them. Unpublished paper presented at the annual meetings of the Society for American Archaeology, San Diego.

Carr, C. 1982a. *Handbook on Soil Resistivity Surveying: Interpretation of Data from Earthen Archaeological Sites*. Evanston, IL: Center for American Archaeology Press.

Carr, C. 1982b. Dissecting intrasite artifact distributions as palimpsests. Unpublished paper presented at the annual meetings of the Society for American Archaeology, Minneapolis.

Carr, C. 1983. A design for intrasite research. Unpublished paper presented at the National Park Service Research Seminar in Archaeology. Fort Collins, CO.

Carr, C. 1984. The nature of organization of intra-site archaeological records and spatial analytic approaches to their investigation. In *Advances in Archaeological Method and Theory*, 7: 103-222. New York: Academic Press.

Carr, C. 1985b. Alternative models, alternative techniques: variable approaches to intrasite spatial analysis. In *For Concordance in Archaeological Analysis: Bridging Data Structure, Quantitative Technique, and Theory*, ed. C. Carr, pp. 302-473. Kansas City: Westport Press.

Carr, C. 1985c. Toward a synthetic theory of artifact design. Unpublished paper presented at the annual meetings of the Society for American Archaeology, Denver.

Carr, C. 1986. Dissecting intrasite artifact palimpsests using Fourier methods. In *Method and Theory for Activity Area Research: An Ethnoarchaeological Approach*, ed. S. Kent, Chap. 5. New York: Columbia University Press.

Carr, C. (ed.) 1985a. *For Concordance in Archaeological Analysis: Bridging Data Structure, Quantitative Techique, and Theory*. Kansas City: Westport Press.

Carr, C., and K. Hinkle. 1984. A synthetic theory of artifact design applied to Ohio Hopewell weavings. Unpublished paper presented at the annual meetings of the Society for American Archaeology, Portland.

Christenson, A. L., and D. W. Read. 1977. Numerical taxonomy, R-mode factor analysis, and archaeological classification. *American Antiquity* 42(2): 163-179.

Clark, G. A. 1982. Quantifying archaeological research. In *Advances in Archaeological Method and Theory*, 5: 217-273.

Clarke, D. L. 1972. Models and paradigms in contemporary archaeology. In *Models in Archaeology*, ed. D. L. Clarke, pp. 1-60. London: Methuen.

Cowgill, G. C. 1977. The trouble with significance tests and what we can do about it. *American Antiquity* 33: 367-375.
Cowgill, G. C. 1982. Clusters of objects and associations between variables: two approaches to archaeological classification. In *Essays on Archaeological Typology*, eds. R. Whallon and J. A. Brown, pp. 30-55. Evanston, IL: Center for American Archaeology Press.
Doran, J. E. and F. R. Hodson. 1975. *Mathematics and Computers in Archaeology*. Cambridge, MA: Harvard University Press.
Flannery, K. V. 1973. Archaeology with a capital s. In C. L. Redman (ed.) *Research and Theory in Current Archaeology*. New York: Wiley.
Friedrich, M. H. 1970. Design structure and social interaction: archaeological implications of an ethnographic analysis. *American Antiquity* 35: 332-343.
Gladwin, H. 1975. Looking for an aggregate additive model in data from a hierarchical decision process. In *Formal Methods in Economic Anthropology*, ed. S. Plattner, pp. 159-196. Washington, D.C.: American Anthropological Association (Special Publication).
Greber, N. 1976. Within Ohio Hopewell: Analysis of burial patterns from several classic sites, Appendix A. Unpublished Ph.D. dissertation. Department of Anthropology. Case Western Reserve.
Hanson, N. R. 1972. *Patterns of Discovery*. Cambridge: Cambridge University Press.
Hartwig, F., and B. E. Dearing. 1979. *Exploratory Data Analysis*. Beverly Hills: Sage Publications.
Hemple, C. G. 1966. *The Philosophy of Natural Science*. Englewood Cliffs: Prentice Hall.
Hodder, I., and C. Orton. 1976. *Spatial Analysis in Archaeology*. Cambridge: Cambridge University Press.
Hodson, F. R. 1982. Some aspects of archaeological classification. In *Essays on Archaeological Typology*, eds. R. Whallon and J. A. Brown, pp. 21-29. Evanston, IL: Center for American Archaeology Press.
Hinkle, K. A. 1984. Ohio Hopewell textiles: a medium for stylistic and social information exchange. Unpublished master's thesis. Department of Anthropology. University of Arkansas.
Hoffman, C. M. 1985. Projectile point maintenance and typology: assessment with factor analysis and canonical correlation. In *For Concordance in Archaeological Analysis: Bridging Data Structure, Quantitative Technique, and Theory*, ed. C. Carr, pp. 566-612. Kansas City: Westport Press.
Hole, B. L. 1980. Sampling in archaeology: a critique. *Annual Review of Anthropology* 9: 217-234.
Keene, A. S. 1981. *Prehistoric Foraging in a Temperate Forest*. New York: Academic Press.
Kvamme, K. L. 1985. Determining empirical relationships between the natural environment and prehistoric site locations: a hunter-gatherer example. In *For Concordance in Archaeological Analysis: Bridging Data Structure, Quantitative Technique, and Theory*, ed. C. Carr, pp. 208-238. Kansas City: Westport Press.
Levins, R. 1966. Strategy of model building in population biology. *American Scientist* 54: 421-431.
Limp, W. F. 1983. Rational location choice and prehistoric settlement analysis. Unpublished Ph.D. dissertation. Department of Anthropology, Indiana University.
Marquardt, W. H. 1978. Advances in archaeological seration. *Advances in Archaeological Method and Theory*, 8: 257-314.
Martin, J. 1983. Optimal foraging theory: a review of some models and their applications. *American Anthropologist* 85(3): 612-629.
Meehan, E. 1968. *Explanation in Social Science—A Systems Paradigm*. Homewood, IL: Dorsey Press.
Moore, J. A., and A. S. Keene. 1983a. Archaeology and the law of the hammer. In *Archaeological Hammers and Theories*, eds. J. A. Moore and A. S. Keene, pp. 3-13. New York: Academic Press.
Moore, J. A., and A. S. Keene. 1983b. *Archaeological Hammers and Theories*. New York: Academic Press.

Mueller, J. W. (ed.) 1975. *Sampling in Archaeology.* Tucson: University of Arizona Press.
O'Shea, J. 1981. Social configurations and the archaeological study of mortuary practices: a case study. In *The Archaeology of Death*, eds. R. Chapman, I. Kinnes, and K. Randsborg, pp. 39-52. Cambridge: Cambridge University Press.
Parker, S. 1985. Predictive modeling of site settlement systems using multivariate logistics. In *For Concordance in Archaeological Analysis: Bridging Data Structure, Quantitative Technique, and Theory*, ed. C. Carr, pp. 173-207. Kansas City: Westport Press.
Peebles, C. S. 1971. Moundville and the surrounding sites: some structural considerations of mortuary practices. In J. A. Brown (ed.) Approaches to the Social Dimensions of Mortuary Practices. *Memoirs of the Society for American Archaeology*, 25.
Plog, S. 1976. Measurement of prehistoric interaction between communities. In *The Early Mesoamerican Village*, ed. K. V. Flannery, pp. 255-272. New York: Academic Press.
Plog, S. 1978. Social interaction and stylistic similarity: a reanalysis. *Advances in Archaeological Method and Theory*, 1: 144-182.
Plog, S. 1980. *Stylistic Variation in Prehistoric Ceramics.* Cambridge: Cambridge University Press.
Raab, M. L., and A. C. Goodyear. 1984. Middle-range theory in archaeology: a critical review of origins and application. *American Antiquity* 49(2): 255-268.
Read, D. W. 1974. Some comments on the use of mathematical models in anthropology. *American Antiquity* 39(1): 3-15.
Read, D. W. 1985. The substance of archaeological analysis and the mold of statistical method: enlightenment out of discordance. In *For Concordance in Archaeological Analysis: Bridging Data Structure, Quantitative Technique, and Theory*, ed. C. Carr, pp. 45-86. Kansas City: Westport Press.
Read, D. W., and S. A. LeBlanc. 1978. Descriptive statements, covering laws, and theories in archaeology. *Current Anthropology* 19(2): 307-335.
Reidhead, V. 1979. Linear programming models in archaeology. *Annual Review of Anthropology* 8: 543-578.
Reidhead, V. 1981. *A Linear Programming Model of Prehistoric Subsistence Optimization: A Southeastern Indiana Example.* Indianapolis: Indiana Historical Society.
Renfrew, C., M. J. Rowlands, and B. A. Segraves. 1982. *Theory and Explanation in Archaeology: The Southhampton Conference.* New York: Academic Press.
Salmon, M. H. 1982. *Philosophy and Archaeology.* New York: Academic Press.
Salmon, M. H., and W. C. Salmon. 1979. Alternative models of scientific explanation. *American Anthropologist* 81(1): 61-74.
Scheps, S. 1982. Statistical blight. *American Antiquity* 47(4): 836-850.
Schiffer, M. B. 1975. Factors and "tool kits": Evaluating multivariate analysis in archaeology. *Plains Anthropologist* 20. 61-70.
Schiffer, M. B. 1976. *Behavioral Archaeology.* New York: Academic Press.
Schiffer, M. B. 1983. Toward the identification of formation processes. *American Antiquity* 48(4): 675-706.
Shackley, M. L. 1978. The behavior of artifacts as sedimentary particles in a fluvial environment. *Archaeometry* 20: 55-61.
Smith, E. A. 1981. The application of optimal foraging theory to the analysis of hunter-gatherer group size. In *Hunter-Gatherer Foraging Strategies*, ed. B. Winterhalder and E. A. Smith, pp. 36-65.
Spaulding, A. C. 1953. Statistical techniques for the discovery of artifact types. *American Antiquity* 18: 305-313.
Spaulding, A. C. 1973. Archaeology in the active voice: the new anthropology. In *Research and Theory in Current Archaeology*, ed. C. L. Redman, pp. 337-354. New York: Wiley
Spaulding, A. C. 1977. On growth and form in archaeology: multivariate analysis. *Journal of Anthropological Research* 33: 1-15.

Spaulding, A. C. 1982 Structure in archaeological data: nominal variables. In *Essays on Archaeological Typology*, eds. R. Whallon and J. A. Brown, pp. 1-20. Evanston, IL: Center for American Archaeology Press.

Speth, J. D., and G. A. Johnson. 1976. Problems in the use of correlation for the investigation of tool kits and activity areas. In *Cultural Change and Continuity*, ed. C. Cleland, pp. 35-75. New York: Academic Press.

Stanislawski, M. B., and B. B. Stanislawski. 1978. Hopi and Hopi-Tewa ceramic tradition networks. In *The Spatial Organization of Culture*, ed. I. Hodder, pp. 61-76. Pittsburgh: University of Pittsburgh Press.

Thomas, D. H. 1971. On use of cumulative curves and numerical taxonomy. *American Antiquity* 36: 206-209.

Thomas, D. H. 1978. The awful truth about statistics in archaeology. *American Antiquity* 43: 231-244.

Toussaint, G. T. 1978. The use of context in pattern recognition. *Pattern Recognition* 10: 189-204.

Tukey, J. W. 1977. *Exploratory Data Analysis*. Reading, MA: Addison-Wesley.

Tukey, J. W. 1979. Comment to "nonparametric statistical data modeling." *Journal of the American Statistical Association* 74: 121-122.

Tukey, J. W. 1980. We need both exploratory and confirmatory. *American Statistician* 34(1): 23-25.

Tukey, J. W., and M. B. Wilk. 1970. Data analysis and statistics: Techniques and approaches. In *The Quantitative Analysis of Social Problems*, ed. E. R. Tufte, pp. 370-390. Reading, MA: Addison-Wesley.

van der Leeuw, S. W. 1978. Comment on: Read, D.W., and LeBlanc, S.A., Descriptive statements, covering laws, and theories in archaeology. *Current Anthropology* 19(2): 328-329.

Vierra, R. K. and D. I. Carlson. 1981. Factor analysis, random data, and patterned results. *American Antiquity* 46(2): 272-283.

Voss, J. A. 1980a. Tribal emergence during the Neolithic of northwestern Europe. Unpublished Ph.D. dissertation. Department of Anthropology. University of Michigan.

Voss, J. A. 1980b. The measurement and evaluation of change in the regional social networks of egalitarian societies: an example from the Neolithic of northwestern Europe. Unpublished paper presented at the annual meeting of the Society for American Archaeology, Philadelphia.

Watson, P. J., S. A. LeBlanc, and C. L. Redman. 1971. *Explanation in Archaeology*. New York: Columbia University Press.

Whallon, R. 1972. A new approach to pottery typology. *American Antiquity* 37: 13-33.

Whallon, R. 1973. Spatial analysis of occupation floors I: Application of dimensional analysis of variance. *American Antiquity* 38: 320-328.

Whallon, R. 1974. Spatial analysis of occupation floors II: The application of nearest neighbor analysis. *American Antiquity* 39: 16-34.

Whallon, R. 1979. Unconstrained clustering in the analysis of spatial distributions on occupation floors. Unpublished paper presented at the annual meetings of the Society for American Archaeology, Vancouver.

Whallon, R. 1984. Unconstrained clustering for the analysis of spatial distributions in archaeology. In *Intrasite Spatial Analysis*, ed. H. J. Hietala, pp. 242-277. Cambridge: Cambridge University Press.

Whallon, R. and J. A. Brown (eds.) 1982. *Essays on Archaeological Typology*. Center for American Archaeology.

Wiessner, P. 1983. Style and social information in Kalahari San projectile points. *American Antiquity* 48(2): 253-275.

Winterhalder, B. 1981. Optimal foraging strategies and hunter-gatherer research in anthropology: theory and models. In *Hunter-Gatherer Foraging Strategies*, eds. B. Winterhalder and E. A. Smith, pp. 13-35. Chicago: University of Chicago Press.

Winters, H. D. 1969. The Riverton culture. Illinois State Museum. *Reports of Investigation* 13. Springfield, IL.

Wobst, H. M. 1977. Stylistic behavior and information exchange. In For the Director: Researcher Essays in Honor of James B. Griffin, ed. C. Cleland, pp. 317-342. University of Michigan, Museum of Anthropology. *Anthropological Papers* 61: 317-342.

Zubrow, E. 1975. *Prehistoric Carrying Capacity: A Model*. Menlo Park: Cummings.

11

Reliability, Validity, and Quantitative Methods in Archaeology

Jack D. Nance

Introduction

The last several decades have witnessed significant changes in archaeology. The changes that have occurred have been varied, but one of the more notable trends touching most parts of the research process is a move toward increased quantification. These days we observe regular use of simple quantification, descriptive and inferential statistics, and multivariate and other quantitative methods, applied to almost all aspects of archaeological enquiry.

One significant and welcome effect of the quantification trend is an increased concern about the nature of data recovery methods. For example, methods such as flotation and fine waterscreening of sediment samples to recover small-scale palaeobotanical remains and other bioarchaeological data are now commonplace. Use of probabilistic sampling designs to recover regional samples of archaeological sites is widespread. In some cases these methods have significantly influenced our perception of prehistoric cultures and have radically altered the ways in which we view the archaeological record.

Given trends such as these, it is not unexpected that researchers have begun to ask questions about the quality of the data they collect: Are the samples representative of specified contexts? Are the data retrieved from these samples consistent? Exactly what variables in past cultural contexts do the data measure? If archaeological enquiry is to mature and advance toward its larger objectives, then surely questions such as these must be answered convincingly.

These kinds of questions relate to the *reliability* and *validity* of archaeological observations. These two concepts are crucial in archaeological research because if our observations are unreliable or invalid, then our view into the past will be highly distorted. In turn, this distortion will influence, in a most fundamental way, the formulation of the theory needed to reconstruct lifeways and culture histories and to develop models of culture process.

I think that archaeologists have been attempting to assess the reliability and validity of their measurements and concepts for some time. Indeed, much of what the "new archaeologists" of the 1960s had to say involved a plea for greater emphasis on reliability and validity assessment, without using those words, and the recent literature indicates that archaeologists have begun to seek answers to the kinds of questions posed above. What I wish to show here is that there exists a body of theory and methods that may be of use in our search for meaningful answers to some of these questions. From my knowledge of the literature it appears that most attempts at assessing the reliability and validity of archaeological measurements have been undertaken ad hoc, purely within an archaeological context, without reference to any general guiding principles (see Cowgill 1970, Nance and Ball 1986, and Speth and Johnson 1976 for the only exceptions I am aware of). The net result is that, sometimes, these studies have resulted in insufficient use of the analyst's time, perhaps narrow and unconvincing consideration of the data studied, and on occasion, misleading statements about the nature of the data.

The development of methods of assessing reliability and validity took place in the context of the theory of measurement. The literature on measurement theory is extensive, and much of it is highly mathematical (see Stanley 1971, for example), so my discussion will of necessity deal with basics. Numerous complexities and subtleties relating to these two concepts could be explored.

Reliability and Validity

Intuitively, we all know what the words reliability and validity mean. If something is reliable, it is dependable. If you own a reliable automobile, then time after time, when you turn the key in the ignition, the engine will start. The reliable car responds similarly on different occasions.

By the same token, if we make the same observation on several occasions and the observation is reliable, the result will be consistent; all the values obtained will be similar—indeed, the basic definition of reliability involves *consistency*. A measurement or observation is reliable if repeated attempts to make the measurement yield the same or similar results. An observation is unreliable if it does not yield consistent data.

Estimating reliability, then, involves estimating how consistent, or replicable, the results of observations are. More specifically, measuring reliability entails estimating the amount of *random error* inherent in measurements. The reliability of a measurement is inversely related to the amount of random error present in that measurement (Figure 11.1).

But reliability isn't everything. Continuing with the automobile example, if there is a short in the electrical system that drains the car's battery, when you turn the key, you'll get a consistent response all right, but it won't be a satisfactory response. In one sense, *valid* observations yield satisfactory responses or data. Satisfactory data tell you what you want to know, not something else. Intuitively then, to say that an observation is valid means that the observation doesn't lie to you—valid observations do not mislead the observer. Put another way, an observation is valid if it measures what you think it measures.

Whereas reliability relates to random error, validity relates to nonrandom, or *systematic error*. Thus an invalid observation is a biased observation—degree of validity is inversely related to the amount of systematic error present in measurements. Low validity results from the presence of a lot of systematic error. A perfectly valid measurement is one without any systematic error. Repeated invalid observations will be biased as a whole, all in the same direction. This observation leads to the conclusion that measurements may be reliable (i.e., consistent) but, at the same time, invalid for a given purpose.

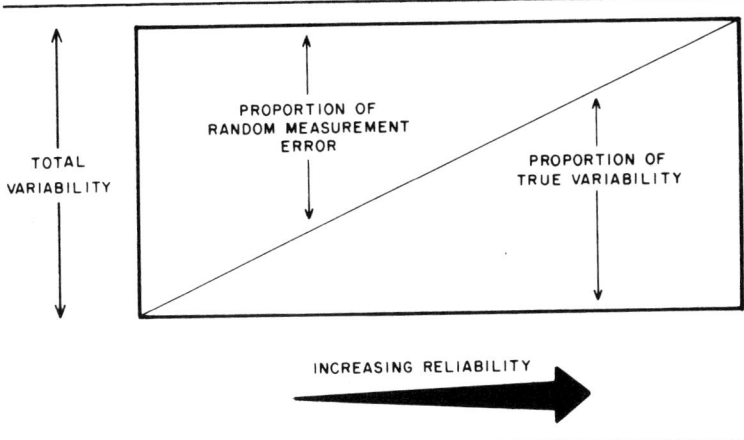

Figure 11.1 Reliability in terms of the relative proportions of true and error variance. As variability due to measurement error decreases, reliability increases.

It would be very difficult to overemphasize the importance of these two concepts in archaeology or any science. They relate to our ability to make meaningful observations about the phenomena we study. It is a universal truth of science that if we cannot measure a phenomenon properly, we can never truly understand that phenomenon. Reliability and validity lie at the very heart of the science of prehistory.

Measurement

The concepts of reliability and validity originate in the context of measurement theory. For this reason it is useful to briefly consider the basic nature of the idea of measurement and some ways in which it relates to archaeological research.

Measurement is a concept that describes the basic process for gathering information about "things." The things being studied may be concrete (an artifact, for example) or abstract (a time sequence, for example). Information is obtained by making observations about or measuring these "things." In what follows the terms "observation," "measurement," and "score" are used in a generic sense and interchangeably to refer to the value of the datum that results from making an observation or measurement of some phenomenon. The experiment by means of which the data are acquired will be referred to as a "test."

Elementary definitions of measurement deal with assigning numbers to the results of observations. For example, "Measurement is the assignment of numbers to objects or events according to rules" (Stevens 1951: 22). For many archaeological research operations this definition is reasonably accurate. We often measure the dimensions of objects or count things, for example. The "rules" are normally those relevant to distinguishing continuous from discrete variables and quantifying observations in terms of nominal, ordinal, interval, or ratio scales. This kind of measurement for the most part appears fairly straightforward: measuring the size of a mussel shell, determining the abundance of thorium in a piece of obsidian, recording the presence or absence of a design element on a potsherd, measuring the thickness of a stratum in a site deposit, estimating the density of artifacts in that stratum, etc. Archaeologists spend a lot of time making more or less *direct measurements* on objects and events.

Often, however, measurement of archaeological variables is not quite so straightforward. Rather, we are frequently faced with the necessity of taking *indirect* measurements of the variable we really wish to study. For example, in the absence of absolute dates we may resort to constructing seriated sequences of time-sensitive artifacts or attributes to measure time. In the absence of dated, stratigraphic contexts (e.g., "surface" sites), in order to estimate site occupation span, we are required to attempt to derive some index of time as represented in the assemblage of material remains from the site. When attempting to study social status, we cannot interview informants directly but must attempt indirect measurement of status, perhaps by determining which ages or sexes of human remains are associated with certain kinds of burial goods, for instance. In short, we frequently find ourselves in the position of having to determine the correlates (Schiffer 1976: 13) of some variable in physical finds populations (Cowgill 1970: 163) and measuring the correlate rather than the phenomenon we really want to know about. Often the phenomenon is really an abstract concept which can never be measured directly, as is the case in the social sciences generally (Carmines and Zeller 1979: 9-10).

Much archaeological measurement is probably even more error-prone than the above comments might apply. *Reconstructed* measurements are routinely required when fragmentary artifacts are encountered in archaeological analyses, for example, estimating vessel volumes or lengths and/or weights of broken projectile points. Sometimes even seemingly precise technical measurements (e.g., use of spectroscopy or other methods to identify unknown substances or sources of materials, i.e., "fingerprinting") probably leave a substantial amount of room for error.

All kinds of archaeological measurement are riddled with perils. Achieving reliable direct measurements, although seemingly simple, even has its surprises (Cowgill 1970). The artifact (or other) taxonomy used in a specific instance will have an effect on the value of most measurements; and when it is necessary to aggregate or partition archaeological finds, questions arise about which means of aggregation or partitioning should be used (see Grayson 1984, for example). We cannot, at this point, even guess at the reliability of most indirect measurements, and the science of prehistory is absolutely impoverished when it comes to assessing the validity of measurements, especially those of the indirect variety. In part, what is required to remedy the situation is development of the body of "midrange" theory linking the physical properties of the archaeological report with past cultural contexts, as several (e.g., Binford 1964, 1971, 1978a, 1978b, 1979, 1980, 1982; Schiffer 1972, 1975, 1976, 1979) have been telling us for some years. It is within the contexts of reliability and validity that the assertion that "the maturity of a discipline is gauged by the sophistication of its measurement systems" takes on real meaning.

A Formal Definition of Reliability

As pointed out above, assessing the reliability of measurements involves estimating the amount of random error in those measurements. It is a fact of life that if almost any observation or measurement, say X, is made on the same object or event on different occasions, the results on the different measurement occasions will not be identical. That is, assume that a measurement, $X(1)$ is taken at time $T(1)$. If we then repeat the measurement, on the same object, to obtain $X(2)$ taken at time $T(2)$, while $X(2)$ is expected to be similar to $X(1)$, the two measurements are also expected, under normal circumstances, to differ from each other somewhat because of measurement (observation) error. Random errors are ubiquitous, and they result from a host of sources. It may be possible to minimize random error, but it can never be totally eliminated. All measurements and observations contain measurement error.

Assuming measurement errors are random, a fundamental relation in classical test theory states

$$X = t + e. \qquad [1]$$

X is an observed score or value on a variable, t is the "true" value, and e is a random error. In words, an observed score is composed of two parts: a true score and a random error component.

True scores are unknowable quantities, but they are central to the development of reliability theory. For most purposes a true score may be thought of as the average of an infinitely large number of observed values.

Random errors are just that, random. That is, "positive" errors in measurement are assumed to be just as likely to occur as are "negative" deviations from the true value. Moreover, the deviations are of similar magnitude. Random positive and negative errors cancel each other, and so, in the long run, have an average or expected value of zero.

Because reliability deals with the study of repeated measures over events or objects, it is necessary to note that observed values $X(i)$, errors $e(i)$, and true scores $t(i)$ will be variable. Figure 11.2 illustrates by showing observed values of X, each being the sum of a true score $t(i)$ and a random error $e(i)$ for each of n objects or events. Variability in these quantities is usually expressed as the variance (VAR) of the quantities over the n objects or events.

An elementary theorem of statistics states that the variance of a sum (in this case X is the sum) may be expressed as

$$VAR(X) = VAR(t) + VAR(e) + 2COV(t,e). \qquad [2]$$

In words, for the quantities in Figure 11.2, the total variance VAR(X) in observed values is the sum of true variance, VAR(t), and error variance, VAR(e), plus double the covariance of true and error scores. But if, as assumed above, errors are random, the covariance term in (2) will be zero, so that

$$VAR(X) = VAR(t) + VAR(e). \qquad [3]$$

TRUE SCORES		ERRORS		OBSERVED SCORES
$t(1)$	+	$e(1)$	=	$x(1)$
$t(2)$	+	$e(2)$	=	$x(2)$
$t(3)$	+	$e(3)$	=	$x(3)$
⋮		⋮		⋮
$t(n)$	+	$e(n)$	=	$x(n)$

Figure 11.2 n observed values of X represented as the sum of a "true score" $t(i)$ and a random error $e(i)$.

The reliability of X as a measure of t is the ratio of the true score variance [VAR(t)] to the observed variance [VAR(X)]:

$$p(X) = VAR(t) / VAR(X). \qquad [4]$$

Equation (4) can be rewritten to express the reliability terms of the error variance:

$$p(X) = [VAR(X) - VAR(e)] / VAR(X),$$
$$p(X) = 1 - [VAR(e) / VAR(X)]. \qquad [5]$$

The reliability is 1.0 minus the proportion of the variance of observed scores that is due to error. Thus a reliability coefficient measures the proportion of variance in observations that arises because of *true differences among the objects or events being measured*, exclusive of random measurement error. If we can estimate the error variance, then we can estimate the reliability because the total variance can be estimated directly from observed scores.

Reliability varies between 0 and 1.0. If observed scores are swamped by random error, reliability will be low. If there is little or no random error, reliability will be high. By rearranging equation (3), one of the truly remarkable findings of classical true score theory becomes apparent:

$$VAR(t) = VAR(X)p(X). \qquad [6]$$

So, if we can estimate the reliability of X, we can easily estimate the *unobservable* variance of the true scores because true variance is the product of observed variance and the reliability.

Parallel Measurements

In general, empirical estimates of reliability may be obtained by measuring the correlation $p(XX)$ between *parallel measurements*. Briefly, two measurements are parallel "if they have identical true scores and equal variances" (Carmines and Zeller 1979: 32). In symbols, $X(1)$ and $X(2)$ (two measurements) are parallel if

a. $X(1) = t(1) + e(1)$;
b. $X(2) = t(2) + e(2)$;
c. $t(1) = t(2) = t$; and
d. $VAR\ e(1) = VAR\ e(2)$.

"Parallel [measurements] are functions of the same true score and the differences between them are the result of purely random error" (Carmines and Zeller 1979: 33).

For practical purposes parallel measurements are repeated, comparable measurements on the same object or event, all made under the same conditions. When the assumptions of random errors and zero correlations and covariations apply, then *repeated* measurements of a variable on the same object or event may be characterized as follows (Carmines and Zeller 1979: 30):

(1) the expected error is zero;
(2) the correlation between true scores and errors is zero;
(3) the correlation between the error on one measurement and the true score on a
(4) second measurement is zero;
    the correlation between errors on distinct measurements is zero.

Under these conditions (especially 2) the "expected" value of X is t. Moreover, it can be shown that the correlation between parallel measurements measures the proportion of variance in observed scores that is true score variance (Schuessler 1971: 352-358) because this correlation is the square of the correlation between observed and true scores (Magnusson 1967: 67-68). Thus the correlation between parallel measurements measures the proportion of variance in observed scores that is explained by their relationship to true scores.

Empirical reliability estimates may be obtained by obtaining at least two parallel measurements on a number of items or events and calculating the correlation between these paired observations. The usual sample estimate of p(XX) is Pearson's product-moment correlation coefficient [r(XX)]. In general, reliability coefficients below about 0.8 are considered undesirable.

Estimating Reliability

Many different ways of estimating reliability are known. Each has strengths and weaknesses, and each requires a somewhat different interpretation. Below I describe several, but not all, of them and present brief samples illustrating their use. The approach to reliability presented here arises from classical true score theory. Recently developed approaches are less restrictive in required assumptions, but limitations of time preclude a discussion of these methods here.

Test-Retest Reliability

The test-retest method of assessing reliability probably corresponds most closely to what we intuitively feel a reliability test should be. In this method a person is first asked to make a measurement or observation on some variable, and the result X(1) is recorded. After some time has elapsed, the person is asked to make exactly the same measurement under the same conditions as the first. The result of this second attempt at measuring the variable is X(2). The results of the two measurement episodes may be written:

$$X(1) = X(t) + e(1)$$
$$X(2) = X(t) + e(2)$$

Presumably the two results will be similar because exactly the same object or event is being measured by exactly the same person at two different points in time (Figure 11.3): We are controlling interobserver error and insuring the same true score at times 1 and 2. The only reason for differences between X(1) and X(2) is assumed, therefore, to be the presence of random error. If the results at time 1 and time 2 are identical, then the correlation, over persons, between $X_i(1)$ and $X_i(2)$ will be equal to 1.0. But the results are not likely to be identical because of random errors of measurement. The larger the random errors, the lower the correlation between the observed measurements, and the lower the reliability.

Table 11.1 presents the results of reliability calculations from a test-retest experiment conducted by B. A. Nicholson (1980) while carrying out a study of growth rings on freshwater bivalves. In this experiment, a graduate student who was himself engaged in growth-ring research was asked to count the number of annuli on the external surface of specimens of *Lampsilis siliquoidea* shells at two points in time. The results of the two tests are correlated at $r(XX) = .74$, suggesting, according to the mathematical definition of $r(XX)$, that about 26% of the variability in the counts is due to random error. About 74% of the variability between counts can be attributed to true differences in the number of rings on the shells being examined.

In the above study measurements of the dimensions of the specimens were found, predictably, to be much more reliable. The same was the case for an experiment I conducted that involved measurement of the dimensions of chipped-stone projectile points. In this experiment I measured a sample of projectile points initially, and then had occasion to measure the same sample of points one year later. The reliability of the measurements, all taken with (the same) vernier calipers (hand-held), are in line with expectations (Table 11.2): All the test-retest correlations are above .9, so the measurements may be considered quite reliable. That is to say, the measurements apparently contain little random error. The least reliable is stem length. The probable reason for the lower reliability of this measurement lies in the fact that the depth feeler of the calipers was used to obtain the measurement. Location of indistinct landmarks on the artifact is difficult, and consistent orientation of the artifact and measuring instrument is not easy to achieve when both are hand-held.

The test-retest method of estimating reliability may not always be practical or even appropriate in many cases. For example, if the interval between times 1 and 2 is short, memory may play a role in determining test results. If this interval is long, changes in the

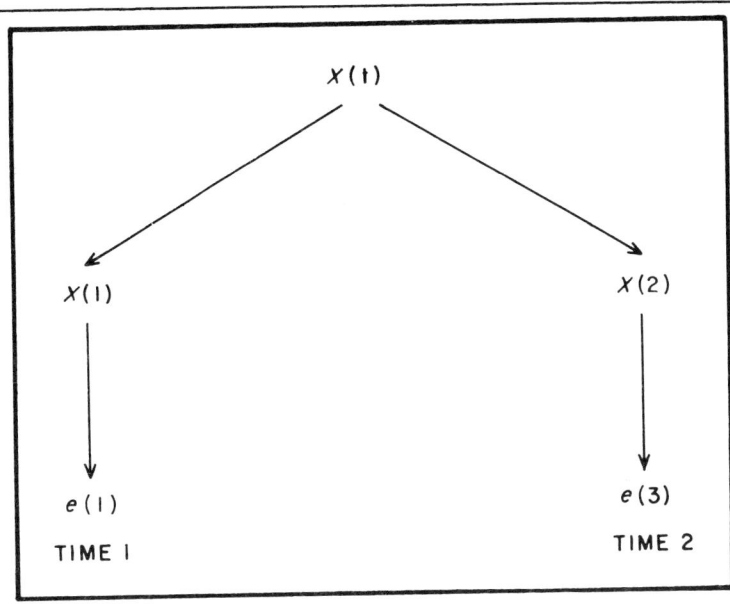

Figure 11.3 Test-retest method of assessing the reliability of a measurement. Two measurements $X(1)$ and $X(2)$ are made at times 1 and 2. Because the true score $X(t)$ is the same at times 1 and 2, differences between $X(1)$ and $X(2)$ are attributed to random error (after Carmines and Zeller, 1979: Fig. 1).

observer, or the subject of observation, may affect the results. Such changes might involve perceptual changes on the part of the observer to certain issues relating to the phenomenon being measured, for example, the process being known as "sensitization." Similarly, it may not be economical or possible to assemble the same set of observers at two different points in time; or, as is often the case with our data base, the subject of observation, a site for instance, may experience radical change or even disappear during that interval. Many of these difficulties may be overcome by administering a properly designed experiment only once.

Split-Halves Reliability

In a split-halves experiment a set of n observations is obtained at a single point in time. n is the length of the test. The sample of

TABLE 11.1
Replicate Annulus Counts on Freshwater Bivalve Shells

Specimen	Annulus Count	
	Aug. 29	Nov. 20
A045	8	11
A207	8	10
CA003	9	8
CA016	10	12
CM006	11	11
M004	5	4
M032	7	11
M103	6	7
M104	9	10
M106	9	10

SOURCE: Nicholson 1980, Table 4.
r(XX) = .74.

observations is then divided, randomly perhaps, into two halves, each n/2 in length. The reliability estimate is obtained by calculating the correlation between scores from the first and second sample halves over a number of subjects.

An example of the use of split-halves reliability is given by Nance and Ball (1986). The experiment was undertaken to examine the reliability of the use of shallow, subsurface testing to locate archaeological sites in probabilistic regional survey. Nance and Ball's procedure involved excavating and screening a number, n, of 25 × 25 × 10 cm test pits on the surface of 18 sites of varying surface artifact density and spatial clustering to estimate the likelihood of the occurrence of "productive" (containing artifacts) test pits over sites (Table 11.3).[1]

In this case n = 30, so that the samples of test pits were randomly divided into halves of n/2 = 15 test pits. The values of X(1) and X(2), the counts of productive test pits in respective half-samples, were then correlated. The resulting reliability estimate was r(XX) = .948, suggesting a reasonably small amount of random error between measurements in different half-samples. Test pit sampling appears to be fairly reliable in the sense that replicate samples of test pits produce similar results on known sites. A strong note of caution is required here, however, because "reliable" has a very special meaning. Reliable means that replicate tests produce similar results. If a first

TABLE 11.2
Test-Retest Reliabilities for Projectile Point Dimensions

Variable	Test-Retest Reliability
Length	.999
Maximum width	.999
Maximum thickness	.932
Neck width	.964
Stem length	.916

SOURCE: Nance, unpublished.

sample of test pits produces a fair number of productive test pits, then so will a second sample. But *if the first sample of test pits are all sterile, then it is very likely that all of those in the second sample will also be sterile* (see remark on the *validity* of Test Pit Sampling [TPS] below).

Actually, the reliability coefficient of r(XX) = .948 above is the reliability of each half-sample. By means of another remarkable finding (Spearman 1910; Brown 1910) this coefficient may be "corrected" so that it measures the reliability of the entire 30 unit samples rather than the 15 unit half-samples. The correction is accomplished by means of the Spearman-Brown prophecy formula (don't you just love the name?):

$$t(XX') = 2r(XX) / 1 + r(XX). \qquad [7]$$

The corrected estimate of r(XX) from above is r(XX') = .974.

In Nance and Ball's study a general version of the Spearman-Brown formula (see Carmines and Zeller 1979: 42) proved very useful. The generalization of the Spearman-Brown finding permits one to estimate the reliability of a test of *any* length, based upon an observed value of r(XX). By means of this approach Nance and Ball were able to show (Figure 11.4) how the reliability of TPS decreases as the number of test pits intersecting the surface of a site decreases (and varies with other properties of sites). From this finding it was concluded that TPS will be less reliable in helping to discover sites with small surface exposures than it will be in the discovery of sites with larger surface areas. It follows that the *validity* of TPS as a site

TABLE 11.3
Split-Half Counts of Productive Test Pits

Sample	X (First)	X (Second)
DkLt 18A	2	0
DkLt 18B*	3	1
HbRf 62	3	1
FgQm 6	7	8
HhOu	1	1
Dry Island 1	11	10
Dry Island 29	13	12
ASA 05	1	2
Trail A	15	15
Trail B*	14	11
Lv 49	14	15
Lv 98A	9	11
Lv 98B	14	14
LCAP 72	13	12
LCAP 77	13	9
Cw 35	15	19
LCAP 17	1	3
LCAP 16	11	10
Gordon I	11	14
Gordon II	15	15

SOURCE: Nance and Ball, 1986, Table B.
* = replicate sample.
$r(XX) = .974$.

discovery method varies with the properties of the archaeological record.

The results of another example of the use of split-halves reliability testing are shown in Table 11.4. The data utilized are part of those originating in an experiment in which my students and I asked several archaeologists to sort a number (n = 20) of specimens of different classes of chipped-stone artifacts using two different forms of presenting the definition of the classes into which the artifacts were to be sorted. In one test a "type specimen" was provided to aid the analyst in deciding to which class a given artifact belonged. In a second experiment a written definition of each category was provided instead of the type specimen.

In each test for each artifact class "correct" scores were recorded when artifacts were sorted into the proper classes, predetermined by the experiment administrators to exist in the collection of artifacts. If

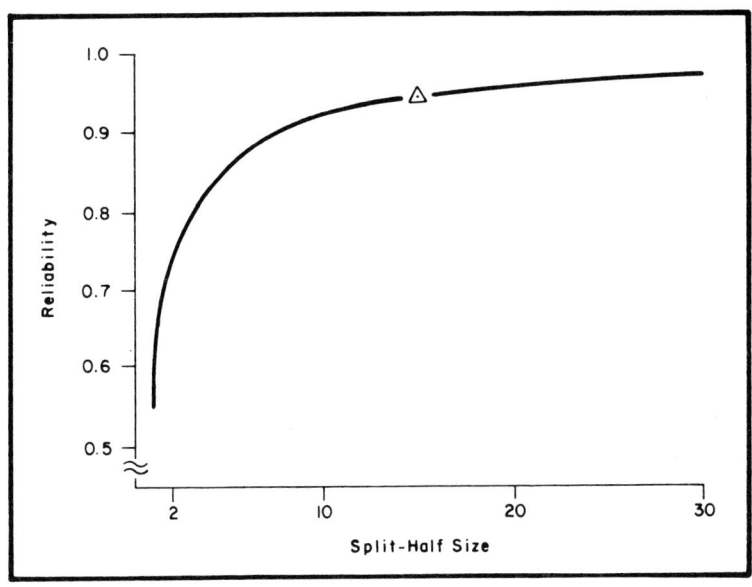

Figure 11.4 Spearman-Brown curve for the reliability of test pit sampling. The curve was generated from data obtained by employing the split-halves method to assess the consistency of the content of small text pits excavated on 18 known archaeological sites. The triangle indicates the reliability level of a sample of 30 test pits. As the number of test pits intersecting a site's surface exposure decreases, so does the reliability of the method (after Nance and Ball, 1986: Fig. 3).

an artifact was placed in a class other than the one to which we had assigned it membership, an "incorrect" score was recorded.[2] The 20 items were then split on an odd-even basis, the 10 odd-numbered items being assigned to the first half-test. The remaining 10 items were assigned to the second half-test. The number of correct responses was then summed for each half test, and the half-scores were correlated and corrected using Spearman-Brown. Results for two classes of artifacts (unhafted bifaces and retouched flakes) are presented in Table 11.4.

The reliabilities recorded in the first row of Table 11.4 appear somewhat contradictory in terms of the effects of the form of presentation of artifact class definition. That is, the written description seems to have produced the more reliable results for bifaces, whereas it produced less reliable results for retouched flakes. Taken

TABLE 11.4
Estimated Reliabilities of Biface and Flake Classifications

	Bifaces		Retouched Flakes	
	Written	Specimen	Written	Specimen
Reliability (A)	.916	.645	.639	.924
Reliability (B)		.933	.810	
Variance	23.4	4.5	21.6	41.0

SOURCE: Nance, unpublished.
A = uncorrected reliabilities.
B = adjusted reliabilities.

at face value, the data suggest the existence of an "interaction effect" between the form in which artifact class definition is presented and the artifact class itself, because the correlations change in magnitude and the changes reverse direction moving from one form of presentation to another and from one artifact class the other. This may be a truly provocative finding. However, another explanation for the nature of the results may be more accurate.

It should be noted that somewhat (but not entirely) different groups of archaeologists participated in the two experiments. Also, the exact same set of artifacts was not used in both tests. Because of methodological naivete on my part, a smaller number of archaeologists participated in the second experiment than in the first. Now, it is a well-known fact that the "restriction of range" phenomenon (Blalock 1960: 291; Guilford and Fruchter 1973: 419-20) may act to reduce the magnitude of a correlation coefficient due to reduced variability (variance) in observations. This can be quickly appreciated by examining equation (5). This equation shows that reliability is a function of the relative sizes of error variance [VAR(e)] and total variance [VAR(X)]. Thus, holding error variance constant, if total variance is restricted, reliability must decrease.

The variances in the bottom row of Table 11.4 suggest that the design of our experiment produced a restriction of range effect on some of the reliability coefficients, because lower reliability estimates are associated with smaller variances. In the test where a written definition was provided, the scores for bifaces were slightly more variable than were those for retouched flakes. In the test where the type specimen was provided, the reverse obtains: Scores for retouched flakes were much more variable than those for bifaces. Direct comparison of the reliability coefficients may not be advisable.

A way out of this predicament is available, however. Guilford and Fruchter (1973: 420) show how a correlation may be corrected to an estimate of its value had it been obtained from a distribution of scores with a given variance. The second row of Table 11.4 provides adjusted correlations for the biface-specimen and retouched flake-written test results from the artifact classification experiment that are predicted to have been obtained had they originated from data with total score variances comparable to the biface-written and retouched flake-specimen results, respectively. The adjusted values seem less contradictory and suggest that overall recognition of the class "biface" may be a little more consistent (i.e., less error-prone) than is the case for "retouched flake," and that for both, a type specimen may communicate artifact class definition a little better (i.e., reduce perceptual error a little more) than the written word, at least for the data at hand. Because our samples of artifacts and archaeologists were not random samples, perhaps these results should be viewed as suggestive rather than conclusive.

Archaeological researchers are often faced with large quantities of data or remains. It is not always necessary, nor is it very efficient, to examine massive amounts of data to achieve one's research objectives. Moreover, improper or uninformed design of experiments may result in loss of information critical to examination of the results of the research. I shall use data collected by Schaaf (1981: Tables 3 and 4) to illustrate.

The data arise from an experiment carried out to test the consistency of counts of palaeobotanic remains recovered from flotation processing of bulk sediment samples. Briefly, Schaaf took the entire fill from a shallow pit feature at a site in Minnesota, homogenized the total by hand, and then removed 18 one-liter subsamples. These were set aside for later flotation processing and analysis in "Trial 1."

The remainder of the feature fill was then further homogenized and reduced in volume by processing through a mechanical sample-splitter to recover a 25% sample of this remainder. This procedure was repeated to recover a second set of 18 one-liter subsamples from "Trial 2." Both sets of 18 subsamples were then processed by the same flotation process and sorted, and the remains were identified. This process yielded 14,132 carbonized and noncarbonized seeds distributed over 26 different genera.

The counts for each genus were statistically examined to ascertain their consistency over all subsamples and to compare "Trial 1" and "Trial 2" results. The subsamples processed through the sample-splitter appear to have produced the more homogeneous counts.

I calculated reliability coefficients to estimate the split-halves reliability from Schaaf's data, using counts subtotaled for families rather than genera. Reliability was estimated in two ways. First, counts were summed, for each family, for the first nine subsamples for a trial, yielding a count X(First), and for subsamples 10-18, yielding a second count X(Second). These counts were correlated over families to estimate r(XX') for both Trials 1 and 2. Results are entered as "Reliability 1A" and "Reliability 2A" in Table 11.5.

I then calculated similar reliability estimates, but this time based on counts from only two subsamples (subsample 1 and 2 from Schaaf's Tables 3 and 4) rather than total counts from all subsamples (see Table 11.6). These results are entered in Table 11.5 and "Reliability 1B" and "Reliability 2B" respectively. All the estimates are identical when rounded.

Schaaf provides some data (1981: 225) about the time required to sort different sample fractions. Based on these data I calculate that 11.5 hours of effort were required to sort a single subsample. For two subsamples (Reliability Bs above) the time investment for processing would be 23 hours. For 18 subsamples (Reliability As above) the time required is 207 hours or a ninefold increase in effort, yielding the same estimate of reliability.

To be sure, Schaaf's study is an interesting and useful one, illustrating the benefits of using sample preprocessing to improve the consistency of archaeological observations. It must be kept in mind also that Schaaf examined aspects of her data not considered here. It is not my mission to downgrade the value of Schaaf's study. At the same time, it is necessary to note that because Schaaf did not take "control" samples before the whole process began, we have no data to which the final results can be compared to determine just how effective the homogenization procedures were. It is not possible to measure the gains in consistency, etc., resulting from different sample treatments because no data were collected on untreated samples. Thus it cannot be determined whether or not possible improvements in data quality were great enough to offset the extra effort required to achieve those improvements. The reliability estimates cited above suggest that these issues might be candidates for examination.

TABLE 11.5
Seed Count Reliability Coefficients

Trial	Reliability	
	A	B
1	.999	.999
2	.999	.999

SOURCE: Schaaf, 1981, Tables 3 and 4.
A = reliabilities based on 18 subsamples.
B = reliabilities based on 2 subsamples.

Internal Consistency Reliability

One of the shortcomings of the split-halves method of estimating reliability is that samples can be split in a variety of ways. For example, in calculating r(XX) for the artifact classification data considered earlier, I split the observations into odd-numbered and even-numbered halves. I could have split the items randomly. Had I followed that course of action, the reliability coefficients generated would have been slightly different than those presented in Table 11.4. Moreover, a large number of random splits is possible, and each of them would have produced a slightly different value for r(XX). In short, the split-halves reliability is not unique; a somewhat different estimate will result depending on the way in the which the data are subdivided. While these different estimates will all be similar, it is desirable to have a unique estimate of reliability for a given set of observations. Researchers in educational and psychological testing have developed methods (e.g., Cronbach 1951; Kuder and Richardson 1937) that yield unique reliability estimates. These methods aim at quantifying the internal consistency of a set of test results.[3] I shall illustrate with one widely used method (Cronbach's ALPHA; Cronbach 1951) as applied to a portion of the artifact classification data discussed earlier.

Although ALPHA may be calculated for scores recorded in other forms, I shall use observations that are expressed as dichotomies. The data from the biface classification experiment (written definition) are conveniently presented in an item-score matrix that represents the responses of several individuals to a number of test items (Table 11.7). In Table 11.7 items (artifacts; total = 20) are listed along the left side of the matrix while individuals (i.e., 14 archaeologists) are listed

TABLE 11.6
Seed Counts

Family	Subsample 1	Subsample 2
Graminae	26	28
Cyperacae	4	0
Juncaceae	5	0
Liliaceae	1	0
Juglandaceae	0	1
Polygonaceae	0	0
Chenopodiaceae	88	84
Amaranthaceae	9	1
Azioaceae	258	223
Portulacacae	19	16
Rubiaceae	0	0
Rosaceae	4	8
Ericaceae	1	0
Solanaceae	3	2

SOURCE: Schaaf, 1981, Tables 3 and 4.
$r(XX) = .99$.

across the top of the matrix. The Xs within the box represent incorrect responses. Test scores (i.e., the number of correct responses) for each archaeologist are given along the bottom margin of the matrix, and the column on the far right of the box presents the proportion of correct responses (out of 14 attempts) for each artifact, bearing in mind my noted comments regarding the correctness/incorrectness of responses in this experiment. Using the $SPSS^X$ program RELIABILITY (SPSS Inc. 1983: 717-732), Cronbach's ALPHA was calculated for this matrix. The value of ALPHA so obtained is ALPHA = .898 (Table 11.8). This value suggests that the biface classification responses are fairly reliable. Comparable calculations for the retouched flake test in the same experiment yielded a value of ALPHA = .828.

The relative magnitude of the ALPHA values are commensurate with the adjusted reliabilities for these artifact classes (i.e., Reliability B estimates for the biface-written and retouched flake-written tests) presented in Table 11.4. It is, however, important to understand that Cronbach's ALPHA measures different properties of the responses than do the split-halves reliability coefficients. ALPHA monitors the internal consistency of the "response pattern" to an item-score matrix in the following way.

TABLE 11.7
Item-Score Matrix Displaying Scores Obtained by
14 Archaeologists in Classifying 20 Bifaces Each

	ARCHAEOLOGISTS														PROPORTION "CORRECT"
ARTIFACT	8	3	4	14	9	11	13	5	6	1	7	12	2	10	
10														x	.93
8														x	.93
4					x										.93
18												x	x		.86
17												x		x	.86
2													x	x	.86
1											x		x		.86
20								x				x		x	.78
11											x		x	x	.78
13								x				x	x	x	.78
14											x		x	x	.78
5										x		x	x	x	.78
6											x	x	x		.78
9						x		x	x					x	.71
7			x								x	x	x	x	.64
3									x	x	x	x	x	x	.64
15						x		x	x		x		x	x	.64
12						x		x		x	x	x	x	x	.50
19			x		x	x	x	x			x	x	x	x	.42
16	x	x	x			x				x	x	x	x		.42
	20	19	19	19	18	18	17	16	16	13	12	11	7	4	

INDIVIDUAL SCORES

SOURCE: Nance, unpublished.
NOTE: Xs indicate incorrect responses. The "internal consistency" of the responses as measured by Cronbach's *ALPHA* is .89.

In Table 11.7 responses are arranged horizontally in decreasing order of individual scores, from left to right. Responses for items (artifacts) are arranged vertically according to the proportion of times the artifact was correctly classified, proportions being recorded in the column to the far right of the matrix. Each of these proportions may be interpreted as a "difficulty index" associated with each item. Thus artifact number 10, correctly classified in 93% of attempts, may be considered "easier" than artifact number 12, with an index of .5.

A set of responses for an archaeologist in the matrix is internally consistent if easier items were classified correctly while "harder" items were not. Responses are not internally consistent if, for a given individual, more difficult items were done correctly while easier items were "missed." For example, archaeologists 3 and 4 in Table 11.7

TABLE 11.8
Cronbach's *ALPHA* for Internal Consistency of
Biface and Retouched Flake Classifications

Item Class	Alpha
Bifaces	.898
Retouched Flakes	.828

both missed item 16, with a difficulty value of .42, and got all other items right. Similar results are apparent for archaeologist number 9. Thus the responses for these persons are internally consistent.

In contrast, archaeologist number 6 got items 15 and 19 (difficult ones) correct but missed artifacts 9 and 20, items of lesser difficulty. Therefore the responses of archaeologist 6 exhibit internal inconsistencies. ALPHA measures internal consistency in the terms just illustrated.

Thus the value of ALPHA = .898 calculated for Table 11.7 indicates a fair degree of internal consistency. For comparison, ALPHA for Table 11.9 (from Ferguson 1971: 354) which exhibits a perfectly consistent pattern is .91.

The form of one formula for estimating ALPHA is instructive:

$$\text{ALPHA} = np/[1 + p(n-1)] \qquad [8]$$

where

n = number of test items, and
p = average interitem correlation.

This formula shows that the value of ALPHA varies as a function of the average correlation (here the phi coefficient) among item scores. If scores are assigned to items randomly, then ALPHA will be small. As the response pattern becomes more structured, i.e., as the responses become increasingly correlated, the value of ALPHA increases, although never reaching unity because of "interaction" between abilities of the testees and item difficulties (Winer 1971: 295-296). Analysis of variance methods may be used to study these interaction effects (Winer 1971).

TABLE 11.9
A Perfectly Consistent Item-Score Matrix

		\multicolumn{10}{c}{Individuals}	
		1	2	3	4	5	6	7	8	9	10	p(i)
I	1	1	1	1	1	1	1	1	1	–	–	.8
T	2	1	1	1	1	1	1	–	–	–	–	.6
E	3	1	1	1	1	1	1	–	–	–	–	.6
M	4	1	1	1	1	–	–	–	–	–	–	.4
S	5	1	1	1	1	–	–	–	–	–	–	.4
	X (j)	5	5	5	5	3	3	1	1	0	0	

Cronbach's ALPHA = .91

SOURCE: Ferguson, 1971: 354.

Before this section is closed, it should be noted that there are many different ways of measuring reliability that have not been discussed here. These various methods are applicable under a variety of circumstances depending on the nature of the variables being studied and the experimental design employed in gathering the data. For example, Cohen (1960) illustrates a "coefficient of agreement" (rather than correlation) for nominal scale data. Robinson (1957) deals with similar issues, while Rulon (1939) illustrates a simplified procedure for handling split-halves data. Harper (1964) has developed a method of studying misclassification. Repeated measures (more than two replicates per object or event) may be studied by means of analysis of variance models (Winer 1971).

Correcting Correlations for Attenuation

As Cowgill (1970) has discussed, one of the important findings of reliability theory is that if observations on a variable X are unreliable due to the presence of random error, then the observed correlation of that variable with any other variable will be *attenuated*, or lowered, because of the large amount of random error associated with measurement of X. In fact, it can be shown that the reliability of a variable is an upper limit on that variable's correlation with any other variable (Guilford and Fruchter 1973: 401). The reason for this attenuation can be made clear if we think about the extreme case.

Consider two variables X and Y. Suppose X has a reliability of zero. By definition variable X is composed entirely of random error and measures nothing but random error. Therefore X cannot provide any information about Y. X's correlation with Y must therefore be zero.

If the reliabilities of two variables X and Y, r(XX) and r(YY), are known, then the correlation between the two variables r(XY) can be corrected for attenuation, i.e., to estimate the value of r(XY) that would be attained under conditions where both variables are measurable with perfect reliability (Spearman 1904). The correction for attenuation is:

$$r(XYT) = r(XY)/\sqrt{r(XX') r(YY')} \quad\quad [9]$$

where

r(XY) = observed correlation between X and Y;
r(XX') = reliability of X;
r(YY') = reliability of Y;
r(XYT) = correlation between X and Y corrected for attenuation.

From (9) it can be seen that the correction will not change the sign of r(XY) but that it will increase this correlation in an amount that depends on the reliability with which X and Y are measured. When both variables are measurable without error, r(XY) will be unaffected by the correction.

In the only discussion of this effect that I have been able to find in the archaeological literature, Cowgill (1970) has argued that counts of item classes that occur with low frequency in archaeological populations (i.e., "rare" item classes) are inherently unreliable because counts of such item classes are effectively "swamped" by sampling error. Counts of rarely occurring items will exhibit small total variance. Therefore error variance will appear relatively large in proportion to total variance. Theoretically then, counts of infrequent item classes can be expected to exhibit high degrees of unreliability.

Because of this phenomenon correlations among rare item classes will suffer from attenuation more than similar correlations among counts of more common items. Cowgill (1970) has demonstrated this with empirical data. It follows that when these counts are used in multivariate procedures such as factor or principal components analysis that rely on correlation matrices, the pattern of intercorrelations in such a matrix may be significantly altered, because some (larger) counts are more reliable than others (smaller ones). Analyses based on such correlation matrices may, then, provide misleading results, so that correlations should be corrected for attenuation before they are used for these analyses. Archaeologists are still ignoring, or are unaware of, Cowgill's warning.

I shall illustrate the correction for attenuation using data from a study of gastropods by Bobrowsky (1982: Tables 27 and 28). I will then consider a property of the archaeological record that could produce the effects discussed by Cowgill.

The snail samples studied by Bobrowsky were collected from test excavations at the Gordon Site, a late Mississippian farmstead located on a terrace near the Ohio River in Livingston County, Kentucky. To collect the gastropod samples two test pits at the site were excavated in 10-cm levels. From each 10-cm level a bulk sediment sample was collected and waterscreened. Gastropods were then extracted from the residue and identified, and species were tabulated over 10-cm levels. The counts for two species, *Campeloma decisum* and *Pupoides albilabris*, are given in Table 11.10.[4]

Ten-centimeter levels are assumed to be stratigraphically and temporally equivalent between units. Under this assumption, the counts for a given level of the two test pits may be viewed as parallel measurements on the same object (site). Therefore the data in Table 11.10 may be used to estimate the reliability of counts of C. decisum and P. albilabris by calculating the reliabilities r(CC') and r(PP') between species counts over levels. The resulting correlations are r(CC') = .464 and r(PP') = .777, suggesting that the reliability of the Campeloma counts is somewhat less than those for Pupoides, all in conformance with Cowgill's expectations regarding the relative reliabilities of commonly and less commonly occurring phenomena. It is suspected that it is the marked difference in total variance between the two species that produces the observed difference in reliabilities, rather than the inherent properties of the species themselves.

The correlation between the two species counts, r(CP) = .188, may be corrected for attenuation by applying formula (9). The value of r(CP) corrected for attenuation is r(CPT) = .313. Had the reliabilities of Campeloma and Pupoides counts been higher, the difference between r(CP) and r(CPT) would have been less than that observed.

At this point it is of interest to ask what property or properties of

TABLE 11.10
Excavation Species Counts

Species	Unit 1	Unit 2	Level
Campeloma decisum	7	0	1
	9	0	2
	9	3	3
	8	3	4
Pupoides albilabris	243	269	1
	735	685	2
	642	98	3
	58	26	4

SOURCE: Bobrowsky, 1982, Tables 27 and 28.

the archaeological context are influential in determining the above reliabilities. We may note first that counts are not just reliable or unreliable, they are more or less reliable depending upon the number of sampling units examined (i.e., the "length" of the test). This is true because as the length of the test is increased k times, increases in error variance are directly proportional to k, while true variance increases as the square of k (Magnusson 1967: 68-74). The Spearman-Brown formula (Equation 7) makes this clear. The gastropod count reliabilities were based on two test pits. Had they been based on larger numbers of observations, they would have been higher. Thus the important "sample size" here is the length of the test, or the number of observation units examined, not the number of specimens collected. I have shown elsewhere (Nance 1981) that this principle holds in site sampling generally. Because specimens are collected in "clusters" (from test pits), rather than as random element samples, the number of specimens is only indirectly important. While number of specimens will be (linearly) correlated with the number of sampling units examined, *one cannot rely on the number of specimens in a sample as an indicator of sample adequacy.*

Beyond the influences of test length ("sample size"), the general answer to the question of what determines reliability is that any factor that will increase the amount of random error in the counts will lower their reliabilities. Relevant factors include within-site sampling error, errors that might arise in sample processing, and others involving possible errors in species identification, etc. If it is assumed that recovery and identification errors are nil (not realistic, but convenient), then sampling error becomes the prime suspect. I have shown elsewhere (Nance 1981, 1983) that intrasite variation in item density resulting from spatial aggregation of items is one of the major factors contributing to within-site sampling error.

To illustrate this for the Gordon Site snail study, I calculated reliabilities, as described above, for all species having minimum counts of five in each level of both test pits. I then calculated the average number of specimens per level over all levels to measure the ABUNDANCE of each species. To measure spatial aggregation for a species I calculated the coefficient of variation (CV = standard deviation divided by ABUNDANCE) over all levels for both units. I then performed a multiple, least squares regression of RELIABILITY x 100 on ABUNDANCE and CV, to determine the way and the degree to which overall abundance and spatial clustering affect the reliability estimates. The results of the regression (Table 11.11) show that with such a small number of observations (12 species), the results are not highly significant (p = .07) but have an *R-square* value of .438.

Accordingly, the regression was recalculated using all species regardless of minimum count, but eliminating or combining species (within genera) to rid the data of sets of observations exhibiting zero variability. Observations exhibiting zero variability are constants. The reliability of a constant is undefined.

Table 11.12 presents the results of the second regression with 18 taxa, significant at p = .03. From the regression coefficients (COEFF) in the lower part of the table it would appear that reliability varies negatively with both abundance and spatial aggregation. However, the effects of density (ABUNDANCE), adjusted to account for the effects of spatial clustering, are not significant (i.e., the regression coefficient, COEFF = –0.01, attached to species density could easily have arisen in a population where a random relationship exists between species abundance and reliability). The square of the partial correlation (–0.24) shows that, after controlling for the effects of spatial clustering as measured by CV, species abundance accounts for only about 6% of the residual variation in the reliability coefficients. These statistics suggest that at least in the present context, the commonness or rarity of species does not influence the reliability of counts of these species unduly.

Why this should be the case demands explanation, especially in light of Cowgill's (1970) observations cited earlier. First, it is possible

TABLE 11.11
Analysis of Variance of Reliability for 12 Taxa

Source	DF	Sum Sqrs	Mean Sqr	F-Stat	Signif
Regression	2	2256.9	1128.5	3.5115	.0746
Error	9	2892.3	321.36		
Total	11	5149.2			
Mult R = .66205		R-Sqr = .43831			

Variable	Partial	Coeff	Std Error	T-Stat	Signif
Constant		130.37	22.356	5.8314	.0002
Dens	.00017	.26433 −4	.52413 −1	.50432 −3	.9996
CV	−.66205	−66.147	24.960	−2.6501	.0265

Dens = average density.
CV = coefficient of variation.

that the "rare" species in the data at hand are not rare enough for sampling error to be a problem. At the same time it may be pointed out that Cowgill's (correct) arguments were put forward independent of the actual spatial context from which the counts arise.

Now, I have argued elsewhere (Nance 1981: 153-60) that abundance or rarity within archaeological contexts should not be measured in terms of simple numerosity of a given class of items or elements. Rather, the "perceived abundance" (Nance 1981: 154) of an item class depends on the probability that specimens of that item class enter a sample. Because we sample most archaeological populations by means of spatially defined sampling units, that probability is highly conditioned by the spatial distribution of members of that item class. For example, if very numerous items exhibit significant spatial clustering, they may appear rarely in small to moderate-sized samples of collection units, and/or counts of these items may be highly variable from one locus to another within a site. On the other hand, elements occurring in small or moderate population proportions may appear common and/or counts may be less variable if they are uniformly distributed over the context being sampled. These factors influence the amount of sampling error expected in counts of a given item class and hence the reliability of those counts. Thus, as the above regression results show, the spatial clustering of items affects the

TABLE 11.12
Analysis of Variance of Reliability for 18 Taxa

Source	DF	Sum Sqrs	Mean Sqr	F-Stat	Signif
Regression	2	2834.3	1417.1	4.4114	.0311
Error	15	4818.6	321.24		
Total	17	7652.9			
Mult R = .60857		R-Sqr = .37035			

Variable	Partial	Coeff	Std Error	T-Stat	Signif
Constant		103.38	13.726	7.5318	.0000
Dens	−.24060	−.10808 −1	.11258 −1	−.96004	.3523
CV	−.59173	−34.390	12.097	−2.8429	.0123

Dens = density.
CV = coefficient of variation.

reliability of item counts, and this influence may be stronger than that of overall abundance.

The general nature of these relationships may be illustrated with data from the study by Nance and Ball (1986) cited earlier. For each of the samples of test pits used in that study I randomly selected two and then randomly assigned one of them to a first sample. The other test pit was assigned to a second sample. Total artifact counts for each test pit were then recorded. These counts are designated X(FIRST) and X(SECOND) respectively.

I then calculated a least square regression of the first test pit count on the second, over all sites, and obtained predicted X(FIRST) values based on the associated X(SECOND) counts. The correlation between the two count is $r(XX) = .472$. Hence the reliability of the counts (over sites) for two test pits is $r(XX') = .641$. Using the Spearman-Brown formula, the needed number of test pits required for 95% reliability would be about 22, or around three-quarters the number of subsurface tests actually conducted at each site.

I then compared the observed first sample counts with values predicted from the regression, obtaining residuals, or differences between the observed and predicted values. The magnitude of the residual for a given site is proportional to the amount of sampling error inherent in the artifact counts for that site and is, therefore, inversely related to the reliability of the count for that site. I then performed a second regression of these residuals against estimates of average item density (abundance) and variance (related to the degree of within-site spatial clustering) to estimate the relative influence of these two variables in determining sampling error and, by extension, the reliability of the counts. Item densities and variances were estimated from all 30 test pits at each site.

The results of all this work with mirrors are shown in Table 11.13. It can first be noted that the regression is highly significant ($p = .0013$). The R-square value of .522 indicates that over half of the variability in residuals can be related to variability in artifact abundance and spatial clustering. The partial correlation coefficients indicate that (1) as spatial clustering increases, so does sampling error, hence reliability decreases; (2) about 46% of the increase in a residual can be attributed to spatial clustering of artifacts, adjusted to account for change in artifact abundance; (3) the effects of spatial clustering are significant ($p = .001$); (4) as artifact abundance (density) increases, sampling error decreases, hence reliability of artifact counts increases; (5) only about 1.8% of the decrease in a residual can be attributed to changes in artifact abundance, adjusted for the effects of changes in spatial clustering; (6) the influence of changes in artifact abundance is not statistically significant ($p = .572$) for these data.

My interpretation of Cowgill's discussion in conjunction with the above analyses is this. Counts of "rare" item classes may be unreliable because of small *total* variance in counts of these items. Spatially clustered distributions nearly always will result in lowered reliability of counts of a given item class. The reliability of counts of uniformly or randomly distributed items normally should be relatively high. When cluster sampling designs are utilized to sample the archaeological record, the "sample size" that is important in estimating the reliability of counts is the number of *collection units* examined.

Reliability, Attenuation, and the Structure of the Archaeological Record

The idea that counts of item classes that occur in small population proportions may be unreliable and exhibit attenuation effects carries with it a number of implications that may have farther-reaching significance than is currently appreciated. In general, the implications of the attenuation effect are that:

TABLE 11.13
Analysis of Variance of Residuals for 21 Samples

Source	DF	Sum Sqrs	Mean Sqr	F-Stat	Signif
Regression	2	2659.4	1329.7	9.8500	.0013
Error	18	2429.9	134.99		
Total	20	5089.2			
Mult R = .72287		R-Sqr = .52255			

Variable	Partial	Coeff	Std Error	T-Stat	Signif
Constant		−6.7417	3.2749	−2.0586	.0543
Dens	−.13433	−.19707	.34264	−.57514	.5723
Var	.67798	.95889 −1	.24505 −1	3.9131	.0010

Dens = average artifact count per test pit.
Var = variance in artifact counts over test pits.

(1) Intercorrelations among items expected to occur in reduced proportions in physical finds populations will be attenuated because of the low reliability of both of any two counts being correlated. Because of this, intercorrelations among counts of rare items will suffer most from attenuation effects, and are expected to be "low."
(2) Correlations among counts of more abundant elements, counts that are more reliable, should show small attenuation effects and are expected, therefore, to be "high."
(3) Correlations between counts of rare and abundant elements will be attenuated to a fair degree due to the lower reliability of the rare item count, but less so by the reliability of the abundant item count. Thus correlations between rare and abundant item classes should have "moderate" and/or variable values.

Let me now try to translate these observations into substantively meaningful statements about what I think are some significant aspects of the structure of the archaeological record.

For some time now I have been conducting research into the Archaic occupation of extreme western Kentucky. One of the seemingly significant facts about the Archaic prehistory of this region is that sometime during middle to late Archaic times (perhaps around 5000 years ago), a change in settlement and subsistence patterns seems to have occurred that resulted in the establishment of numerous small, limited-activity camps, often located at higher elevations, that apparently were but briefly occupied or utilized. These camps give the impression of having resulted from the activities of mobile groups and yield only lithic artifacts. In short, the sites represent "plowzone" contexts, some of which could be called "lithic scatters." One of the primary objectives of my fieldwork and long-standing theoretical musings has been to improve our understanding of the cultural processes that influence the composition of the simple, limited-content assemblages that occur at these small hunter-gatherer sites.

At the same time, some archaeologists, notably Binford (1978a, 1978b, 1979, 1980, 1982) and Schiffer (1972, 1976), have been attempting to construct behavioral models to account for the ways in which various kinds of cultural items become a part of the archaeological record, what happens to these items subsequent to disposition, and what kinds of structure should be expected in the archaeological record in different contexts. It is now recognized, theoretically, that a certain behavioral structure exists in small lithic assemblages such as those mentioned above. Elements of that structure that appear important include the potential occurrence of (portable) curated implements, improvised or opportunistically acquired or produced tools, and by-products of lithic reduction activities that occurred at various sites. Although other variables such as the length of time a site was utilized must also be considered, this taxonomic framework appears generally useful in characterizing the content of the small lithic assemblages under consideration.

Curated artifacts are those that require some expenditure of energy to acquire or produce, and they are regularly maintained or repaired in an effort to keep them in the system for some time. Effectively, these artifacts have long "use-lives." Because of this, these items will be transported about from site to site within a "system" of small, temporary camps and generally will be deposited only when they are lost, eventually wear out, or are broken, etc. It may be suggested then, that curated tools will occur as the result of relatively "rare" depositional events, occurring almost at random.

Similar expectations may be suggested for the deposition of improvised or opportunistically acquired implements, for different reasons. Because such tools may be required only irregularly and occasionally, they should be introduced into the cultural residue at small, limited-activity camps irregularly and occasionally. These artifacts will be acquired, used briefly, and then will be discarded or "abandoned." Therefore these artifacts should result from "rare" depositional events, but should have a different distribution among sites than curated items because improvisational tools have effectively short use-lives. It follows that both classes of artifacts named above enter the archaeological record at temporary camps in small numbers as a result of largely independent depositional events, and that counts of these items should be low and unreliable.

While by-products of lithic reduction activities may enter the record at irregular, perhaps random, intervals, these artifacts will be deposited in large numbers, as clusters of individual items, deposited during individual lithic reduction episodes. These items will constitute abundant occurrences, and counts of them should be reliable.

Now, when the expectations of attenuation due to variable reliability are recalled, the following expectations seem reasonable. First, correlations among curated items and between improvised and curated item counts should be "low." Intercorrelations among lithic by-products counts should be "high." Correlations of counts of curated and improvisational classes with counts of lithic by-products should be "low" to "moderate" and variable. These effects are expected to be most well-defined in small samples of artifacts from the sites. Finally, rotated principal components should isolate "curated/improvised" and "lithic working" factors that are essentially independent of each other. Specifically, high density lithic by-products should be closely associated on a single component, while curated and improvised implements should be rather loosely correlated, perhaps independent, and distributed over more than one factor.

Table 11.14 presents summary data from surface collections acquired from 15 small campsites located along a spring-fed creek in Trigg County, Kentucky. I am aware of the problems with surface collections—they produce biased samples and unreliable counts. Classes of larger items, including some curated elements, are overrepresented in surface collections, while smaller item classes, e.g., small flakes, are underrepresented. Nevertheless, the data in Table 11.14 are generally in line with the expectations expressed above. Specifically, curated tools occur in low quantities and have somewhat random distributions over sites. The improvised class 'crude chopping tool' also occurs in low abundance but shows considerable clustering presumably because on the occasions when these tools were required, they might have been required in some numbers. Other possible explanations for the marked clustering of these items is that some sites were utilized longer than others, or that

TABLE 11.14
Distributions of 6 Classes of Surface-Collected Artifacts

Variable	Mean	Variance	Variance/Mean
1. Cutting Tools*	1.2	2.46	2.04
2. Projectile Point*	0.8	1.12	1.29
3. Scraping/Incising*	1.2	1.92	1.52
4. Crude chopper*	1.2	6.31	5.26
5. Utilized/retouched flake	10.2	79.74	7.82
6. Unmodified flakes	22.3	612.36	27.42

SOURCE: Nance, unpublished.
* = curated classes.

they have been misclassified. Lithic reduction by-products (flakes) occur in much higher densities, as do utilized and retouched flakes. Both classes exhibit significant clustering within sites.

Table 11.15 shows a matrix of correlations among counts of these different item classes over the 15 sites. In general, the predicted relationships are evident in the correlation matrix. A varimax rotated principal components solution on three factors (Figures 11.5 and 11.6) shows that the expectations arising from the foregoing considerations are met, at least approximately. High density flake counts are tightly associated on the first component, and these are largely independent of all other item classes. Curated item classes are generally loosely associated; and two of them, projectile points and formed scraping/incising tools, appear to be totally independent of the high density flake classes and each other, being highly associated with components two and three, respectively. Overall, the interpretation that component I represents a lithic working factor, while components II and III largely measure curation seems reasonably valid, assuming that the artifact taxonomy employed here is meaningful. The apparent association between formed cutting tools (CUTT) and chopping tools (CHOP), a curated and an improvised class in Figures 11.5 and 11.6, is just that: apparent. These item classes were isolated on fourth and fifth factors accounting for 13.8 and 12.9% of variance respectively. These two components are unique; no variables other than the two just noted are associated with them.

The fact that it is possible to deduce the factors expected to manifest themselves in quantitative analyses of archaeological data

TABLE 11.15
Correlation Matrix for Counts of Artifact Classes in Table 11.14

	CUTT	PJPT	SCIN	CHOP	UTRF	UMFL
CUTT	1.000					
PJPT	.533	1.000				
SCIN	.401	.123	1.000			
CHOP	.606	.600	.291	1.000		
UTRF	.599	.221	−.010	.590	1.000	
UMFL	.740	.361	.182	.684	.883	1.000

should not be surprising. Here, I have been able to do this with some accuracy, based on limited theoretical considerations coupled with some knowledge of how the reliability of archaeological measurements affects behavior of correlations among archaeological variables under certain circumstances, and a simple data set. When we are capable of making such predictions regularly, in widely varying, more complex contexts, we will have made substantial progress in establishing the *validity* of the theoretical concepts we work with. I now turn to a brief consideration of the validity of archaeological measurements.

Validity and Archaeological Measurement

The topics I have touched on so far are wide-ranging. The varied issues and ideas relating to assessing the validity of archaeological measurements and concepts are no less wide-ranging in content but appear in many ways to be much thornier than those relevant to reliability assessment. This is true for a number of reasons. First, there are a number of different ways in which validity may be considered, and empirically demonstrating validity of any sort seems in general a more intricate and difficult task than assessing reliability. Similarly, the task of empirical validation becomes more difficult as one moves from more concrete to more abstract ideas and concepts. Finally, it appears that the more abstract measurements, ideas, and concepts, the most important to the goals of anthropological archaeology, may require measurements on several different variables, these to be combined into some sort of composite measurement of the phenomenon about which information is sought. In short, we

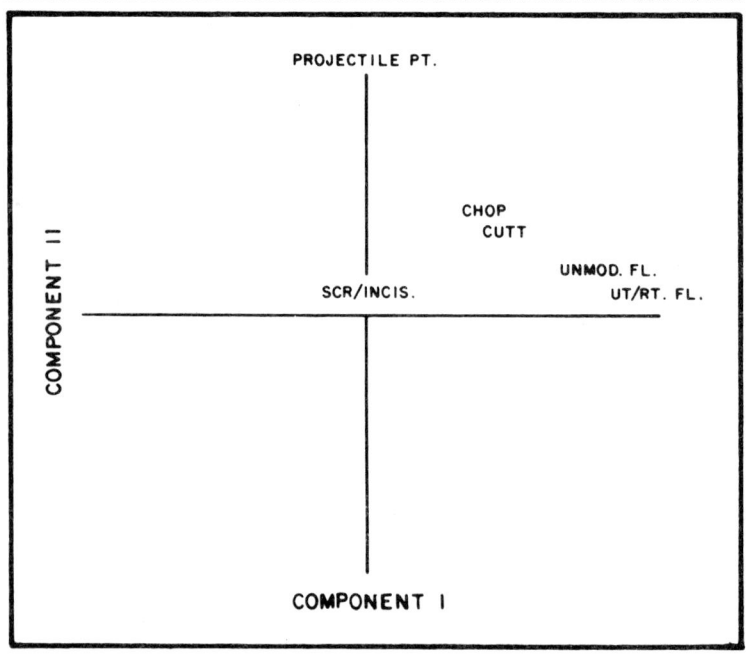

Figure 11.5 *Varimax* rotated principal components solution (components I and II) for counts of six classes of surface-collected artifacts from 15 small Archaic campsites in western Kentucky. PJPT = projectile point; CHOP = chopping tool; CUTT = formed cutting tool; UNMOD. FL. = unmodified flake; UT/RT. FL. = utilized and retouched flake; SCR/INCIS = formed scraping and incising tool. Component I appears to measure lithic-reduction activity, while Component II measures curation.

will have to construct composite scales to measure those variables that cannot be measured simply and directly.

In general, a measurement is *valid* if it measures what it purports to measure. This definition seems straightforward and simple, and it is. If it were the case that observations on most archaeological variables measured what they appear to, assessing the validity of these measurements would be reasonably easy. But it is one of the unfortunate truths of archaeology generally that most of the measurements we deal with do not measure the phenomenon they appear to, or at best, they measure that phenomenon imperfectly. An example, from zooarchaeology, will clarify.

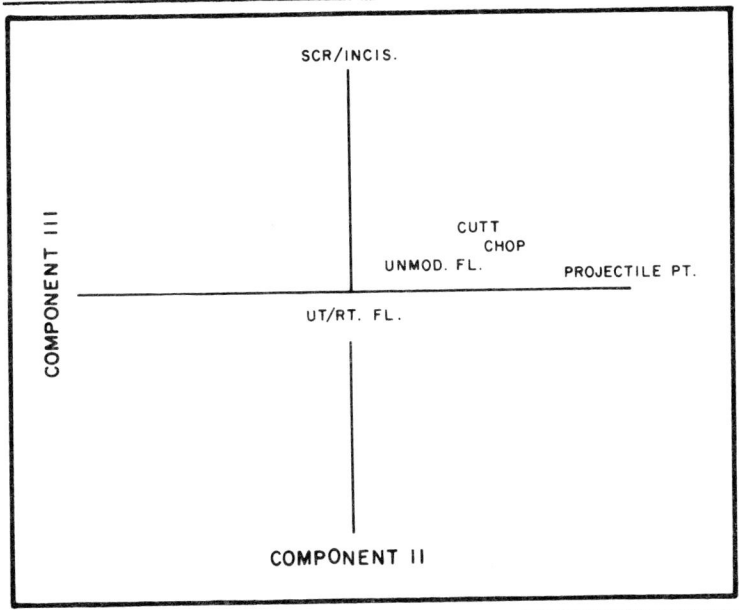

Figure 11.6 *Varimax* rotated principal components solution (Components II and III) for counts of six classes of surface-collected artifacts from 15 small Archaic campsites in western Kentucky. See Figure 11.5 for definitions of individual artifact classes. Both components appear to measure curation behavior.

If it were the case that the counts or proportions of bones of different species in archaeological sites yielded direct information about the relative importance of those species in prehistoric diet, then such counts would be valid measures of the relative dietary importance of the species observed. But they don't. Several factors interfere (see Cowgill 1970: 161-63 for a discussion in general terms). First, not all bones of animals preyed upon by prehistoric hunters were transported to their habitation sites. Similarly, of those bones that were actually present at the site, some will have disappeared as a result of differential preservation. Some bones may weather more and/or be chemically affected by soil conditions more than others, and some may be removed by scavengers such as domestic dogs, for example. Others will have been utilized to manufacture artifacts that might have been deposited at some other location in the settlement system. Also different animals have different numbers of skeletal elements and/or incomparable anatomical structures, and different species yield different amounts of food. Finally, natural processes may result in addition of bones of certain species to the archaeological assemblage, and different bones from various species have different diagnostic values. These factors, and others, act together to insure that simple bone counts do not measure relative dietary importance directly.

These counts do yield some information about dietary importance, but they also contain information about numerous other processes, and are therefore less than perfectly valid measures of dietary importance of different taxa. The tricky part is to find out the *degree of validity* of bone counts as a measure of relative dietary importance. Zooarchaeologists have spent a lot of time on this problem. If it could be shown that the degree of validity of this application of bone counts is high, then such counts could be used to measure dietary importance. If, on the other hand, it is shown than validity is unacceptably low, then these counts should not be used as a measure of dietary importance of species.

Some measurements also may be reliable but at the same time of low validity. For example, in attempts to bypass some of the problems cited above, several varieties of the *Minimum Number of Individuals* (MNI) index have been proposed. Grayson (1979, 1984) has discussed MNI at length and demonstrates, among other things, that details of MNI will vary depending on how an assemblage of bones is aggregated or subdivided over collection units or stratigraphic contexts. In Table 11.16 I present reliability coefficients calculated from the data presented by Grayson (1984: 37). These reliabilities were obtained by correlating MNI indices over different taxa and show (as does Grayson, using different methods) that the MNI counts are consistent (within limits) over different aggregation methods. But MNI indices are not valid measures of relative dietary importance of species (and have other problematic properties).

Another example of a reliable but somewhat invalid measurement may be found in the results of regional, probabilistic site survey. One of the reasons for using probabilistic sampling designs in regional surveys is to obtain estimates of the total numbers of sites (population total) in a given sampling area. In its simplest form, the procedure normally employed entails subdividing the area to be sampled into small areally defined sampling units. A certain proportion of these sampling units is selected for examination. The frequencies of sites in

TABLE 11.16
Reliability Coefficients for MNI Indices

Comparison	MNI Correlation
10 cm/Stratum	.977
10 cm/Site	.962
Stratum/Site	.985

NOTE: For raw data see Grayson, 1984: 37.

the sample units provide the data for estimating the population total.

Through various experiments on known site "populations" (e.g., Judge 1981; Plog 1976) it has been found that estimates of population totals derived in the above fashion usually overestimate the total number of sites in a given area, because of "edge" and "size" effects resulting from an interaction between the geometric properties of arbitrarily defined sampling units and variability in the sizes of the surface exposure of archaeological sites (Plog 1981; Nance 1983). Estimates so derived will be consistent (reliable), but if not corrected, will be upwardly biased, that is, they will suffer from somewhat lowered validity.

Some measurements may be valid for some purposes but less so for others, or their validity may shift from one context to another. For example, from the principal components analysis discussed earlier, associations among counts of lithic artifact classes appear, within limits, to be valid measures of curation, improvisation, and lithic working behavior. In past times it was fashionable to interpret associated sets of artifacts as representing "toolkits." Given my discussion of the concepts of curation, improvisation, and lithic reduction behavior, and the context under scrutiny, the toolkit interpretation of artifact associations appears to be invalid, although it might be more valid in other contexts, intrasite spatial analysis, for instance. The validity of measurements must, therefore, be evaluated relative to the purpose for which they are being taken. Thus one does not say that a given measurement is valid or invalid, rather one questions whether or not the given measurement is valid for obtaining the information required to investigate a stated problem.

The ideas and methods of validation have been developed mainly within the context of education and psychological testing, as is the case for reliability studies. Some of the methods that have been developed may be less useful in archaeology than in other fields of enquiry, because of differences in the phenomena studied, and because educators and psychologists, unlike archaeologists, work with living populations. Effective validation in archaeology may, therefore, require some originality and innovation on our part, either to adapt these methods to our discipline or to develop methods more appropriate for our purposes. Nevertheless, the framework developed within the educational/psychological testing context should be of value to us because the concepts are basic to all forms of scientific enquiry. In what follows I have simply tried to transfer ideas from the educational-psychological context more or less directly to archaeology and have attempted to identify parallel or analogous situations where those ideas may be applicable.

Content Validity

"*Content validity* is established through a rational analysis of the content of [an observation or series of observations], and its determination is based on individual, subjective judgement" (Allen and Yen 1979: 95). Thus assessment of content validity involves the application of individual knowledge to judge whether or not the information yielded by an archaeological measurement is in fact the information being sought.

"*Face validity*, sometimes called 'armchair' validity is established when a person examines [a measurement or series of measurements] and concludes that [they provide the relevant information]. . . . *Logical* or *sampling validity* is a more sophisticated version of face validity . . . [and] . . . involves the careful definition of the domain of behaviors to be measured . . .[and] . . . the logical design of [measurements] to cover all the important areas of this domain" (Allen and Yen 1979: 76). The salient feature of assessing content validity is subjective evaluation, without employing any external, objective criteria in the assessment. I engaged in subjective evaluation of content validity above when considering the validity of using bone counts to measure dietary importance, with negative results. Because it is subjective, content validation is the most error prone way of assessing validity.

Criterion-Related Validity

Criterion-related validity is tested by assessing the relationship between a measurement and some external criterion (or criteria) to determine the nature of information contained in the measurement. In educational/psychological testing the thing evaluated is usually a test of some sort, and the criterion is usually some measure of human performance in a relevant context. For example, if scores on university entrance examinations are shown to correlate highly with university grade point averages, then the entrance exam would be a valid predictor, or measure, of academic success.

In archaeology, we employ a similar approach not infrequently. For example, to assess whether or not a given ceramic type may be a valid temporal marker, we may seek to establish that that type's distribution in a proper stratigraphic context conforms to certain expectations, or we may use external standards such as radiocarbon dates to establish that type's temporal sensitivity. Another (simple) example can be provided by examining the data in Table 11.17. C. R. Nance and D. C. Hurst (1981), in investigating a certain "plowzone" site in Alabama, proposed that stratigraphically associated variability in certain classes of lithic waste represented a change in lithic working activities with time. As the data in the table show, however, the average size of flakes is highly, negatively correlated with excavation level ($r = -.995$), suggesting that the information contained in their data relates to postdepositional disturbance (by plowing, i.e., another "size effect"), not temporal change. In this case, the relationship of the criterion of artifact size to stratigraphic level was used to assess the validity of Nance's and Hurst's interpretation.

An important limitation to assessing criterion-related validity in archaeological enquiry is the difficulty experienced in identifying suitable criteria that can be used for validation. In the above simple examples stratigraphy and absolute dating were employed as useful criteria. In other cases identification of behavioral correlates in the data is an arduous and difficult task. Turning to ethnoarchaeology to facilitate the search for validation standards is a reasonable step recently employed by some (e.g., Binford 1978a, 1978b, 1979, 1980; Yellen 1977; and others). Finally, it must be noted that the reliability of the criterion itself is as important in validation as finding a criterion. If the criterion cannot be measured reliably, then it can never function as an adequate standard for validating any measurement.

In an effort to place the idea of criterion-related validation and its relation to archaeology in perspective, let me note that when one considers the sources of criteria for validation, there appear to be two elementary types of criterion-related validation process in archaeology: internal and external (Figure 11.7). *Internal* criteria are those

TABLE 11.17
Frequencies of Flakes of Varying Dimensions Over
Excavation Levels at the O'Neal Site, Alabama

Flake Dimension (mm)	Excavation Level					
	1	2	3	4	5	6
0.6-1.19	669	253	134	74	26	23
1.2-1.39	783	216	102	31	9	3
1.4-1.69	1011	222	90	44	15	6
1.7-2.09	849	162	88	33	3	4
2.1-6.49	793	144	52	17	3	1
Mean	2.00	1.78	1.68	1.56	1.37	1.24

SOURCE: Nance and Hurst, 1981: Table 5.1.
NOTE: The correlation between level and average flake size is $r = -.99$.

originating within the discipline itself; *external* criteria are "borrowed" from our sister disciplines in the "hard" and social sciences. As the incomplete trial formulation in Figure 11.6 shows, when archaeological enquiry is examined from the point of view of the origin of criteria for validation, we must consider the entire structure of the discipline itself.

Internally there appear to be two significant kinds of sources of validation criteria. *Contextual* criteria are those that can be identified using the archaeological method per se. This method can be used to search the (pre)historic record itself for validation criteria, or ethnographic and/or modern contexts. *Replicative* sources lie in those approaches that rely on "experimental" attempts to replicate past behaviors to account for observed archaeological configurations.

Finally, as Figure 11.7 implies, archaeologists are extraordinary borrowers. We employ validation criteria from numerous sciences (including some not shown in Figure 11.7), reflecting the fact that anthropological archaeology is committed to "holistic" study of cultures. However, a phenomenon that characterizes modern archaeology is the development of specialists (e.g., zooarchaeologists, palaeoethnobotanists, geoarchaeologists), heralding the continuing maturation of the discipline. Thus the subdivisions implied in Figure 11.7 are drawn with fuzzy lines; we are in the process of "internalizing" many of these external sources of validation criteria.

INTERNAL	EXAMPLES
CONTEXTUAL	
Historic Record	stratigraphy, seriation
Ethnoarchaeology	functional organizations
Modern Refuse	recycling behaviors
REPLICATIVE	
Flint Knapping	lithic working patterns
Kinematics	artifact usewear
Earthworks	taphonomy, soil movement
EXTERNAL	
Physical Sciences	absolute dating
Biological Sciences	animal/plant ecology, evolutionary theory
Mathematics	simulation, probability theory
Earth Sciences	sedimentary processes, paleoenvironment
Social Sciences	ethnographic analogies

Figure 11.7 Sources of validation criteria in archaeology.

Construct Validity

A measurement's construct validity can be thought of as the degree to which that measurement reflects a given theoretical construct. Construct validation is an on-going, cyclical process that embodies the very essence of scientific enquiry in any discipline. In general, construct validation proceeds as follows: First, based on theoretical ideas about the phenomenon of interest, certain predictions or expectations are formulated. These expectations state how measurements should behave under specified circumstances. Relevant data are then collected and examined in an appropriate manner. If the expectations of the theory are met, then the validity of the theoretical construct is enhanced. If not, several conclusions must be considered: the data examined were not collected properly, the theory is wrong, or the measurement employed does not measure the phenomenon of interest.

Because assessing construct validity is the very process of defining the building blocks from which general theory is constructed, an in-depth exploration obviously cannot be undertaken here. An important point should be made, however. The maturity of any discipline is directly proportional to the abundance of valid theoretical constructs available in that discipline. Thus assessment of construct validity is an activity that should assume more importance in archaeology as time goes on.

Multitrait-Multimethod Validity

It may sometimes be possible to measure two or more phenomena by two or more methods. If so, then the pattern of relationships among the reliabilities of the measurements, correlations between two different methods of measuring the same phenomenon, and correlations between measurements of unrelated phenomena using the same method may provide useful information about how well different measurements methods "converge" on the same phenomenon, how well different methods of measurement "discriminate" between different phenomena, and whether or not "method bias" is present in the measurements. The reader is referred to Campbell and Fiske (1959) and Sullivan and Feldman (1979) for discussion of this and related methods.

Factorial Validity

Factorial validity assessment is a form of construct validity testing made possible by the use of "factor analysis." In seeking factorial validity, factors, hypothetical variables that are thought to influence values of one or more observed variables, are defined. Empirical measurements on relevant variables are then obtained, and patterns of intercorrelations among them are analyzed using factor or principal components methods.

If the sample data sort out into clusters of correlated variables that correspond in a meaningful way to the underlying factors that are hypothesized to exist in the data, then the validity of the constructs employed in the analysis may be accepted. The earlier discussion of the curation factor in small lithic assemblages is a simple example of seeking factorial validity.

Factor-analytic techniques are widely employed in archaeology. For the most part, however, they seem to have functioned primarily as descriptive, data-reduction, structure-seeking devices, employed in serendipitous ways, rather than as a general method of studying the possible existence of higher-order, more abstract relationships in archaeological data. Although assessing factorial validity may be a tricky business (see Carmines and Zeller 1979: 59-70), it may turn out that more sophisticated use of factor analysis may be helpful in assessing the validity of archaeological measurements under the right conditions.

Conclusion

The above discussion indicates that assessing the reliability and validity of archaeological measurements is a complex undertaking, and my treatment of these topics here has been far from adequate. I have dealt mostly with fairly obvious issues and have concentrated more on reliability than validity, mainly because validity assessment, as noted above, is a vastly more intricate and involved task than is assessment of reliability. Adequate determination of the reliability and validity of archaeological measurement is something that will take some time to achieve.

Although I have not surveyed it here, the recent literature does provide reason for optimism, however, because it appears that archaeologists are beginning to give these issues some thought (e.g., Daniels 1980; Dibble and Barnard 1980; Fish 1978; McGuire et al. 1982). At the same time, although I have no empirical data to validate it, my impression is that most archaeologists are simply not consciously aware of the issues of reliability and validity and/or have no formal knowledge about how to go about assessing reliability and validity. That the latter is true is attested to by the fact that the term "reliability" is often misused (e.g., Nicholson 1983). Also, formal methods of testing are of course statistical, and traditionally many archaeologists and students seem to have some inbred fear of numbers. I think that this attitude is changing, however. Many more of the archaeology undergraduate and graduate students I am seeing these days are computer literate and appear to be much more favorably disposed toward "sadistics" than was the case ten years ago.

From my point of view there appear to be at least two things that can be done to stimulate activity in this important area. First, we can introduce ourselves and our students to formal methods of reliability and validity assessment and to the principles of experimental design. Second, we can collect data in ways that permit reliability and validity to be assessed from them and make these data widely available, either through publication or other means.

Notes

1. By selecting replicate samples at two sites where large numbers of test pits were excavated, the total number of samples was increased to 20.

2. Although I have used the terms "correct" and "incorrect" to describe the two possible outcomes for an artifact assignment, it should be noted that it is really not the correctness or incorrectness of the outcomes that is at issue here. What was really under investigation in our experiment was how well the two forms of presenting definitions communicated our perception of the content of several different artifact classes. We would like to think that our classes for the artifacts were correct in the strict sense, but this is not a position I would care to defend to the death. In the long run, however, the correctness of the classes used by us is irrelevant. It is how the participants responded to our means of communicating with them that is at issue.

3. The reader will have noted that the split-halves method also measures the internal consistency of a set of observations. In fact, the statistics used in this section can be calculated for data in split-halves form (Allen and Yen 1979: 79). The split-halves method may be related to the internal consistency methods discussed in this section in the following way. Consider splitting a sample of data not into just two halves but into quarters, eighths, etc., until the data are totally subdivided into n parts, so that each part corresponds to a single observation. If the correlation between each item and every other item is calculated, one obtains an interitem correlation matrix. The essential information required for deriving measures of internal consistency reliability is contained in this matrix.

4. It is important to note a problem here. In calculating reliabilities for the snail counts, correlations between counts were calculated over levels of test pits. Thus the experimental design employed was split-halves, each sample half consisting of a single test pit. The "length" of the test is, therefore $n = 2$. The problem arises because the assumption of independence of counts is violated. That is, a count for a given level of a test pit is not totally independent of counts in under- and overlying levels. Thus pairs of measurements are properly *parallel*, but different parallel measurements do not represent random selections. The net effect of this is to restrict total variance in the counts and to cause correlations among errors within a test pit. Thus the calculated reliabilities are not necessarily good estimates of reliability. However, all coefficients are affected equally, and so as long as the reader bears this in mind no harm will be done.

The problem becomes more acute in examining the behavior of the reliability coefficients, where there is a need to talk about statistical significance. But because there is an important point to be made, I have proceeded with the analysis. I demonstrate that the relationships of interest also exist in data that do not suffer from the shortcoming noted above, so apparently it is not the lack of independence that produces these relationships.

Acknowledgments

This paper is a revised version of a paper presented in the quantitative methods symposium which was a part of the 50th annual meeting of the Society for American Archaeology held in Denver, Colorado in May 1985. I wish to thank Mark Aldenderfer for the invitation to participate in that symposium. I am also grateful to George Cowgill for his thoughtful comments and discussions on the topic of reliability. I express my gratitude to Heather Dumka and Gerry Conaty who administered the artifact classification experiments described herein, and to those who participated in those experiments. Several people were of assistance in obtaining the data for the test pit sampling studies and I am grateful for their help. Finally, practically all of the research that made this paper possible was supported by grants from the Social Sciences and Humanities Research Council of Canada. I am grateful to S.S.H.R.C. for their generous support of my research.

References

Allen, M. J., and W. M. Yen. 1979. *Introduction to Measurement Theory*. Monterrey: Brooks-Cole Publishing Company.

Binford, L. R. 1964. A consideration of archaeological research design. *American Antiquity* 29: 425-41.

Binford, L. R. 1971. Mortuary practices: their study and their potential. In Approaches to the Social Dimensions of Mortuary Practices, ed J. A. Brown, pp. 6-29. Society for American Archaeology *Memoir* No. 25.

Binford, L. R. 1978a. *Nunamuit Ethnoarchaeology: A Case Study in Archaeological Formation Processes*. New York: Academic Press.

Binford, L. R. 1978b. Dimensional analysis of behavior and site structures: learning from an Eskimo hunting stand. *American Antiquity* 43: 330-71.

Binford, L. R. 1979. Organization and formation processes: looking at curated technologies. *Journal of Anthropological Research* 35: 255-73.

Binford, L. R. 1980. Willow smoke and dogs' tails: hunter-gatherer systems and archaeological site formation. *American Antiquity* 45: 4-20.

Binford, L. R. 1984. The archaeology of place. *Journal of Anthropological Archaeology* 1: 5-31.

Blalock, H. M. 1960. *Social Statistics*. New York: McGraw-Hill.

Bobrowsky, P. T. 1982. The quantitative and qualitative significance of fossil and subfossil gastropod remains in archaeology. Unpublished Master's thesis. Department of Archaeology. Simon Fraser University.

Brown, W. 1910. Some experimental results in the correlation of mental abilities. *British Journal of Psychology* 3: 296-332.

Campbell, D. T. and D. W. Fiske. 1959. Convergent and discriminant validation by the multitrait-multimethod matrix. *Psychological Bulletin* 56: 85-105.

Carmines, E. and R. Zeller. 1979. *Reliability and Validity Assessment*. Beverly Hills: Sage.

Cohen, J. 1960. A coefficient of agreement for nominal scales. *Educational and Psychological Measurement* 20: 37-46.

Cowgill, G. L. 1970. Some sampling and reliability problems in archaeology. In *Archeologie et Calculateurs: Problemes Semiologiques et Mathematiques*, pp. 161-175. Paris: Editions du Centre National de la Recherche Scientifique.

Cronbach, L. 1951. Coefficient alpha and the internal structure of tests. *Psychometrika* 16: 297-334.

Daniels, S. G. H. 1972. Research design models. In *Models in Archaeology*, ed. D. L. Clarke, pp. 201-29. London: Methuen.

Dibble, H. L. and M. C. Bernard. 1980. A comparative study of basic edge angle measurement techniques. *American Antiquity* 45: 857-65.

Ferguson, G. A. 1971. *Statistical Analysis in Psychology and Education*. New York: McGraw-Hill.

Fish, P. R. 1978. Consistency in archaeological measurement and classification: a pilot study. *American Antiquity* 43: 86-89.

Grayson, D. 1979. On the quantification of vertebrate archaeofaunas. *Advances in Archaeological Method and Theory*, 2: 199-237.

Grayson, D. 1984. *Quantitative Zooarchaeology*. Orlando: Academic Press.

Guilford, J. P. and B. Fruchter. 1973. *Fundamental Statistics in Psychology and Education*. New York: McGraw-Hill.
Harper, D. 1978. Misclassification in epidemiological surveys. *American Journal of Public Health* 54: 1882-86.
Kuder, G. G. and M. W. Richardson. 1937. The theory of the estimation of test reliability. *Psychometrika* 2: 151-60.
Magnusson, D. M. 1967. *Test Theory*. Reading: Addison-Wesley.
McGuire, R. H., J. Whittaker, M. McGuire, and R. Swain. 1982. A consideration of observational error in lithic use wear analysis. *Lithic Technology* 11: 59-63.
Nance, J. D. 1981. Statistical fact and archaeological faith: two models in small sites sampling. *Journal of Field Archaeology* 8: 151-65.
Nance, J. D. 1983. Regional sampling in archaeological survey: the statistical perspective. *Advances in Archaeological Method and Theory*, Vol. 6, ed. M. B. Schiffer, pp. 289-356. New York: Academic Press.
Nance, J. D. and B. F. Ball. 1986. No surprises? the reliability and validity of test pit sampling. *American Antiquity* (in press).
Nance, C. R. and D. C. Hurst. 1981. Statistical approaches to shallow site archaeology: analysis of the O'Neal site, Jefferson County, Alabama. In *Plowzone Archaeology: Contributions to Theory and Technique*, eds. M. J. O'Brien and D. E. Lewarch, pp. 159-86. Nashville: Vanderbilt University Publications in Anthropology, No. 27.
Nicholson, B. A. 1980. An investigation of the potential of freshwater mussels as seasonal indicators in archaeological sites. Unpublished Master's Thesis. Department of Archaeology. Simon Fraser University.
Nicholson, B. A. 1983. A comparative evaluation of four sampling techniques and of the reliability of microdebitage as a cultural indicator in regional survey. *Plains Anthropologist* 28: 273-81.
Plog, F. 1981. *Managing Archaeology: A Background Document for Cultural Resource Management on the Apache-Sitgreaves National Forests, Arizona*. U.S. Department of Agriculture, Forest Service, Southwest Region, Report No. 1, Albuquerque.
Plog, S. 1976. Relative efficiencies of sampling techniques for archaeological surveys. In *The Early Mesoamerican Village*, ed. K. V. Flannery, pp. 136-58. New York: Academic Press.
Robinson, W. S. 1957. The statistical measurement of agreement. *American Sociological Review* 22: 17-25.
Roulon, P. J. 1939. A simplified procedure for determining the reliability of a test by split-halves. *Harvard Educational Review* 9: 99-103.
Schaaf, J. M. 1981. A method for reliable and quantifiable subsampling of archaeological features. *Midcontinental Journal of Archaeology* 6: 219-48.
Schiffer, M. B. 1972. Systemic context and archaeological context. *American Antiquity* 37: 156-65.
Schiffer, M. B. 1975. The effects of occupation span on site content. In *The Cache River Archaeological Project: An Experiment in Contract Archaeology*, assembled by M. B. Schiffer and J. H. House, pp. 265-69. Arkansas Archaeological Survey, Research Series, No. 8.
Schiffer, M. B. 1976. *Behavioral Archaeology*. New York: Academic Press.
Schiffer, M. B. 1979. The place of lithic use-wear in studies of behavioral archaeology. In *Lithic Use-Wear Analysis*, ed. B. E. Hayden, pp. 15-25. New York: Academic Press.
Schuessler, K. 1971. *Analyzing Social Data: A Statistical Orientation*. Boston: Houghton-Mifflin.
Spearman, C. 1904. The proof and measurement of association between two things. *American Journal of Psychology* 15: 72-101.
Spearman, C. 1910. Correlation calculated from faulty data. *British Journal of Psychology* 3: 271-95.
Speth, J. D. and G. A. Johnson. 1976. Problems in the use of correlation for the investigation of tool kits and activity areas. In *Cultural Change and Continuity: Essays in Honor of James B. Griffin*, ed. C. E. Cleland, pp. 35-57. New York: Academic Press.
SPSS Inc. 1983. $SPSS^x$ User's Guide. New York: McGraw-Hill.

Stanley, J. 1971. Reliability. In *Educational Measurement*, ed. R. Thorndike, pp. 356-442. Washington: American Council on Education.
Stevens, S. S. 1951. Mathematics, measurement and psychophysics. In *Handbook of Experimental Psychology*, ed. S. S. Stevens, pp. 1-49. New York: Wiley.
Sullivan, J. L. and S. Feldman. 1979. *Multiple Indicators: An Introduction*. Beverly Hills: Sage.
Winer, B. J. 1971. *Statistical Principles in Experimental Design*. New York: McGraw-Hill.
Yellen, J. E. 1977. *Archaeological Approaches to the Present: Models for Reconstructing the Past*. New York: Academic Press.

12

Quantitative Burial Analyses as Interassemblage Comparison

James A. Brown

Introduction

In the past 20 years that have transpired since computers first engaged in quantitative analysis of archaeological remains, considerable experience with substantial data sets has afforded us with a perspective on analytical utility that should have placed us in an excellent position to evaluate archaeological practice. We must have learned something from the experience of these years. However, one may even ask, given the emphasis on quantitative analysis that has become standard in the computerized world of contemporary science, has such analysis in archaeology lived up to expectations?

No better basis for such a review exists then in the basic enterprise of interassemblage comparison. The formalization of such comparisons started with Petrie's (1899) chronological solution to the variability of predynastic Egyptian grave lot assemblages. From these simple beginnings students of archaeological comparison have developed a series of methods to cover such diverse problems as the taxonomic differences among cultures, functional differences in settlement assemblages, and even degrees of social ranking among burials. Central to this development has been the refinement of Petrie's problem to become what we recognize today as seriation. With this refinement has come an enlargement of the problem into the general study of sequence ordering. Although seriation has retained a pride of place in interassemblage comparison, it remains only one aspect of interassemblage analysis.

In the past interassemblage comparisons have been almost entirely conceived of as analyses of whole assemblages. When phylogenic, historical, and evolutionary relationships between cultures were central research questions, the very generality in which these relationships were conceived called for little more than measures of gross relative similarity. These measures could be supplied by a quantitative methodology in which the total assemblage of traits, artifact types, or cultural elements were cast into a single matrix. Since then, the basic warrant for this "omnibus" approach to interassemblage analysis has gone the way of the culture-historical paradigm. Past approaches that involved large interassemblage matrix comparisons no longer attract archaeologists as they once did. The question remains, however, whether growth in theory in the meantime has outstripped methods of whole assemblage comparison, and to what extent have these methods lagged behind theoretical developments?

Background

Interassemblage analysis of the type described above dominated the archaeological literature in the early period of quantification (cf. Clarke 1968; Doran and Hodson 1975; Hodson et al. 1971). Some of the earliest computerized applications were whole assemblage comparisons (Binford and Binford 1966; Deetz 1965; Freeman and Brown 1964; Hole and Shaw 1967). Early applications centered on matrix ordering techniques, factor analysis, and cluster analysis, which were methods that dominated the solution of seriation problems and the analysis of settlements, activity areas, and toolkits (Cowgill 1968).

Since this flush of early work two developments have taken place. First, the old archaeological stand-by, seriation, has been affected by both a methodological sophistication (Kendall 1971; Cowgill 1972) and a maturation in our understanding of the theory of temporal ordering (e.g., de Barros 1982; Dunnell 1971; Marquardt 1978; Read 1979). Our view of seriation as a method has been tempered by the knowledge that variability among assemblages is affected by spatial and functional factors, sampling and measurement error, inadequate typological separation, and variability in the span of site occupation (de Barros 1982). These factors affect the fidelity of the mathematical applications to the changes that occur with the passage of time and render untenable the simplistic chronological assumption behind the comparison of whole assemblages (Cannon 1983).

As a consequence, analytical problems have shifted away from casting an entire assemblage into a matrix "solution" and toward the application of specific mathematical methods to better controlled problems that require a selection of variables. Most frequently, these variables are not in the form of counts and percentages of archaeological objects. In this respect, the theory-guided research problems of today have turned their back on the basic conceptualizations of interassemblage analyses of the past (Clark 1982).

A recognition of the theoretical necessity of a shift in emphasis came early. In place of the use of interassemblage variation to express differences in cultural affiliation arose the position that such differences expressed either social change (Deetz 1965) or social structure (Longacre 1966). These shifts in problem led to a battery of techniques that have become more closely gauged to the anthropological conceptualizations of the archaeological problems (e.g., Plog 1980). The result was development of many new methods: network analysis, diversity analysis (Kintigh 1984), spatial analysis (Hodder and Orton 1976), and graph theory approaches (Renfrew and Cooke 1979). A relatively small number of whole assemblage approaches remain. One of these is the analysis of burial assemblages.

Problem

Discussion of interassemblage analysis should take into account recent criticisms of multivariate methods, considering the strength these methods have in such analysis. Criticisms of multivariate applications in archaeology have directed attention toward the necessity of (a) fitting our mathematical models more carefully to the analytical problems, and (b) rethinking our analytical problems to escape the straight jacket imposed by the structure of established mathematical models (Christenson and Read 1977). The former admonition is directed toward the obvious shortcomings of borrowed models in any discipline. But the latter raises a more subtle problem in the constraints that the structure of borrowed mathematical models impose on the approach to the problem in the first place. The rush to methodological application before theory has been adequately developed has led repeatedly to spurious quantification (Binford 1977).

For instance, most of the popular multivariate methods, such as factor and cluster analysis, are widely acknowledged to impose a structure on the solution. The imposition is particularly forced when the input data are not structured compatibly (Vierra and Carlson 1981; Aldenderfer and Blashfield 1984). As a result, not only are misleading solutions reported, but the very conceptualization of the archaeological problems is easily distorted to conform to the structure of a particular mathematical model. But despite these drawbacks, factor and cluster analysis continue to enjoy great favor—perhaps because archaeologists have persuaded themselves that the solutions to archaeological problems are expressed as factors and clusters to be found in the form dictated by the mathematical models (Benfer 1972; Binford and Binford 1966).

The most commonly advocated remedy is to insist on simple univariate and bivariate analyses before undertaking multivariate computations (Christenson and Read 1977; Thomas 1976). Exploratory data analysis represents a formal approach to preanalysis screening of variables that substantially helps to clean up the technical problems of multivariate analysis (Lewis n.d.). However, the basic question of theoretical support for these methods remains problematical if not very questionable.

Burial Analysis

Of the various types of interassemblage analysis the more interesting are those having to do with variables that can range in variety and quantity from 0 to n. When all variables are represented in a matrix, zero entries typically predominate. The distribution of variables per site or burial is typically very skewed with a modal, and even median value, of around 1. The "Reverse J" distributions that result are incapable of transformation to anything approaching a normal distribution. Variables are typically sparse in the matrices generated from such distributions. Consequently, these matrices are difficult to analyze from a parametric statistical standpoint. Techniques for circumventing some of the problems created by skewed distributions have been developed (Speth and Johnson 1976). On the other hand, the strength of these distributions is the simplicity of the underlying structure. Methods for accessing this underlying structure are key to the success of any analysis.

Of this category of interassemblage comparisons I will restrict my attention to burial analysis because this category represents a special case in which the collection of graves constitutes the sampling population. Because all the variability is conceived of as a product of a deliberate set of acts, variance otherwise consigned to error first must be considered as variance to be explained. Differential absences of specific attributes, whether rare or common, must be treated as products of deliberate burial treatment rather than as the byproducts of sampling or excavatory strategy (O'Shea 1981). For instance, grave goods typically are unevenly distributed in even the rich cemeteries. At Moundville only 36% of the 1975 burials were accompanied by grave goods of any kind (Peebles and Kus 1977). This figure is not much better than Middle Archaic Period hunter-gatherer cemeteries. At the Black Earth site in southern Illinois, 27% of 124 burials had grave goods (Jefferies and Lynch 1983). The only exceptions are situations where differential preservation and/or recovery of attributes of burial treatment or grave furnishings varies within a single site. In addition to highly skewed attribute distributions, the comparison of grave lots is complicated by the conditional potential association of attributes to each other (Goldstein 1980; O'Shea 1984). All of these characteristics constitute features of the data that are inherent in burial analysis. The high amount of cultural information that must be assumed to be contained within the variability of co-associational matrices makes burial analysis a demanding type of interassemblage analysis. The consequences of these difficulties are problems that must be considered when specific studies are conducted.

Standard multivariate methods have constituted the mainstay of burial analysis from the beginning. The computational strengths of computers lend themselves to the comparison of burial attributes and grave furnishings in large samples. Both principle components analysis and cluster analysis have been popular, and with few exceptions there has been little critical examination of the suitability of these methods (Braun 1977, 1979; Hatch 1976; O'Shea 1984; Peebles 1974; Tainter 1975b). In fact, most criticism has been directed toward the relative utility of factor and cluster analysis (O'Shea 1984; Tainter 1975b) and to detailed critiques of attribute coding procedures (Braun 1981). Critical though these problems can be, they are small compared to the basic issue of how well these multivariate methods serve the research goal.

How important is revealed by the role that the monothetic-divisive approach in cluster analysis has in the works by analysts following the Saxe-Binford theory of mortuary studies (Goldstein 1980; King 1976; Mainfort 1979; Peebles 1972, 1974; Rothschild 1979; Tainter 1975a). This particular method conforms well to certain critical expectations of that theory. As Saxe (1970) has developed the theory, discrete burial types are viewed as expressions of the critical social identities of the persona of the dead that are recognized as requiring separate treatment. Thus each burial type is regarded as having been socially warranted by the dead's possession of a critical set of social identities. These identities could be as diverse as a political office, circumstance of death, social maturity, and membership in kin unit or sodality.

Given these expectations, cluster analysis naturally fits this theoretical perspective as a technique for grouping individuals by qualitative social characteristics (Figure 12.1). Of the different techniques possible in cluster analysis the monothetic-divisive technique suggests itself because of the analogy that can be made to the decision tree approach adopted by Saxe. The approach is important because it is a method for detecting the degree of hierarchical organization in the system. In line with this decision tree approach, the monothetic-divisive method starts with a single division of the burial population and divides in half each cluster of burials so created until each burial is its own cluster, or subdivision is halted by some criteria, such as sudden drop in information (Peebles 1972). At each step the clusters are divided into daughter clusters according to the criterion that maximizes the dissimilarity between these subdivisions. As a result, each cluster is a division of a larger cluster based on the presence or absence of a single defining nominal attribute (Goldstein 1980; Peebles 1974; Tainter 1975a, b). Thus the cluster diagram

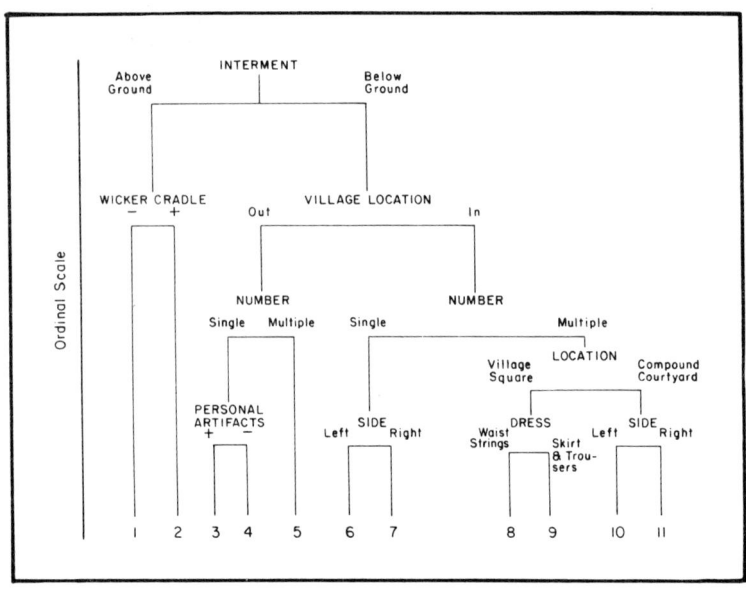

Figure 12.1 Key diagram of LoDaaga disposal of the dead classes with defining criteria for the eleven recognized disposal types (modified after Saxe, 1970: Figure 8).

mimics Saxe's decision tree in certain key respects that facilitate the application of Saxe's criteria for quantifying the degree of hierarchical organization in the structure of mortuary practices. As a result, the strings of ordered attributes that define each burial treatment type can be thought of analogically to correspond to a similar ordered string of identity distinctions. Ideally, the cluster diagram could be represented by a decision tree—if all information on burial practices of a society were known. In practice, there are many reasons why this ideal is not likely to be approached, but the point remains nonetheless that monothetic-divisive techniques in burial analysis have some theoretical warrant.

While monothetic-divisive techniques give priority to order in the string of attributes defining a cluster, polythetic-agglomerative techniques accord all attributes equal weight. These techniques build clusters by attachment, and a large number of procedures are available (Aldenderfer and Blashfield 1984). Both average linkage (Rothschild 1979) and single linkage (Hodson 1977) have been employed, usually with a Jaccard coefficient that ignores mutual absences of attributes between two graves (Hodson 1977; Peebles 1974). The strength of the polythetic-agglomerative techniques is their conservative expectations: Assumptions respecting the attributes are kept to a minimum, and large-order expectations respecting the structure of attribute interrelationships are shied away completely. The weakness of these techniques is that structures underlying variability are unlikely to emerge from an analysis that distances itself as much as possible from encoding measures that potentially relate to such structures in the first place. Polythetic and monothetic procedures have generally provided confirmatory support of each other. They have coincided best where wealth and symbols of status provide a mutually confirmatory redundancy of artifacts (Mainfort 1979, 1985; Hatch 1976; Peebles 1974).

Support for the use of polythetic-agglomerative techniques comes largely from the relatively uncomplicated way in which burials are grouped into clusters of progressively decreasing homogeneity as one moves from the grouping of burials to higher order arrangements (Hatch 1974, 1976; Hodson 1977; Mainfort 1979; O'Shea 1984; Pearson 1981; Peebles 1974; Rothschild 1979). For the most part polythetic-agglomerative techniques offer an easy-to-understand solution to clustering—much as it could be achieved on the laboratory sorting table, if such a physical arrangement could be achieved in practice. In this regard such analyses have followed a general, loosely warranted direction prevalent in cluster analytical applications generally.

All methodological differences aside, so much of the results depend upon what is included or excluded from the input matrix that it is surprising so little attention has been devoted to this problem. Although most studies take the grave goods as the universe for comparative study, there is no anthropological rationale for so restricting comparison. Goldstein (1980) showed how different were the clusters when burial and limb position was included along with grave goods. An analysis of cemetery data that included both limb positioning and grave associations was not only markedly different in cluster structure than an analysis on grave associations alone, but the inclusion of limb position revealed them to be far more critical in defining clusters at the higher levels than associations alone (Figure 12.2). Her findings open up the whole matter of what constitutes the universe of burial attributes in any particular case, and in so doing lay bare a weakness of cluster analysis of interassemblage variability that is strictly empirical in task orientation.

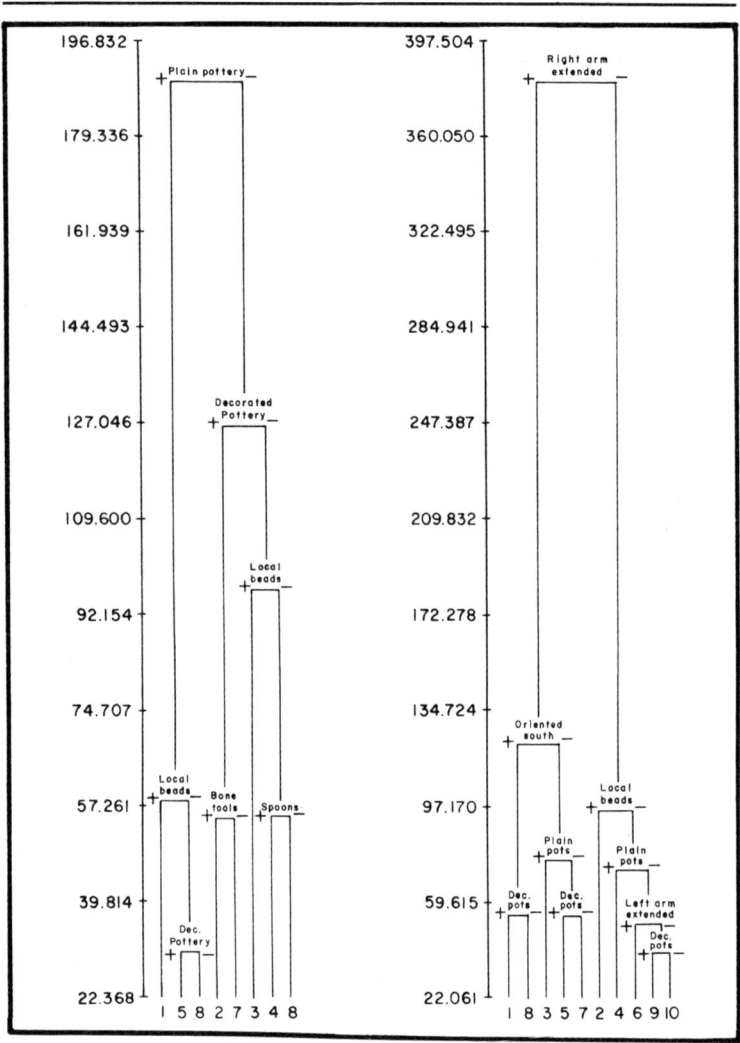

Figure 12.2 Key diagram of Schild archaeological site disposal of the dead classes. Key diagrams are generated by monothetic-divisive cluster analysis using the information statistic. The left-hand key is generated from artifact associations only; the right-hand key is from both associations and skeletal positioning (after Goldstein, 1980: Figures 22, 23).

Factor Analysis

The strength of cluster analysis should not blind us to its deficiencies. They require a restriction to nominal categories, and they limit the extraction of all the covariation in the data set. Spaulding (1982), Cowgill (1982), and others have delved into some of the shortcomings of object clustering as opposed to variable association, and their insights apply to burial analysis as well as to artifact classification. In practice it is possible to overcome some of these limitations through preanalysis of the variables in a R-mode form. This mode examines the interactions among variables alone or in combination as against the interburial interactions of Q-mode. Although many different procedures are potentially useful in this regard, all preanalysis basically boils down to a screening procedure for filtering out cross-cutting variability exhibited by variable associations and substituting newly created "clean" attributes for the single observationally given attributes. Factor analysis is commonly employed for this purpose in burial analysis (Braun 1979; Mainfort 1979; O'Shea 1984). Where factor analysis and related techniques have been employed in the Q-mode form, the search for factors or underlying dimensions leads in a direction that is truly obscure. The covariation among grave lots results in patterns that are entirely post hoc, while being without the benefit of a set of attributes to act as defining criteria.

Problems and Solutions

Although there are limitations to the extent that filtering can be successful, the ideal objective is clear—to recover attributes most faithfully conforming to expectation of the corresponding social identities and to include in the input matrix as many of these as possible. The pursuit of this ideal brings us to a critical juncture in this retrospect. The close approximation of monothetic-divisive techniques to a single theoretical stance alerts us to the incapacity of that technique to distance itself from the Saxe-Binford theory. Thus it does not allow us the freedom to quantify alternative theoretical postures. The Saxe-Binford theory assumes that burials and grave associations are directly representative of the important social statuses of the community to which the cemetery belonged. Since this assumption has been criticized, it is fair to conclude that what is regarded as an assumption is a problem to be determined analytically. However, I might add that the growth of criticism of this theory has not gone hand in hand with the construction of methodologies that serve the alternative theoretical perspectives (Pader 1982).

As partial solution to the technical problems of Q-mode analysis some researchers have advocated a strategy of multiple analyses using different techniques to overcome a problem that intercorrelation among social identities could have in masking the importance of any one of them in the definition of social rank or other indicators of organizations behind burial practices. This solution, partially taken up by Hatch (1976), Peebles (1974), and O'Shea (1984), tries to address the limitations of Q-mode analysis by comparing as many methods as possible. In line with this strategy, these students of burial analysis accepted as firm those solutions that were replicated by both monothetic-divisive and polythetic-agglomerative techniques. However, this strategy will provide confirmation of most conservative sort—largely in those cases where ample redundancy exists in artifact associational patterns. Where associations are meager or the sample size is small, a conservative position on Q-mode analysis will fail to yield any satisfaction at all.

All of this leads me to conclude that Q-mode analysis necessitates an enlargement of the preanalysis phase and that further progress in alternative analytical strategies will have to concentrate on R-mode analysis instead. The preanalysis phase can benefit from approaches similar to those taken by Braun (1979) in his examination of the distributional pattern of two socially significant categories of artifacts among graves from some Havana Hopewell burial mounds in Illinois. An R-mode factor analysis (PCA) enabled him to conclude that the eigenvectors effectively isolated three sets of variables, one of which was a mortuary set of artifacts. His analysis led to clear separation of status-defining associations with certain grave goods from corporate membership defining associations with grave constructions and furniture. Although the latter had been argued by Tainter (1975a, 1977) to indicate individual status by virtue of energy expenditure principles, R-mode analysis clearly separated out this category as indicators of corporate membership. This result, I might add, did not invalidate his principles, only the bridging argument that applied them. The success of this analysis had more to do with its design than the techniques, and it indicates the necessity for Q-mode analysis to be preceded by a battery of appropriately designed attribute screening procedures.

A more drastic solution can be advocated that side-steps Q-mode analysis as the essential emphasis in burial analysis. The burden of analysis can be more appropriately centered on log-linear methods

(Kerber 1986). Such a shift will, however, necessitate an adoption of robust models of attribute associational expectations. These models will of necessity have to be largely deductive in origin, based on expectations concerning the social significance of differences in burial treatment and grave associations among different ages and between the sexes, for instance. Successful use of demographic characteristics by Kerber (1986), O'Shea (1984), and Palkovich (1980) illustrate the potential for these characteristics for defining useful expectations in a burial model. As a consequence, the limited circle of expectations adopted by Braun (1979) respecting the preferred context of use of status-defining (solely mortuary) versus utilitarian (mortuary and domestic) artifacts will have to be enlarged considerably. Although the empirically oriented archaeologists may feel quite uncomfortable with a deductively derived model as the basis for burial analysis, nonetheless deeper analysis of burial associations will have to depend on a well-formulated model. What I have in mind here is the prospect of a poorly explored approach to burial analysis. Whereas perspectives up to now have mainly conceived the problem of such analysis as an old-fashioned problem of the degree of similarity of culturally given characteristics, the use of such noncultural features as the demographic profile offers the promise of isolating age and sex association in an R-mode framework. Subtle age regressive effects could provide an important conception that moved beyond social identities. But success in these R-mode studies has depended largely on breaking out of the confines of an attribute matrix dominated by artifacts by substituting matrices incorporating features of cultural behavior (e.g., limb positioning) and human demography.

Conclusion

To return to my original question, I think that experience with Q-mode analysis in burial studies is a mixed bag. Although the Q-mode perspective has successfully isolated the ranking of status in burial assemblages, it has performed this task crudely and not necessarily with any deeper perspective than can be provided by an informal analysis with low-powered statistics. Interassemblage analysis in the Q-mode form has measured up to the expectations of the Saxe-Binford decision-making perspective to burial treatment organization better than most cluster analysis applications. However, continued prime reliance on cluster analyses, in particular those that are polythetic and agglomerative in procedure, satisfies the desire for direct manipulation while resorting to the methods of mathematical procedure. Although the results will benefit from the unrelenting application of formal rules, I predict they will fail to satisfy other questions having to do with underlying structures to data sets that are less obvious and demand prior stands on certain demographically founded expectations concerning the distribution of wealth, status symbols, tools, and other categories of objects.

Intrinsically beguiling and as directly manipulative as cluster analysis is in burial analysis, little technical and methodological progress has been made to overcome major analytical problems inherent in sparse matrices, highly skewed variable distributions, and a solution potential tied to case size or the number of burials. R-mode work is required to help take over some of these deficiencies. Yet one bright spot does remain. Q-mode analysis inherited from the early perspectives toward quantification has found a home with a particular theoretical perspective. Although this niche has not been developed greatly, the next 20 years may see further development that may create a new niche for cluster analysis.

References

Aldenderfer, M. S. and R. K. Blashfield. 1984. *Cluster Analysis*. Sage: Beverly Hills.
de Barros, P. L. F. 1982. The effects of variable site occupation span on the results of frequency seriation. *American Antiquity* 47: 291-315.
Benfer, R. A. 1972. Factor analysis as numerical induction: how to judge a book by its cover. *American Anthropologist* 74: 530-554.
Binford, L. R. 1977. Introduction. In *For Theory Building in Archaeology*, ed. L.R. Binford, pp. 1-10. New York: Academic Press.
Binford, L. R. and S. R. Binford. 1966. A preliminary analysis of functional variability in the Mousterian of Levallois facies. *American Anthropologist* 68: 238-295.
Braun, D. P. 1979. Illinois Hopewell burial practices and social organization: a reexamination of the Klunk-Gibson mound group. In *Hopewell Archaeology: The Chillicothe Conference*, ed. D. Brose and N. Greber, pp. 66-79. Kent, OH: Kent State University Press.
Braun, D. P. 1981. A critique of some recent North American mortuary studies. *American Antiquity* 46: 398-416.
Cannon, A. 1983. The quantification of artifactual assemblages: some implications for behavioral inferences. *American Antiquity* 48: 785-792.
Christenson, A. L. and D. W. Read. 1977. Numerical taxonomy, R-mode factor analysis and archaeological classification. *American Antiquity* 42: 163-179.
Clark, G. A. 1982. Quantifying archaeological research. In *Advances in Archaeological Method and Theory* 5: 217-273.

Clarke, D. L. 1968. Analytical Archaeology. London: Methuen.
Cowgill, G. L. 1968. Archaeological applications of factor, cluster, and proximity analysis. *American Antiquity* 33: 367-375.
Cowgill, G. L. 1972. Models, methods and techniques for seriation. In *Models in Archaeology*, ed. D. L. Clarke, pp. 381-424. London: Methuen.
Cowgill, G. L. 1982. Clusters of objects and associations between variables: two approaches to archaeological classification. In *Essays on Archaeological Typology*, eds. R. Whallon and J. A. Brown, pp. 30-55. Evanston, IL: Center for American Archaeology Press.
Deetz, J. 1965. *The Dynamics of Stylistic Change in Arikara Ceramics.* Urbana: University of Illinois Press.
Doran, J. E. and F. R. Hodson. 1975. Mathematics and computers. In *Archaeology*. Cambridge: Harvard University Press.
Dunnell, R. C. 1971. Systematics. In *Prehistory*. New York: Free Press.
Freeman, L. G. and J. A. Brown. 1964. Statistical analysis of Carter Ranch pottery. *Fieldiana: Anthropology* 55: 126-154.
Goldstein, L. G. 1980. *Mississippian Mortuary Practices. A Case Study of Two Cemeteries in the Lower Illinois Valley.* Evanston, IL: Northwestern Archaeological Program.
Hatch, J. W. 1974. Dallas mortuary practices. Unpublished MA thesis. Pennsylvania State University.
Hatch, J. W. 1976. *Status in death: principles of ranking in Dallas Culture mortuary remains.* Unpublished Ph.D. dissertation. Pennsylvania State University.
Hodder, I. and C. Orton. 1976. *Spatial Analysis in Archaeology.* Cambridge: Cambridge University Press.
Hodson, F. R. 1977. Quantifying Hallstatt: some initial results. *American Antiquity* 42: 394-412.
Hodson, F. R., D. G. Kendall, and P. Tautu (eds.) 1971. *Mathematics in the Archaeological and Historical Sciences.* Edinburgh: Edinburgh University Press.
Hole, F. R. and M. Shaw. 1967. Computer analysis of chronological seriation. *Rice University Studies* 53, no. 3.
Jefferies, R. W. and B. M. Lynch. 1983. Dimensions of Middle Archaic cultural adaptation at the Black Earth site, Saline County, Illinois. In *Archaic Hunters and Gatherers in the American Midwest*, eds. J. L. Phillips and J. A. Brown, pp. 299-322.
Kendall, D. G. 1971. Seriation from abundance matrices. In *Mathematics in the Archaeological and Historical Sciences*, eds. F. R. Hodson et al., pp. 215-252. Edinburgh: Edinburgh University Press.
Kerber, R. 1986. Political evolution in the Lower Illinois Valley: AD 400-1000. Unpublished Ph.D. dissertation. Northwestern University.
King, T. F. 1976. Political differentiation among hunter-gatherers: an archaeological test. Unpublished Ph.D. dissertation. University of California, Riverside.
Kintigh, K. W. 1984. Measuring archaeological diversity by comparison with simulated assemblages. *American Antiquity* 49: 44-54.
Lewis, R. B. n.d. The analysis of contingency tables in archaeology. *Advances in Archaeological Method and Theory* 9.
Longacre, W. A. 1966. Changing patterns of social integration: a prehistoric example from the American Southwest. *American Anthropologist* 68: 94-102.
Mainfort, R. C. 1979. Indian social dynamics in the period of European contact: Fletcher site cemetery, Bay County. *Michigan State University, Publications of the Museum, Anthropological Series* Vol. 1, no. 4.
Mainfort, R. C. 1984. Wealth, space and status in a historic Indian cemetery. *American Antiquity* 50: 555-579.
Marquardt, W. H. 1978. Advances in archaeological seriation. In *Advances in Archaeological Method and Theory* 1: 257-314.
Orser, C. E. 1980. An archaeological and ethnohistorical socioeconomic analysis of Arikara mortuary practices. Unpublished Ph.D. dissertation. Southern Illinois University.

O'Shea, J. M. 1981. Social configurations and the archaeological study of mortuary practices: a case study. In *The Archaeology of Death*, eds. R. Chapman, I. Kinnes, and K. Randsborg, pp. 39-52. Cambridge: Cambridge University Press.

O'Shea, J. M. 1984. *Mortuary Variability: An Archaeological Investigation*. New York: Academic Press.

Pader, E-J. 1982. Symbolism, social relations and the interpretation of mortuary remains. *British Archaeological Reports, International Series, S130*.

Palkovich, A. M. 1980. *Pueblo Population and Society: The Arroyo Hondo Skeletal and Mortuary Remains*. Sante Fe, NM: School of American Research Press.

Pearson, R. 1981. Social complexity in Chinese coastal Neolithic sites. *Science* 213: 1078-1086.

Peebles, C. S. 1972. Monothetic-divisive analysis of the Moundville burials: an initial report. *Newsletter of Computer Archaeology* 8(2): 1-13.

Peebles, C. S. 1974. Moundville: the organization of a prehistoric community and culture. Unpublished PhD dissertation. University of California, Santa Barbara.

Peebles, C. S. and S. M. Kus. 1977. Some archaeological correlates of ranked societies. *American Antiquity* 42: 421-448.

Petrie, W. M. F. 1899. Sequences in prehistoric remains. *Journal Anthropological Institute* 29: 295-301.

Plog, S. 1980. *Stylistic Variation in Prehistoric Ceramics*. Cambridge: Cambridge University Press.

Read, D. W. 1979. The effective use of radiocarbon dates in the seriation of archaeological sites. In *Radiocarbon Dating*, eds. R. Berger and H. E. Suess, pp. 89-94. Los Angeles: University of California Press.

Renfrew, C. and K. L. Cooke (eds.) 1979. *Transformations: Mathematical Approaches to Culture Change*. New York: Academic Press.

Rothschild, N. A. 1979. Mortuary behavior and social organization at Indian Knoll and Dickson mounds. *American Antiquity* 44: 658-667.

Saxe, A. A. 1970. Social dimensions of mortuary practices. Unpublished PhD dissertation. University of Michigan.

Spaulding, A. C. 1982. Structure in archaeological data: nominal variables. In *Essays on Archaeological Typology*, eds. R. Whallon and J. A. Brown, pp. 1-20. Evanston, IL: Center for American Archaeology Press.

Speth, J. D. and G. A. Johnson. 1976. Problems in the use of correlation for the investigation of tool kits and activity areas. In *Cultural Change and Continuity, Essays in honor of James Bennett Griffin*, ed. C. E. Cleland, pp. 35-57. New York: Academic Press.

Tainter, J. A. 1975a. The archaeological study of social change: woodland systems in west-central Illinois. Unpublished PhD dissertation. Northwestern University.

Tainter, J. A. 1975b. Social inference and mortuary practices: an experiment in numerical classification. *World Archaeology* 7: 1-15.

Tainter, J. A. 1977. Woodland social change in west-central Illinois. *Mid-continental Journal of Archaeology* 2: 67-98.

Thomas, D. H. 1978. The awful truth about statistics in archaeology. *American Antiquity* 43: 231-244.

Vierra, R. K. and D. L. Carlson. 1981. Factor analysis, random data, and patterned results. *American Antiquity* 46: 272-283.

About the Authors

MARK S. ALDENDERFER is an Assistant Professor of Anthropology at Northwestern University. His primary research interests are in the archaeology of foraging societies, lithic analysis, including microwear analysis, and quantitative methods as applied to archaeological problems. He is particularly interested in developing theoretical and methodological approaches for the study of the changing adaptive dynamics of foragers through time. Although he has conducted fieldwork in North America, Ethiopia, and Guatemala, his most recent field research has been in southern Peru, where he has directed the Northwestern University Archaic Project since 1984. He received his bachelor's degree from Wake Forest University, where he was Phi Beta Kappa, and his master's and Ph.D. from the Pennsylvania State University.

JAMES A. BROWN is Professor of Anthropology at Northwestern University. He is an archaeologist who has concentrated attention on the development of sedentism and ceremonialism among prehistoric groups of eastern North America. Of particular interest has been the use of burial practices to elucidate features of prehistoric social organization.

Brown is co-author of *Pre-Columbian Shell Engravings from Craig Mound at Spiro, Oklahoma (1975-83)*, with Phillip Phillips, and *Ancient Art of the American Woodland Indians* (1985), with D.Brose and D.Penney. He edited *Approaches to the Social Dimensions of Mortuary Practices* (1971) and co-edited *Essays on Archaeological Typology* (1982) with R. Whallon, *Archaic Hunters and Gatherers in the American Midwest* (1983) with J. Phillips, and *Prehistoric Hunters and Gatherers: The Emergence of Cultural Complexity* (1985) with D. Price.

CHRISTOPHER CARR is an Assistant Professor at Arizona State University and former Director of the Institute for Quantitative Archaeology, University of Arkansas. He has worked on geographic and general statistical problems since 1972. His more recent quantitative research has focused on the role of analysis in the logic of science, intrasite spatial analysis, predictive modeling of settlement location choice, artifact style analysis and seriation, and geophysical surveying statistics. Carr has had published two books and many journal articles that focus on quantitative archaeology, including *For Concordance in Archaeological Analysis*. He is a member of the Society for American Archaeology, the American Anthropological Association, and Sigma Xi. Carr has received a variety of national fellowships and grants.

G. A. CLARK was born in Philadelphia in 1944 and completed his formal education at the Universities of Arizona (BA, MA) and Chicago (PhD). His degrees are all in anthropology (prehistoric archaeology). Clark is the author or co-author of about 100 publications concerned with quantitative research designs in archaeology and anthropology, Old World prehistoric hunter-gatherer adaptations, human evolution and the social aspects of mortuary analysis. He has done fieldwork in France, Spain, Turkey, Jordan, and Mexico, as well as in the Southwestern United States. A Professor in the Department of Anthropology at Arizona State University, he is the current Editor of ASU's *Anthropological Research Papers* monograph series (since 1974). His devotion to the preservation of Austin-Healey roadsters is widely known, and he frequently can be seen at classic sports car rallys and gymkhanas in central and southern Arizona.

JIM DORAN initially studied mathematics and statistics at Hertford College, Oxford and after research work at the University of Edinburgh is now a Senior Lecturer in the Department of Computer Science at the University of Essex, Colchester, England. Although a computer scientist specializing in artificial intelligence studies, he has a long-standing interest in the application of mathematical and computing techniques in archaeology and has published a number of papers related to this interest in addition to being co-author of the book *Mathematics and Computers in Archaeology*.

About the Authors

LARRY R. KIMBALL is a Ph.D. candidate in anthropology at Northwestern University. He has conducted archaeological research in North Carolina, Tennessee, and Kentucky. He is currently undertaking microwear analysis of Upper Paleolithic stone tools from the Dordogne region of France. Among his principal research interests are hunter-gatherer adaptations, statistical evaluation of intersite functional variation, spatial analysis, and microwear analysis.

KEITH W. KINTIGH is now Associate Professor of Anthropology at the University of California at Santa Barbara. In 1974 Dr. Kintigh earned a Master of Science degree in computer science at Stanford University, and he received a doctoral degree in anthropology from the University of Michigan in 1982. In 1980 he was appointed Associate Archaeologist at the Arizona State Museum, University of Arizona, a position that he held until joining the faculty at the University of California at Santa Barbara in 1985.

Professor Kintigh's field research has been focused on the late prehistoric period in the Zuni area of New Mexico and Arizona, although he has also done extensive field work in Peru and Morocco. His publications cover a variety of topics, many of them concerned with the use of quantitative methods in archaeology. Subjects of particular interest have been the analysis of archaeological diversity and spatial analysis.

JACK D. NANCE is Associate Professor of Archaeology at Simon Fraser University. He received a PhD from the University of Calgary in 1972. His field research has centered on the prehistory of the lower Tennessee-Cumberland-Ohio region of western Kentucky and Tennessee. His major publications in archaeostatistics have been in the area of statistical sampling.

DWIGHT W. READ is Professor of Anthropology at UCLA with degrees from Reed College, the University of Wisconsin, and UCLA. He is a mathematician/anthropologist who has worked extensively on the application of formal methods of reasoning to anthropological and archaeological problems. His work in archaeology has centered on conceptual issues involved in the application of statistical methods and the development of a rigorous foundation for a theory and method of classification. His numerous publications in these areas include articles and book chapters on sampling methods, the method and theory of classification, statistical modeling and models, and the construction of archaeologically based formal systems of reasoning. Dr Read was a co-Principal Investigator on the Chevelon Archaeological Research Project, has done ethnographic work with the !Kung San and has been serving as a consultant on a number of archaeological projects.

A. VOORRIPS is Director of the Group for Applied Information Science in Archaeology at the Institute for Pre- and Protohistory, University of Amsterdam, the Netherlands, and has been involved with quantitative methods, data base management, and computer applications in archaeology since 1974. He is the Secretary of Commission 4, "Data management and mathematical methods in archaeology" of the Union Internationale des Sciences Préhistoriques et Protohistoriques, and, with Susan H. Loving, co-edited *To Pattern the Past* (1985), the proceedings of an international symposium on mathematical methods in archaeology held in Amsterdam, 1984.

ROBERT WHALLON is Professor of Anthropology at the University of Michigan and Curator in the University of Michigan Museum of Anthropology. In addition to his interests in quantitative methods, he is concerned with the archaeology of hunter-gatherers, in particular the Paleolithic and Mesolithic periods in Europe. He has conducted field work and research in North America, the Near East, and Europe, with his most recent project focused on Paleolithic research in Yugoslavia.